MULTILITERACY CENTERS

Writing Center Work, New Media, and Multimodal Rhetoric

NEW DIMENSIONS IN COMPUTERS AND COMPOSITION
Gail E. Hawisher and *Cynthia L. Selfe*, editors

Multiliteracy Centers

Writing Center Work, New Media, and Multimodal Rhetoric

edited by

David M. Sheridan
Michigan State University

James A. Inman
University of Tennessee

HAMPTON PRESS, INC.
CRESSKILL, NEW JERSEY

Printed in the United States of America

Library of Congress Cataloging-in-Publication Data

Multiliteracy centers : writing center work, new media, and multimodal rhetoric / edited by David M. Sheridan, James A. Inman.
    p. cm. -- (New dimensions in computers and composition)
  Includes bibliographical references and indexes.
  ISBN 978-1-57273-898-0 -- ISBN 978-1-57273-899-7 (pbk.)
  1. English language--Rhetoric--Study and teaching--Computer network resources.
2. Report writing--Study and teaching--Computer network resources. 3. Mass media and education. 4. Creative writing (Higher education) 5. Writing centers. 6. Literacy. I. Sheridan, David M. II. Inman, James A.
  PE1404.M83 2010
  808'.0420785--dc22
                                    2009047192

Hampton Press, Inc.
23 Broadway
Cresskill, NJ 07626

CONTENTS

v

PRODUCTION

REALITY CHECK

ACKNOWLEDGMENTS

David wishes to thank all of the MSU Writing Center folks he has had the honor of working with over the years, including Patti Stock, Janet Swenson, Troy Hicks, Stephanie Sheffield, Dean Rehberger, Michael Fegan, Scott Pennington, Jim Oliver, Vince Vatter, Jackie Frens, Scott Schopieray, Michael McLeod, Timothy Gunn, Chad O'Neil, Luis Rosero, Amy Diehl, Seth Morton, and many others. While he never worked with her there, he inherited Dànielle DeVoss' innovative work at the MSU Writing Center and benefited from the record of that work in her publications. Dwayne Overmyer (University of Michigan) shaped David's understandings of expertise and disciplinarity in key ways. Dickie Selfe first introduced David to the word and concept of "multiliteracy center" at the 1999 CIWIC. Lisa Ede was an early supporter of this project and offered useful comments on what would become the Introduction and Chapter 4 of this collection. Bill Hart-Davidson offered useful comments on an early draft of Chapter 9. The anonymous reviewer for this project offered useful guidance that shaped the entire collection. Gail Hawisher and Cynthia Selfe, editors of the New Dimensions in Computers and Composition series, have been wonderfully supportive of this project from the beginning, as has Barbara Bernstein, President of Hampton Press. The contributors to this collection deserve hearty thanks for all of their insights, hard work, and perseverance. Finally, David wishes to thank his wife Joy and sons Elijah and Levi for their endless patience and support. This book is for them.

James thanks David for his exceptional work as co-editor, enthusiasm, and good humor. Additionally, James thanks the terrific team at Hampton Press for being so professional and kind. Finally, James thanks his family and his friends and colleagues at the University of Tennessee.

INTRODUCTION

WRITING CENTERS
AND THE MULTIMODAL TURN

David M. Sheridan

Michigan State University

My advice is probably the same advice we very often offer our students: Know your possibilities.

—DeVoss (2002, p. 177)

Change is difficult, mostly because we just don't know how to change.

—George (1995, p. 331)

CHANGES IN THE LANDSCAPE
OF COMMUNICATION

As Gunther Kress (1999) observed a decade ago, "the landscape of communication is changing fundamentally" (p. 67). Salient among the many changes currently transpiring is the increasing reliance on the integration of multiple semiotic components that span across aural, visual, and verbal modes: written words, spoken words, music, still images, moving images, charts, graphs, illustrations, animations, layout schemes, navigation schemes, colors, ambient noises, and so on. Further, these components are not neatly separable; communication is not the result of one element merely being added to another, but of the *interaction* among the different elements. Semiotic resources "cooperate" (Barthes, 1977a, p. 16) with each other or, even better, "interanimate" (Blakesley, 2004, p. 112) each other, resulting in a whole that is decidedly greater than the sum of its parts. This collection explores the ways that writing centers might position themselves in the context of this shift to "multimodal" rhetoric.

The constellation of cultural and technological dynamics that have contributed to or participate in a shift to multimodality include:

- *Increasing proliferation of multimodal media.* "Old media" forms like radio, TV, and film—and ever-more sophisticated print media—flourished beginning in the early 20th century, to be joined at the century's end by "new media" forms, such as web pages, digital videos, and digital animations.
- *Increasing access to the tools of multimodal production and distribution.* Many entry-level computers now come bundled with easy-to-use digital video applications. These applications enable a kind of video production that only a few years ago would have required expensive and arcane equipment. Moreover, videos can now be distributed over the Internet at little or no cost (cf. YouTube).
- *Increasing cultural acceptance of multimodal compositions as "serious" and useful forms of communication.* In public, professional, and personal contexts, multimodal forms are increasingly understood to be not just for entertainment, but essential ways of getting work done, whether that work is publicizing a nonprofit organization or presenting a proposal to the board of directors.

These transformations have affected language-related fields in substantial ways. More than two decades ago, for instance, Robert Scholes (1985) warned those involved in English studies that

> This rickety, demanding English apparatus has important work to do in our society, but it will do this work well only if we can rebuild it. The essential change—the one that will enable all others—must be a change in the way we define our task. To put it as directly, and perhaps as brutally, as possible, we must stop "teaching literature" and start "studying texts." Our rebuilt apparatus must be devoted to textual stud-

ies with the consumption and production of texts thoroughly intermin-
gled. . . . All kinds of texts, visual as well as verbal, polemical as well
as seductive, must be taken as occasions for further textuality. (p. 16)

Scholes' reconfiguration of English studies calls for a broadening of mission. His embrace of "all kinds of texts" (not just literary and written) opens
the door for English studies to claim as its domain (in addition to novels,
poems, and plays) TV shows, magazine ads, and films, as well as "new
media" artifacts that Scholes couldn't have imagined in 1985: web pages,
digital videos, digital animations, and so on.

Indeed, the proliferation of new media forms has brought new urgency
to Scholes' call for a reconfigured English studies. For example, noting the
visual nature of the Web, Craig Stroupe (2000) offers a map for "visualizing
English," proposing a "hybrid approach" characterized by "dialogically constitutive relations between words and images—in a larger sense, between
the literacies of verbal and visual cultures—which can function as a singly
intended, if double-voiced, rhetoric" (p. 609). Stroupe claims,

> the practice and teaching of this hybrid literacy will require that those
> of us in English studies reexamine our customary distinctions and judg-
> ments about literacy in light of this historical challenge of the visual—
> not just in the extracurricular, top-down media of television and film,
> but in the more commonly accessible media of textual production and
> academic communication. (p. 609)

Likewise, Gunther Kress (1999) claims that "if English is to remain relevant
as the subject which provides access to participation in public forms of
communication, as well as remaining capable of providing understandings
of and the abilities to produce culturally valued texts, then an emphasis on
language alone simply will no longer do" (p. 67).

Even more relevant for writing centers, however, are the changes that
have occurred in the fields of literacy studies, rhetorical studies, and composition studies. The New London Group famously popularized the now
ubiquitous "multiliteracies" with the publication of "A Pedagogy of
Multiliteracies: Designing Social Futures" in 1996. Since then, we have seen
official statements by professional organizations like National Council of
Teachers of English (2005), which endorse the teaching of "multimodal literacies" in the language arts classroom. Likewise, rhetorical theory is being
reformulated to account for multimodality (see Barthes, 1977b; Blair, 1999;
Blakesley, 2003; Foss, 1994; Handa, 2004; Hill & Helmers, 2004; Kenney,
2002; Lucaites & Hariman, 2001; McComiskey, 2004; Welch, 1999).

Numerous compositionists have called for those of us involved in teaching writing to take up the challenge of preparing students to be producers of multimodal compositions (e.g., George, 2001; Hawisher & Sullivan, 1999; Selfe, 2007; Sheridan, Ridolfo, & Michel, 2005; Shipka, 2005; Westbrook, 2006; Williams, 2001; Yancey, 2004). Cynthia Selfe (2004) nicely sums up the urgency of attending to multimodality within composition studies:

> To make it possible for students to practice, value, and understand a full range of literacies—emerging, competing, and fading—English composition teachers have got to be willing to expand their own understanding of composing beyond conventional bounds of the alphabetic. And we have to do so quickly or risk having composition studies become increasingly irrelevant. (p. 54)

In short, our culture is changing; the academy is changing; English studies, rhetorical studies, literacy studies, and composition studies are all changing. Nearly every sector and institution is participating in a shift that involves a more capacious embrace of semiotic possibility: an embrace that comprehends images, words, and sounds. What about writing centers? How are we responding to these changes? What is the range of possible responses and which ones are most compelling?

EVERYTHING FROM PROJECT REPORTS TO POSTER DESIGN: POSSIBLE DIRECTIONS FOR WRITING CENTERS

In the "first millennial edition" (Mullin & DeCiccio, 2000, p. 5) of *The Writing Center Journal*, John Trimbur (2000) offers a vision of writing center work that reflects the turn to multimodality discussed earlier. Borrowing the term *multiliteracies* from the New London Group, Trimbur writes:

> I think it's fairly indicative of recent trends in writing center theory and practice to see literacy as a multimodal activity in which oral, written, and visual communication intertwine and interact. This notion of multiliteracies has to do in part with new text forms and new means of communication associated with the information age and knowledge economies of the globalized markets and societies of late capitalism. . . . [T]he notion of multiple literacies offers a way to think about working on everything from essays and project reports to PowerPoint presentations to webpage and poster design.

> My guess is that writing centers will more and more define them-
> selves as multiliteracy centers. (pp. 29–30)

Trimbur's millennial prognosticating notwithstanding, I think it is accu-
rate to say that the shift to multimodality has not instilled in writing centers the kind of we-have-to respond-quickly urgency expressed by Cynthia
Selfe on behalf of composition studies. In "Planning for Hypertexts in the
Writing Center . . . Or Not," Michael Pemberton (2003) notes that, although

> writing centers . . . have been influenced by advances in computer
> technology . . . most of the interactions between students and tutors
> still center on the handwritten or printed texts that are placed on a
> table between them or, perhaps, shared in a word-processed file. These
> texts are structured linearly and hierarchically, moving along a single
> path from beginning to end, following well-known and universally
> taught discourse forms that have emerged from a print-based rhetori-
> cal tradition. (p. 9)

Although the literature on multimodal literacies and rhetoric continues to
grow apace, there have only been a handful of articles that explore the
implications of multimodality and new media for writing centers (see e.g.,
Griffin, 2007; McKinney, in press; Pemberton, 2003; Sheridan, 2006). As
the "Or Not" in his title suggests, Pemberton seems ambivalent about the
need for centers to make major shifts in light of new media and multimodality. Although he outlines a range of possible approaches centers
might take, he concludes:

> Although it would be easy to pursue this trail of possible resources fur-
> ther, identifying an assortment of sites and texts that could be used to
> teach tutors HTML and JavaScript, or how to use Microsoft FrontPage
> or Netscape Composer, we should stop and think carefully about how
> far we are really willing to go down this path in our quest to create "bet-
> ter" writing tutors. Ultimately, we have to ask ourselves whether it is
> really the writing center's responsibility to be all things to all people.
> There will always be more to learn. There will always be new groups
> making demands on our time and our resources in ways we haven't
> yet planned for. And there will never be enough time or enough money
> or enough tutors to meet all those demands all of the time. If we diver-
> sify too widely and spread ourselves too thinly in an attempt to encom-
> pass too many different literacies, we may not be able to address any
> set of literate practices particularly well. (p. 21)

How far are we willing to go? This collection is an attempt to explore that question. A look at the table of contents reveals that nearly all areas of writing center practice are potentially open to transformation in light of multimodality: the configuration of physical and virtual spaces, tutor training and tutoring practices, outreach initiatives, and, indeed, centers' identities and missions. Before turning to those more specific discussions of how writing center practice might be transformed, however, I would like to say a few more general words about what writing centers might look like if they are reconceived as "multiliteracy centers."

THE IDEA(L)
OF A MULTILITERACY CENTER

A full articulation of a multiliteracy center necessitates a bit of utopian thinking—thinking unfettered by limits imposed by scarcity of resources and various institutional practices. Before we get to the work of deciding what kinds of spaces we are *able to create* (given the pressures that bear at our respective institutions), we need to consider what spaces are *possible to imagine*, even if we ultimately will not be able to fully realize such imaginings. I would argue that a fully realized multiliteracy center would be defined by the following characteristics:

> *Multiliteracy centers should be spaces equal to the diversity of semiotic options composers have in the 21st century.* Students working on web pages, digital slide presentations, desktop-published documents (flyers, posters, brochures, chapbooks), digital videos, and digital animations would all be welcome. Indeed, one of the questions that multiliteracy centers will need to face is what forms of communication, if any, would be excluded from such a center. Would a student working on a painting be welcome? A student designing a video game? What about a student expressing his or her ideas through a performance such as a song or a dance? Would we say yes to the song if it had lyrics, but no if it were strictly instrumental? If we said yes to the lyrics, would we examine the words in isolation or would we confront their relationship with the music? What would happen if we never turned away anyone?

Multiliteracy centers should be staffed by consultants who have the rhetorical, pedagogical, and technical capacities to support this diversity of semiotic options. In order to meet this goal, multiliteracy consultants would need to be recruited from a range of backgrounds and experiences: students majoring in TV and video, art history, graphic design, film studies, cultural studies, computer science, English, professional writing; and students with backgrounds as amateur photographers, freelance web designers, and closet illustrators. Consultants would model good composing practices for their clients by producing media artifacts themselves and by representing those artifacts in meaningful ways to the public. They would be given venues for collaboration, inquiry, and dialogue so that they and their clients could benefit from the diversity of paradigms operating at any given moment. Multiliteracy centers would become what Rolf ⟵ Norgaard (1999) has called a "disciplinary contact zone"—institutional and intellectual sites "that place students at the margins of their own fields or that have them straddle organizational ⟵ boundaries" so that the conventions and perspectives we nor- ⟵ mally take for granted are made visible" (p. 48).

Multiliteracy centers should facilitate the competent and critically reflective use of technologies and other material, institutional, and cultural resources. Those involved in literacy instruction are increasingly asked to confront the material and the technical, to help students be sophisticated users of communication tools. We can no longer adopt what Haas and Neuwirth (1994) have called a "computers are not our job" (p. 325) attitude. As Stuart Selber (2004) argues, we need a "professionally responsible" (p. 470) approach to functional computer literacy. The challenges of composing in the 21st century, DeVoss, Cushman, and Grabill (2005) warn us, call for us and our students to confront "infrastructure"—the material and human resources of composing. Technologies are no longer incidental, no longer distractions from the symbolic or cognitive work of composing. They are integral.

As technology-rich spaces populated with what Richard Selfe calls, "advanced literacy practitioners" (see chap. 5, this volume), multiliteracy centers can play an important role in helping student composers be both competent and critically reflective users of infrastructural resources.

Multiliteracy centers would, therefore, invest in the technological resources that citizens as media producers increasingly exploit: high-end desktops for processor-intensive tasks and wireless laptops for portability, but also scanners, microphones, mixing boards, digital still cameras, digital video cameras, analog to digital video-conversion equipment, drawing tablets, oversized monitors, data projectors, digital voice recorders, DVD burners and players, external hard drives, and web servers, as well as a range of applications for media production: graphics editors, audio editors, HTML editors, desktop-publishing software, digital animation software, screen-capture software, various collaboration tools, and a library of print resources ranging from back issues of *Communication Arts* to Sontag's *On Photography*, from Tufte's *Envisioning Information* to Chion's *Audio-Vision*.

Does this vision for multiliteracy centers sound excessive? Does it seem idealistic to think that writing centers, always underresourced, could continue to provide all of the forms of support that they have traditionally provided and heap this new set of services on top of everything, with the demands in personnel, space, and technology that such services imply? Do writing centers become unrecognizable in this morass of wires and monitors—something more akin to a media production studio than the comfortable spaces defined by soft couches, leafy plants, and copious amounts of scrap paper?

It is important to remember, when confronting questions like these, that the choice between a multiliteracy center and a traditional writing center is not an either-or choice, but a matter of finding a set of locations along various continua (see McKinney, chap. 10, this volume). Many readers will have already protested on reading these words that writing centers have always been multiliteracy centers. Writing centers have long helped students think about the visual design of their resumes and have explored issues of aurality and performance when working with writers on papers meant to be presented orally. Writing centers have invested in and helped students use communication technologies for decades, whether those technologies were electronic typewriters or desktop computers. This volume argues that writing centers might productively travel a little farther down a road that they have been on for some time.

We begin this journey with explorations of the kinds of spaces needed to facilitate multiliteracy consulting. James Inman (chap. 1) examines the ways that the physical space of the multiliteracy center can support multimodal composing practices. Inman suggests that the concept of *use zoning*, borrowed from city planning, can provide an effective methodology for designing multiliteracy center spaces. The needs of multiliteracies, with their emphasis on visual, aural, and verbal production in multiple media formats, introduce new complexities into the use of writing center spaces. Video and audio production, for instance, introduce challenges that are different from those related to conversations about paper-based writing. Zoning offers a way of confronting these complexities, forcing center planners to begin with "what clients will actually be doing" and to seek out designs that can accommodate that activity. Inman goes on to explore the design of spaces within the center, the relationships of those spaces to each other, and the relationship of center spaces to those outside of it.

Morgan Gresham (chap. 2) examines the way virtual spaces can be used to facilitate multiliteracy consulting. Gresham's story of developing an online studio to complement the work of the Class of '41 Studio for Student Communication at Clemson University is at once an account of concrete exigencies and solutions and a reflection on the metaphors and tropes that shape our thinking about our work. She discusses Clemson's experimentation with multiple platforms for delivering online support to students working on multimodal compositions: a Writing Studio space, a MOO, a Moodle space, and a fourth, multifaceted space fashioned by cobbling together a number of "common tools." Gresham's account is, in its content and in its form, a playful exploration of process: how things evolve within an ecology of ideas, metaphors, needs, resources, and limitations. By assembling the fragments of this experience—e-mail artifacts, keywords, figures, interfaces, maps, quotations from technorhetorical theory and popular music— Gresham provides both practical wisdom about our work and a chance to interrogate the various frames we use to make sense of that work.

After this exploration of space, we turn our attention to the day-to-day operations of a multiliteracy center, asking what it means to carry out the work of supporting composers who are making meaning through sounds, images, and words. All three of the chapters in this section are preoccupied (in part) with confronting the nature of technology and the roles that it might play in centers. As Michael Pemberton (2003) has observed, writing centers have historically been ambivalent about technology. These three chapters do not attempt to dissolve that ambivalence, but they do offer new ways of confronting it. Drawing on her experience with Clemson's Class of '41 Studio, Teddi Fishman (chap. 3) explores the theory and practice of multiliteracy consulting. She begins with the fundamental tension between students' desires for efficient answers to technical questions and the writing center's goals of helping students become more critically reflective composers. Fishman describes three areas of practice in which tutors or "associates" receive preparation: "orientation practices," which include an inquiry into theoretical foundations for multiliteracy work; "technology practices," which include "goal-driven" exploration of technical resources;

and "tutoring practices," which include the principles that guide associates' interactions with student composers. Fishman then turns to a discussion of values, which involve a kind of diplomacy whereby associates acknowledge the "how-to" exigencies that student composers bring to the Studio, but also find ways to foster attention to the "why" and "to what purpose" questions that are so important to writing centers.

Beginning with this same complex diplomacy, I attempt to refigure the work of multiliteracy consulting through the trope of "materiality" (chap. 4). A focus on the material forces us to account for what DeVoss, Cushman, and Grabill (2005) call *infrastructure*—a term that includes all of the necessary evils that we usually attempt to hide under the rug or behind a plant: firewire cables, monitors, USB drives, DVD + Rs, external hard drives, scanners, printer stands, pixels, and memory chips. This stuff is so dehumanizing! It is so not what writing centers are about! Yet I argue we need to increasingly be about it, and, what's more, we need to confront the diverse material forms that compositions—the cold hard products of rhetorical labor—take. Our insistence that we are about processes, not products, is no excuse for failing to grapple with the reality that a photograph, a digital animation, and a paper-based essay do not mean in the same ways. Accounting for this semiotic alterity will force writing centers to develop sophisticated models of interdisciplinarity as we integrate knowledge from fields and practices like studio art, graphic design, video production, and music.

Richard Selfe (chap. 5) asks us to step back from our minute-by-minute interactions with student composers and examine the big picture. In a move that might at first seem shocking to those involved with writing center work, Selfe reverses the usual question—What is the place of technologies in human-centered institutions like writing centers?—by invoking Bernard Stiegler (1998), who asserts that "to know the essence of the machine . . . is also to know the place of the human in 'technical ensembles' " (p. 66). Drawing on Bruno Latour and Actor Network Theory, Selfe asks us to "listen carefully" not just to the "human," but also to the "nonhuman agents in our communicative dramas." Doing so might change the scope and quality of our work; we might find ourselves, for instance, recruiting "advanced literacy practitioners" as peer "coaches" who cannot only engage peer composers in conversations about digital videos, but can help composers conduct focus-group research about the effectiveness of those videos, can help them inventory the technological resources across campus that might facilitate the composing process, and can work with others to create systems for storing and accessing the large files that accompany video projects. In short, MLCs and the advanced literacy practitioners who work in them might intervene fundamentally in what Bruno

Latour (2004) calls "political ecologies" that all of us—human and nonhuman agents alike—inhabit.

George Cooper (chap. 6) begins a section of the book called "Connections," which is concerned with how multiliteracy centers can build bridges with people and units across and beyond campus. Cooper explores a sustained partnership between University of Michigan's (UM) Sweetland Multiliteracy Center (SMC) and his section of first-year writing. Taught as part of UM's Community Scholars Program, this course adopted a service-learning approach, in which students produced websites for nonprofit organizations—an approach that would have been impractical without the support of the SMC. In many ways, this partnership reveals the expanded notion of writing center work that Selfe discusses: Sweetland's multiliteracy consultants' relationships with Cooper's students extended way beyond the single session and text to include rhetorical analyses of example compositions, sustained engagement with various technologies, whole-class workshops, and so on. Cooper demonstrates the role that multiliteracy centers might play in facilitating innovative teaching practices.

Troy Hicks (chap. 7) looks at connections between multiliteracy centers and K–12 schools. In his account of the Michigan State University's (MSU) Red Cedar Writing Project, a site of the National Writing Project based in MSU's Writing Center, Hicks argues that writing centers can be powerful sites of professional development for K–12 teachers confronting the literacy challenges of the 21st century. In seeking to adopt an approach that fully accounts for the complexities of a critical and multifaceted literacy at a time of rapid technological change, teachers struggle against numerous limitations related not only to software and hardware, but to larger social and institutional structures. Despite this, Hicks points out, universities stand to learn a lot from the new knowledge being produced by teachers and students working in public school settings. Outreach efforts need to adopt a "model [that] respects teacher knowledge and invites them into a conversation, rather than giving them a lecture." After establishing this global context, Hicks turns to the local context of the MSU Writing Center and its mission, philosophy, and history. Long traditions of technology work and outreach work inform two multiliteracy projects that illustrate the potential of center–school partnerships. In the first project, teachers produce digital portfolios that consist of multimodal representations of their professional experiences. In the second, teachers capture their experiences at the 2005 NCTE convention in Pittsburgh in blogs, wikis, and podcasts. Hicks unpacks the lessons learned from these experiences in terms of three of MSU's outreach goals: collaboration, capacity building, and cross-disciplinarity.

Until this point, the chapters in this collection have largely been concerned with the resources and practices that writing centers can harness to enable multimodal composing practices of learners near and far. But will these changes transform other areas of writing center work or will their effect be limited to a minority of composers experimenting with technology-intensive projects? Will day-to-day interactions between tutors and writers change in the proximity of new technologies and knowledge bases? If centers are populated by Selfe's "advanced literacy practitioners"—who can produce web pages and digital videos, who understand interface design and usability testing—what reverberations will this send out through the rest of center practices? Christina Murphy and Lory Hawkes (chap. 8) ask us to consider a new model that positions centers squarely in the center of the university, empowered to change the paradigm of learning across campus. In this new model, "peer tutors" become "digital content specialists" who "use the principles of e-literacies, cognitive theory, and composition pedagogy" to design multimodal learning environments customized to the needs of individual learners. Digital content specialists can produce new tools of learning that integrate images, words, and sounds to address multiple learning styles. To embrace this model, however, centers will need to situate themselves within "new cultural narratives" that go beyond the "marginalization and rebellion" that have traditionally characterized their identity.

I attempt (in chap. 9) to illustrate the work of digital content specialists by describing an interactive learning module produced by MSU's Writing Center. *Getting Started: Analytical Writing in the Humanities* is a collection of learning tools that address some of the challenges writers face as they sit down to begin analytical papers in literature, art history, American studies, and other humanities courses focused on the interpretation of cultural texts and artifacts. This module uses digital video and interactive components such as writing prompts, discussion forums, and graphical interfaces to implement an online pedagogy informed by principles that centers have traditionally embraced. I attempt to demonstrate that the affordances of new media technologies allow the creation of learning environments that are process-oriented, student-centered, and dialogic.

Having outlined major transformations for writing centers that involve all areas of writing center work—changes in space, mission, and identity—it is time for a reality check. In the final chapter of this collection, Jackie Grutsch McKinney (chap. 10) brings us back to earth with a more cautious examination of practical challenges that centers will need to face as they contemplate these transformations. McKinney makes the important point that there is no single, universal model for what a multiliteracy center should be; different centers will need to make decisions that reflect their different contexts. Through a reflective reading of her own institutional context at Ball State, McKinney outlines a process for negotiating the limitations that all centers face—limitations of funding, time, and staffing. This negotiation brings us back, once again, to our various understandings of literacy and technology, and the complex relationship between the two. Drawing on the work of Stuart Selber and others, McKinney helps us understand and assess our options, revealing what's at stake in each one.

JUST BEGINNING

Writing in 1989, Cynthia Selfe observed that

> we are just beginning to get an idea of how radically our definition of literacy changes when communication activities are mediated by computers. Until we better envision this computer-mediated literacy . . . our profession can hardly expect to provide students with the skills they need to function as literate members of our technologically supported society. (p. 3)

"Nowhere," Selfe continues, "is there greater potential for achieving a degree of success in this exceedingly complex venture than there is in the numerous computer-supported writing centers that have been set up in schools and institutions across the country" (p. 3).

The lesson of the intervening years is that we will always be "just beginning" to confront changes in the landscape of communication occasioned by emergent technologies and by changes in cultural practices that are, in part, shaped by those technologies. In the years during which this collection was conceived and developed, a new set of technologies and practices associated with the label "Web 2.0" have reshaped yet again our understanding of the importance of visual and multimodal rhetoric. YouTube, MySpace, FaceBook, and Flickr are examples of multimodal public spaces that are increasingly important in our culture. As free, easy-to-use technologies, they provide increased access to multimodality. As highly organized public spaces—intricate and densely linked social networks— they introduce new kinds of social interaction.

Gunther Kress (1999) argues that, in a time of constant change, the curriculum should no longer be expected to function "as the site of the reproduction of young people in the image of their society and of its values" because "there are no stable values, no reliable or agreed structures" (p. 66). Instead, we need pedagogical and institutional practices that are transparently about "just beginning"—practices that, instead of introducing learners to a canon of knowledge and skills, ask learners to inventory and critically assess available resources—cultural and material, semiotic and technological, social and cognitive. We hope that the trope of "multiliteracy centers" will provide a generative figure for thinking about writing center work at a time when cultural practices, including rhetorical practices, are always rapidly changing.

REFERENCES

Barthes, Roland. (1977a). The photographic message. *Image, music, text* (S. Heath, Trans.). New York: Hill and Wang.

Barthes, Roland. (1977b). The rhetoric of the image. *Image, music, text* (S. Heath, Trans.). New York: Hill and Wang.

Blair, Carol. (1999). Contemporary U.S. memorial sites as exemplars of rhetoric's materiality. In Jack Selzer & Sharon Crowley (Eds.), *Rhetorical bodies: Toward a material rhetoric* (pp. 1–35). Madison: University of Wisconsin Press.

Blakesley, David. (Ed.). (2003). *The terministic screen: Rhetorical perspectives on film.* Carbondale: Southern Illinois University Press.

Blakesley, David. (2004). Defining film rhetoric: The case of Hitchcock's *Vertigo.* In C. A. Hill & M. Hemlers (Eds.), *Defining visual rhetorics* (pp. 111–134). Mahwah, NJ: Erlbaum.

DeVoss, Dànielle. (2002). Computer literacies and the roles of the writing center. In Paula Gillespie, Byron L. Stay, Alice Gillam, & Lady Falls Brown (Eds.), *Writing center research: Extending the conversation* (pp. 167–186). Mahwah, NJ: Erlbaum.

DeVoss, Dànielle, Cushman, Ellen, & Grabill, Jeff. (2005). Infrastructure and composing: The *when* of new-media writing. *College Composition and Communication, 57,* 14–44.

Foss, Sonja K. (1994). A rhetorical schema for the evaluation of visual imagery. *Communication Studies, 45,* 213–224.

George, Diana. (1995). Wonder of it all: Computers, writing centers, and the new world. *Computers and Composition, 12,* 331–334.

George, Diana. (2001). From analysis to design: Visual communication in the teaching of writing. *College Composition and Communication, 54,* 11–38.

Griffin, Jo Ann. (2007). Making connections with writing centers. In C. Selfe (Ed.), *Multimodal composition: Resources for teachers* (pp. 153–166). Cresskill, NJ: Hampton Press.

Haas, Christina, & Neuwirth, Christine M. (1994). Writing the technology that writes us: Research on literacy and the shape of technology. In C. L. Selfe & S. Hilligoss (Eds.), *Literacy and computers: The complications of teaching and learning with technology* (pp. 319–335). New York: Modern Language Association.

Handa, Carolyn. (2004). *Visual rhetoric in a digital world.* New York: Bedford/St. Martin's.

Hawisher, Gail E., & Sullivan, Patricia A. (1999). Fleeting images: Women visually writing the web. In Gail E. Hawisher & Cynthia L. Selfe (Eds.), *Passions, pedagogies, and 21st century technologies* (pp. 268–291). Logan: Utah State University Press.

Hill, Charles A., & Hemlers, Marguerite. (Eds.). (2004). *Defining visual rhetorics.* Mahwah, NJ: Erlbaum.

Kenney, Keith. (2002). Building visual communication theory by borrowing from rhetoric. *Journal of Visual Literacy, 22*(1), 53–80.

Kress, Gunther. (1999). "English" at a crossroads: Rethinking curricula of communication in the context of the turn to the visual. In Gail E. Hawisher & Cynthia L. Selfe (Eds.), *Passions, pedagogies, and 21st century technologies* (pp. 66–88). Logan: Utah State University Press.

Latour, Bruno. (2004). *Politics of nature: How to bring the sciences into democracy.* (C. Porter, Trans.). Cambridge, MA: Harvard University Press.

Lucaites, John L., & Hariman, Robert. (2001). Visual rhetoric, photojournalism, and democratic public culture. *Rhetoric Review, 20*(1/2), 37–42.

McComiskey, Bruce. (2004). Visual rhetoric and the new public discourse. *JAC, 24*(1), 187–206.

McKinney, Jackie Grutsch (in press). New media matters: Tutoring in the late age of print. *Writing Center Journal.*

Mullin, Joan, & DeCiccio, Albert C. (2000). From the editors. *The Writing Center Journal, 20*(2), 5–6.

National Council of Teachers of English. (2005). *Multimodal literacies.* Retrieved October 2, 2006, from http://www.ncte.org/about/over/positions/category/inst/123213.htm

The New London Group. (1996). A pedagogy of multiliteracies: Designing social futures. *Harvard Educational Review, 66*(1), 60–92.

Norgaard, Rolf. (1999). Negotiating expertise in disciplinary "contact zones." *Language and Learning Across the Disciplines, 3*(2), 44–63.

Pemberton, Michael. (2003). Planning for hypertexts in the writing center . . . or not. *The Writing Center Journal, 24*(1), 9–24.

Scholes, Robert. (1985). *Textual power: Literary theory and the teaching of English.* New Haven: Yale University Press.

Selber, Stuart A. (2004). Reimagining the functional side of computer literacy. *College Composition and Communication, 55,* 470–503.

Selfe, Cynthia. (1989). Redefining literacy: The multilayered grammars of computers. In Gail E. Hawisher & Cynthia L. Selfe (Eds.), *Critical perspectives on computers and composition instruction* (pp. 3–15). New York: Teachers College Press.

Selfe, Cynthia. (2004). Students who teach us: A case study in a new media text designer. In A. Wysocki, J. Johnson-Eilola, C. Selfe, & G. Sirc (Eds.), *Writing new media: Theory and applications for expanding the teaching of composition* (pp. 43–66). Logan: Utah State University Press.

Selfe, Cynthia (Ed.). (2007). *Multimodal composition: Resources for teachers.* Cresskill, NJ: Hampton.

Sheridan, David M. (2006). Words, images, sounds: Writing centers as multiliteracy centers. In Christina Murphy & Byron Stay (Eds.), *The writing center director's resource book* (pp. 339–350). Mahwah, NJ: Erlbaum.

Sheridan, David M., Ridolfo, Jim, & Michel, Anthony J. (2005). The available means of persuasion: Mapping a theory and pedagogy of multimodal public rhetoric. *JAC, 24*(5), 803–844.

Shipka, Jody. (2005). A multimodal task-based framework for composing. *College Composition and Communication, 57*, 277–306.

Stiegler, Bernard. (1998). *Technics and time: 1. The fault of Epimetheus* (R. Beardsworth & G. Collins, Trans.). Stanford, CA: Stanford University Press.

Stroupe, Craig. (2000). Visualizing English: Recognizing the hybrid literacy of visual and verbal authorship on the web. *College English, 62*, 607–632.

Trimbur, John. (2000). Multiliteracies, social futures, and writing centers. *The Writing Center Journal, 20*(2), 29–32.

Welch, Kathleen. E. (1999). *Electric rhetoric: Classical rhetoric, oralism, and a new literacy.* Cambridge, MA: MIT Press.

Westbrook, Steve. (2006). Visual rhetoric in a culture of fear: Impediments to multimedia production. *College English, 68*, 457–480.

Williams, Sean D. (2001). Part 1: Thinking out of the pro-verbal box. *Computers and Composition, 18*, 21–32.

Yancey, Kathleen Blake. (2004). Made not only in words: Composition in a new key, *College Composition and Communication, 56*(2), 297–328.

Space

1

DESIGNING MULTILITERACY CENTERS

A ZONING APPROACH

James A. Inman

University of Tennessee, Knoxville

Historically, writing centers have reflected many different designs based on the institutional context and pedagogical values of each particular center (Kinkead & Harris, 1993). Due to constraints of time and resources, many centers find it challenging to engage in long-term planning about how to utilize available space. Subscribers to WCENTER regularly see posts requesting advice about center design, often along the lines of "Help! Funding just came through, and I have three weeks to tell the dean everything I would want in a new center." Hurried responses follow: "Be sure to include a 35-foot-long table!" The frantic poster of the original message writes everything down, and her new center ends up being a mess with a 35-foot-long table.

Still, over the years, writing center scholars have developed important ideas about writing center design. (Ahern, 2001; Akinci, 2003; Bishop, 1995; Campbell, 1942; Carino, 2001; Cummins, 2002; Ede, 1996; Elmborg, 2006; Hadfield, 2003; Harris, 2000; Haviland, 2001; Hawkinson, 2003; Lerner, 2003; McKinney, 2005; Miller, 2002; Moore, 1950; Rousculp, 2003; Sisk, 2001; Thaiss, 1993; Welch, 1974). For example, James K. Elmborg (2006) articulated important institutional relationships that should exist between libraries and writing centers, including collaborative physical spaces. Muriel Harris (2000) developed categories of technology uses in writing centers to include instructional, administrative, institutional, and research, and then she developed a shopping list for writing center practitioners seeking to advance these uses in their centers. These compelling articles reflect a wide range of ideas, from how to develop writing centers in global contexts to how to design for students with disabilities. All told, however, one idea largely missing from writing center literature is what methodology should be utilized for designing new writing center spaces. We have accounts of such design activities, but few, if any, attempts to articulate a design approach that may be implemented in diverse writing center contexts around the globe.

The move to multiliteracy centers reflects not just a shift in focus and mission, but also an opportunity to articulate center design strategies. We need an advance plan, to put it simply, for designing effective centers. This way, when opportunities arise, we will be ready. This chapter strives to forward one such plan, a methodology for making design decisions.

ZONING FOR DESIGN

Many centers appear to have been designed around furnishings and technologies, rather than what clients will actually be doing. This approach poses a problem because any center exists to provide effective services for clients, not to have the grandest furnishings and technologies. Although a room full of plush leather couches, 35-foot-long hardwood tables, and flat-screen digital TVs might be impressive visually, the clients at the heart of any center's mission and purpose will find somewhere else to go if the space fails to meet their needs effectively. Moreover, staff members will lack opportunities to learn and grow as one-to-one teachers in environments not designed for effective teaching and learning. Administrators will be left the unenviable task of justifying empty rooms full of those couches, tables, and TVs.

City planners have long thought about effective uses of space, both in large, urban areas and in small towns, and we can learn from their ideas.[1] As a general rule, zoning may be understood as the principal type of public land-use regulation that city planners have utilized. Zoning is implemented mostly on the local level in accordance with state statutes that enable local governments to provide for the general welfare of citizens. The idea is that effective zoning enhances the safety, health, and happiness of citizens. Although some local governments zone property to control the

---

[1] Zoning has previously been introduced in composition studies—for instance, in an article by Buttny (2007) and a book chapter by Olson and Goodnight (2004).

density of the population or construction in a given area, other governments focus on "use zoning," which means that the government divides the area into districts based on permitted uses of the land in each district. Readers can no doubt imagine how, if such zoning is not utilized, placing schools next to, for instance, loud manufacturing centers may inhibit safety, health, and happiness. Multiliteracy centers cannot claim much impact from population or construction density, even in the busiest circumstance, so this chapter focuses on use zoning.

The most popular methodology for use zoning has proven to be "Euclidean zoning," originally and famously applied in Euclid, Ohio. As described by Mary W. Blackford (2006),

> This model of zoning seeks to create uniformity throughout cities and rests on the notion that there is "a place for everything, and everything in its place." By dividing properties into different zones based on land use, cities hope to create an organized society fitting neatly into a comprehensive plan. Euclidean zoning provided stability in property development and a roadmap for urban growth. More importantly, Euclidean zoning changed the direction of property rights; "each zoned lot came with a security—a legal guarantee that neighbors would use their lots consistently with tastes, standards and economic goals set by the control group in the local community." (pp. 1229–1390) (citing Claeys, 2004)

Several critiques of Euclidean zoning have emerged, including its general rigidity and the bureaucracy of its administration, but these critiques apply most significantly to larger communities, rather than smaller local contexts, like multiliteracy centers. In a center with one director and a staff of 20 tutors, for example, bureaucracy would hardly hinder approval and implementation of new ideas. Of course, other factors (e.g., a director's unwillingness to listen to or collaborate with staff members) might inhibit development, but no design methodology could reasonably conquer that sort of roadblock.

To implement use zoning, a local government would determine the property uses that need to be considered. From that point, the government would begin to work with an overall map of the district, meeting with citizens in public forums, consulting with experienced practitioners, and developing a proposal for zoning boundaries. Once a final proposal has been established, the government would host additional public forums, seeking approval for the planned zoning of property. After implementation, any changes, including specific variations, to the zoning plan would also need to be addressed at public forums to secure approval. Although multi-literacy centers do not need to gain approval from such substantial publics, the step-by-step approach to design in consultation with stakeholders provides a roadmap for our design in practice. We should begin with a list of the uses that might occur in our spaces and then work with a blueprint or floorplan of our centers to propose areas associated with each use. Having formulated a plan, we should approach stakeholders at various meetings, seeking support and ideas for revision (see e.g., Selfe, 2005).

Although seeking support may seem daunting at first, readers should remember that considerations of space prove far from new in the arts and humanities, even when zoning has not been the particular subject. Across interests, space proves an important enough concern to warrant dialogue and consensus-building. Computers and writing scholars have frequently theorized online spaces. (Bolter, 1991; Johnson-Eilola, 1997; Joyce, 2000; Sullivan & Porter, 1997; Wysocki, 2003). Moreover, postmodernism writ large includes numerous compelling engagements of spatiality (Baudrillard, 1985; Deleuze, 1993; Foucault, 1984; Spivak, 1999; Zizek, 2005). Finally, literary critics have addressed the spatial dimensions of literary works for some time (Barthes, 1970; Derrida, 1974; Hayles, 1999; Jameson, 1972; Said, 1978). Understanding how valuable colleagues have invested in spatial theory should prove reassuring and enable important connections to be made during the development process.

Based on the principle that some spaces should be exclusive of others, use zoning offers an effective means of utilizing space. As outlined in more detail later, this approach to zoning provides a particularly apt methodology for multiliteracy center design. Whether a center has substantial funding or minimal funding, a zoning methodology for design affords an effective way of making smart decisions.

CENTER DESIGN

Based on the prior methodology, the best approach to multiliteracy center design begins with an evaluation of what clients will actually be doing. The key question is what clients will do in multiliteracy centers, and beginning to understand these possible uses requires an understanding of multiliteracy pedagogy. The New London Group (1996)—10 prominent literacy scholars who first met as a group in New London, Connecticut, to discuss the future of literacy pedagogy—has advanced the term *multiliteracies* in two primary ways:

First, we want to extend the idea and scope of literacy pedagogy to account for the context of our culturally and linguistically diverse and increasingly globalized societies, for the multifarious cultures that interrelate and the plurality of texts that circulate. Second, we argue that literacy pedagogy now must account for the burgeoning variety of text forms associated with information and multimedia technologies. This includes understanding and competent control of representational forms that are becoming increasingly significant in the overall communications environment, such as visual images and their relationship to the written word—for instance, visual design in desktop publishing or the interface of visual and linguistic meaning in multimedia. (p. 2)

Since 1996, when the New London Group's first vision was published, scholarship has demonstrated that the group's two goals effectively merge when applied. For instance, Gail Hawisher and Cynthia Selfe's (2000) *Global Literacies and the World Wide Web* presents a series of collaborative global communicative ventures that required sophisticated multiliteracies as applied through Internet technologies. These scholarly perspectives begin to suggest a number of potential uses for multiliteracy centers, including print composing and publishing, oral composing and presentation, audio composing and publishing, video composing and publishing, and webtextual composing and publishing, as well as various forms of reading/listening/interacting with texts.[2]

With the move from writing centers to multiliteracy centers, a hallmark will be the continued development of one-to-one pedagogy as to the various multiliteracy practices that will be evident. Two well-known writing center scholars, John Trimbur (2000) and Michael Pemberton (2003), have accurately foreseen this move. In particular, Trimbur (2000) has noted,

To my mind, the new digital literacies will increasingly be incorporated into writing centers not just as sources of information or delivery systems for tutoring but as productive arts in their own right, and writing center work will, if anything, become more rhetorical in paying attention to the practices and effects of design in written and visual communication—more product oriented and perhaps less like the composing conferences of the process movement. (p. 30)

---

[2] A *webtext* is a project designed specifically for publication on the World Wide Web. This term has been popularized by *Kairos: A Journal of Rhetoric, Technology, and Pedagogy*, which Douglas Eyman and Cheryl Ball edit. See http://kairos.technorhetoric.net for numerous examples of webtexts.

Smartly continuing the conversation, Pemberton (2003) endorsed Trimbur's view: "Trimbur's imagined future may be approaching us more swiftly than we realize, now that the Internet and the World Wide Web have become such pervasive features of our culture and our students' academic lives" (p. 10). In the second half of his article, Pemberton (2003) continued by developing a detailed consideration of how hypertext technologies, in particular, may require different one-to-one teaching and learning practices in centers. Chapters in this collection further reflect the effective teaching and learning practices that will be central to multiliteracy centers in the future.

Following these perspectives, and the definitions of multiliteracies noted earlier, we can work generally with the following uses to zone in multiliteracy centers: one-to-one teaching of print composing and publishing, oral composing and presentation, audio composing and publishing, video composing and publishing, webtextual composing and publishing, and reading/listening/interacting with texts. Each multiliteracy center would need to adapt this list to conform to its own mission and purpose, but the list offers a sense of the uses most often envisioned for multiliteracy centers.

DEDICATED VERSUS FLEXIBLE SPACES

In multiliteracy centers, some uses should have distinct, dedicated spaces. Although the freewheeling, idealist view of multiliteracy centers might be that everything will be open, fluid, and flexible, that view simply does not work in practice. Consider audio composing and publishing, which realistically requires a soundproofed area.[3] Students in any number of disciplines may wish to compose voiceovers, for instance, to accompany PowerPoint presentation materials or self-guided tutorials. How could these students possibly develop a quality voiceover recording if they must work in an area where lots of background noise would be evident? Nothing would sound tackier than a voiceover with someone eating potato chips in the background: "When calculating the length [Crunch!] of a right triangle's hypotenuse, remember to [Crunch!] square the lengths of the two [Crunch!] sides and then [Crunch!] take the square root of the result." Such a recording might make an excellent audio track for a potato chip commercial, but it would hardly be an effective presentation of the intended material.

---

[3]For more on this sort of composing, see webtexts from Rezak (2005) and Wilson (2002).

With the methodology suggested by this chapter, we have to decide which of our uses specifically require distinct, dedicated spaces while reviewing the blueprint or floorplan of the proposed center. As noted, audio composing and publishing qualifies because it requires a silent, perhaps even soundproofed, environment. Similarly, video composing and publishing also requires a dedicated environment.[4] Although these two uses might be able to share an area, the multiliteracy center design team will have to decide how much of each will realistically be done in the center because, if a good bit is imagined, then different spaces may be more likely in order. With live video composing, for instance, you have to think about lighting and shadows, much like a TV studio would, and that requires purchase and installation of the requisite lighting technology. At Furman University, where I helped to design and served as founding director of the Center for Collaborative Learning and Communication (CCLC), we had a dedicated studio sufficient for this sort of video recording, and the student TV station actually made use of the studio for some of its special features.[5] Also, we were able to prepare instructional videos to supplement the overall mission of the center, including website design tutorials (see "Part V: Production," later in this volume). One secondary school group, which attended a 2-week seminar at Furman in the summers, created a sophisticated digital yearbook complete with video segments of the participants. These sorts of applications simply would not have been possible without a dedicated space.

An important consideration should be the relationship of spaces in the center design. Zoning as a practice was created to control relationships among various properties in a community, so we should understand that one of the best applications of zoning to center design will be how we can structure relationships. Consider a seemingly simple design addition, such as a dedicated space for printing, burning, or other production challenges. One might assume that such a space could reasonably be placed anywhere, because printers and burners do not make a lot of noise, and any dedicated multimedia development spaces would have the requisite soundproofing to made proximity acceptable. However, when one thinks further about printing and burning and understands those practices as part of a composing process, the consideration becomes more complicated. For example, if printing and burning end up being considered as the end of any compos-

---

[4]For more on this sort of composing, see articles by Miller (2007), Whithaus (2006), Grigar (2005), and Hickey (2002).

[5]To learn more about the design of the CCLC, readers may wish to consult "At First Site: Lessons Learned from Furman University's Center for Collaborative Learning and Communication," published in 2001 in *Academic Writing: Interdisciplinary Perspectives on Communication Across the Curriculum*.

ing process, good sense indicates creating a space for those activities near
the exit of the center being designed. That way, once clients print or burn
their final product, they will not need to traffic back through the center and
potentially disrupt other clients involved in other activities. However, if a
center design conceives of printing and burning as an earlier part of the
composing process (e.g., if students print drafts before beginning to revise
and edit), then a more central location might be preferable, enabling maximum access to the printing and burning technologies.

As Elmborg (2006) and other scholars have argued, any consideration
of spatial relationships inside a center should also be mindful of relationships that exist and may be forged outside of a center. This consideration
should be particularly important for centers with limited budgets because
partnerships with other campus entities may create exciting opportunities.
For a center located right next to the most high-volume printing center on
campus, the issue described in the previous paragraph sees additional lay-
ers because the printing center's presence may be incorporated into the
design, encouraging students to take advantage of a partner resource that
has already achieved success on campus. More to Elmborg's (2006) particular emphasis, a center designer should consider the instructional
resources available proximate to the center. For instance, if a center will be
located within a campus library, then research experts and potentially
information technology and media experts already reside right next door.
Opening conversations and building collaborative bridges with these talent-
ed neighbors may lead to enhanced services in the center. Moreover, the
library staff involved may benefit from the center designer's knowledge
and expertise with writing, rhetoric, and design. In pursuing opportunities,
center designers should strive to be respectful of the knowledge and experience of faculty, staff, and students with whom they come into contact
because that respectfulness will engender greater willingness to collaborate
and consider future possibilities.

DESIGNING WITHIN THE SPACES

When working with a blueprint or floorplan and designing within the individual spaces of a multiliteracy center, remember again to emphasize the
uses of those spaces, a lesson zoning has reflected since its inception. Too
many times, designers work from a furniture catalog or technology catalog,
find items they like, and then imagine how those items can fit into the center being constructed, but that methodology is absolutely backward.

Within zoned spaces, center designers should remember that much work remains to do. Specifically, setting up productive workstations designed specifically for the intended uses is a large task, often involving a careful consideration of the pedagogical mission of the center. As a simple example, consider whether single-user computer workstations provide one-to-one teaching and learning opportunities or instead turn the center into a standard campus computer lab, effectively devoid of the use-based foundation designed into other spaces in the center. A center designer might set up every computer workstation to seat two individuals side by side, enabling a consultant and a client to work alongside each other on various projects. The downside of such a design would be its awkwardness for single computer users, unless designed effectively for use in consulting and single-use applications.

In zoned spaces, center designers should also remember to dedicate attention to the electronics and data infrastructure. No doubt any designer would assure that electric and data connections will be available in the center; but once the wiring begins to proceed in the ceiling, floor, and walls, the careful consideration has only begun. Construction contractors value completing their jobs on time, which means they appreciate simplicity; along those lines, contractors may suggest simply dropping a standard electricity and data outlet package into every space in the center. Unfortunately, such a standard package neglects to consider the specific uses associated with each of the zoned spaces. Today, students make extensive use of laptops, which means providing extra electric outlets, as well as multiple ways to access the campus network for data connections. In any zoned space, the needs will be different. In a multimedia composing space, center designers should consider all the potential peripherals, such as video cameras, mobile lighting, and mobile sound recording. Moreover, designers should consider the need for particular flexibility because any client filming a segment for digital presentation may need to set up a unique background, affix particular lighting, and establish particular sound recording. Such projects often involve a team atmosphere, where each member of the team will want to have space and infrastructure to enable her or him to participate fully in the project being developed.

A final, but vital, consideration should be the accessibility of any zoned space for individuals with disabilities. In this pursuit, the idea is not just to make spaces minimally accessible, but instead to consider how the disabled may be able to most fully participate in the uses for which the spaces were designed. Drawing up the plans for any center, a professional architect will advise center designers how to comply with the Rehabilitation Act of 1973 and Americans with Disabilities Act of 1990 as interpreted by the courts.

However, an architect simply will not possess the expertise in center pedagogy and application that the designers will, so designer input will be vital. An architect will know how to provide for wheelchairs to enter any zoned space, for instance, and turn around effectively, but an architect will have no idea what sorts of spatial considerations go into effective one-to-one teaching and learning. For assistance, designers may turn to important scholarship published on disability, literacy, and composition studies (Barber-Fendley, 2004; Brueggemann, 2006; Carmichael, 2006; Hamel, 2002; Hewett, 2000; Holly, 2001; Mullin, 2002; Neff, 2001; Slatin, 2006; White, 2002). Moreover, designers should consult with their campus disability services office, asking how to design the best possible environments for client success.

With these special issues addressed, the center designer should be ready to present an initial vision to her or his stakeholders, initiating an important conversation leading to approval or suggestions for revision. Most important, this vision will reflect the uses appropriate for the proposed center, as well as how those uses prove best enacted in the space available. Through the zoning methodology, this vision will further have considered the relationship of dedicated sections of the center to other sections, creating an important holistic design for success.

CONCLUSION

Zoning teaches us that a specific methodology may be utilized for designing center spaces:

- Make a list of important uses of your center;
- Review a blueprint or floorplan of your center, and make decisions about what uses should be supported where;
- Present your plan to stakeholders, soliciting support and ideas for revision;
- Once a final plan has been approved, implement it consistently; and
- Keep an eye out for necessary revisions to the plan, which should also be approved by stakeholders.

Although individual centers will necessarily need to adapt this methodology, it offers a common plan that centers can utilize across geographic and technological boundaries. A zoning methodology should be successful even in centers with fundamentally different views of teaching and learning.

REFERENCES

Ahern, J. S. (2001). *The pedagogy of help at three literacy support sites: Expanding notions of literacy.* Unpublished doctoral dissertation, Florida State University.

Akinci, D. (2003). The birth and the first steps of our writing center at METU, Turkey. *Dangling Modifier, 9.*

Barber-Fendley, K. (2004). A new visibility: An argument for alternative assistance writing programs for students with learning disabilities. *College Composition and Communication, 55*(3), 504–535.

Barthes, R. (1970). *S/Z* (R. Miller, Trans.). New York: Hill.

Baudrillard, J. (1985). *Simulacra and simulation* (S. F. Graser, Trans.). Ann Arbor: University of Michigan Press.

Bishop, W. (1995). Reflections on the sites we call centers. *Focuses: A Journal Linking Composition Programs and Writing Center Practice, 8*(2), 89–99.

Blackford, M. W. (2006). Putting the public's trust back in zoning: How the implementation of the public trust doctrine will benefit land use regulation. *Houston Law Review, 43*, 1211–1240.

Bolter, J. D. (1991). *Writing space: The computer, hypertext, and the history of writing.* Mahwah, NJ: Erlbaum.

Brueggemann, B. J. (2006). Becoming visible: Lessons in disability. In P. Vandenberg, S. Hum, & J. Clary-Lemon (Eds.), *Relations, locations, positions: Composition theory for writing teachers* (pp. 500–34). Urbana, IL: National Council of Teachers of English.

Buttny, R. (2007). Drawing on the words of others at public hearings: Zoning, Wal-Mart, and the threat to the aquifer. *Language in Society, 36*(5), 735– 756.

Campbell, E. M. (1942). The evolution of a writing laboratory. *College English, 3*(4), 399–403.

Carino, P. (2001). Early writing centers: Toward a history. In R. W. Barnett & J. S. Blumner (Eds.), *The Allyn and Bacon guide to writing center theory and practice* (pp. 10–21). Boston, MA: Allyn & Bacon.

Carmichael, S. (2006). The advantages of using electronic processes for commenting on and exchanging the written work of students with learning disabilities and/or AD/HD. *Composition Studies, 34*(2), 43–57.

Claeys, E. R. (1994). Euclid lives? The uneasy legacy of progressivism in zoning. *Fordham Law Review, 73*, 731-801.

Cummins, G. (2002). Standing in the places where we are: What to think about when starting college and university writing centers. In B. B. Silk (Ed.), *The writing center resource manual* (pp. II6.1–II6.7). Emmitsburg, MD: International Writing Centers Association.

Deleuze, Gilles. (1993). *The fold: Leibniz and the baroque* (T. Conley, Trans.). Minneapolis: University of Minnesota Press.

Derrida, J. (1974). *Of grammatology* (G. C. Spivak, Trans.). Baltimore, MD: Johns Hopkins University Press.

Ede, L. (1996). Writing centers and the politics of location: A response to Terrance Riley and Stephen M. North. *Writing Center Journal, 16*(2), 111–130.

Elmborg, J. K. (2006). Locating the center: Libraries, writing centers, and information literacy. *Writing Lab Newsletter, 30*(6), 7–11.

Foucault, M. (1984). Questions on geography. In C. Gordon (Ed.), *Power/knowledge: Selected interviews and other writings 1972–1977* (pp. 63–77). New York: Pantheon.

Grigar, D. (2005). Kineticism, rhetoric, and new media artists. *Computers and Composition, 22*(1), 105–112.

Hadfield, L. (2003). An ideal writing center: Re-imagining space and design. In M. A. Pemberton & J. Kinkead (Eds.), *The center will hold: Critical perspectives on writing center scholarship* (pp. 166–176). Logan: Utah State University Press.

Hamel, C. M. (2002). Learning disabilities in the writing center: Challenging our perspectives? *Writing Lab Newsletter, 26*(8), 1–5.

Harris, M. (2000). Making up tomorrow's agenda and shopping lists today: Preparing for future technologies in writing centers. In J. A. Inman & D. N. Sewell (Eds.), *Taking flight with OWLs: Examining electronic writing center work* (pp. 193–202). Mahwah, NJ: Erlbaum.

Haviland, C. P. (2001). The politics of administrative and physical location. In J. Nelson & K. Evertz (Eds.), *The politics of writing centers* (pp. 85–98). Portsmouth, NH: Boynton/Cook.

Hawisher, G. E., & Selfe, C. L. (Eds.). (2000). *Global literacies and the world wide web.* London: Routledge.

Hawkinson, I. (2003). Wheelchair. *Writing Lab Newsletter, 27*(7), 11.

Hayles, N. K. (1999). *How we became posthuman: Virtual bodies in cybernetics, literature, and informatics.* Chicago: University of Chicago Press.

Hewett, B. L. (2000). Helping students with learning disabilities: Collaboration between writing centers and special services. *Writing Lab Newsletter, 25*(3), 1–5.

Hickey, D. (2002). It's a wrap: Digital video and tutor training. *Writing Lab Newsletter, 26*(6), 13–16.

Holly, J. (2001). Listening more carefully: Working with a person with perception impairment. *Writing Lab Newsletter, 25*(10), 9–11.

Inman, J. A. (2001). At first site: Lessons from Furman University's Center for Collaborative Learning and Communication. *Academic.Writing: Interdisciplinary Perspectives on Communication Across the Curriculum, 2.* Available at http://wac.colostate.edu/aw/articles/inman2001.

Jameson, F. (1972). *Marxism and form: Twentieth-century dialectical theories of literature.* Princeton, NJ: Princeton University Press.

Johnson-Eilola, J. (1997). *Nostalgic angels: Rearticulating hypertext writing.* Norwood, NJ: Ablex.

Joyce, M. (2000). *Othermindedness: The emergence of network culture.* Ann Arbor: University of Michigan Press.

Kinkead, J., & Harris, J. (Eds.). (1993). *Writing centers in context: Twelve case studies.* Urbana, IL: National Council of Teachers of English.

Lerner, N. (2003). Writing laboratories circa 1953. *Writing Lab Newsletter, 27*(6), 1–5.

McKinney, J. G. (2005). Leaving home sweet home: Towards critical readings of writing center spaces. *Writing Center Journal, 25*(2), 6–20.

Miller, A. (2002). Culture and composition: Starting a writing center in East Africa. *Writing Lab Newsletter, 27*(4), 6–8.

Miller, S. M. (2007). English teacher learning for new times: Digital video composing as multimodal literacy practice. *English Education, 40*(1), 61–83.

Moore, R. H. (1950). The writing clinic and the writing laboratory. *College English, 11*(7), 388–393.

Mullin, A. E. (2002). Serving clients with learning disabilities. In B. B. Silk (Ed.), *The writing center resource manual* (pp. IV1.1–IV1.8). Emmitsburg, MD: IWCA Press.

Neff, J. (2001). Learning disabilities and the writing center. In R. W. Barnett & J. S. Blumner (Eds.), *The Allyn and Bacon guide to writing center theory and practice* (pp. 376–390). Boston, MA: Allyn & Bacon.

New London Group. (1996). A pedagogy of multiliteracies: Designing social futures. *Harvard Educational Review, 66*(1), 1–30.

Olson, K. M., & Goodnight, G. T. (2004). Ingenium—speaking in community: The case of the Prince William County zoning hearings on Disney's America. In P. A. Sullivan & S. R. Goldzwig (Eds.), *New approaches to rhetoric* (pp. 31–59). Thousand Oaks, CA: Sage.

Pemberton, M. A. (2003). Planning for hypertexts in the writing center . . . or not. *Writing Center Journal, 24*(1), 9–24.

Rezak, T. A. (2005). Deleting teachers' fears: Audio/visual ICTs and the classroom. *Kairos: A Journal of Rhetoric, Technology, and Pedagogy, 9*(2). Available at http://english.ttu.edu/kairos/9.2/binder.html?praxis/deleting_fears.

Rousculp, T. (2003). Into the community we go: Establishing the SLCC Community Writing Center. *Writing Lab Newsletter, 27*(6), 11–13.

Said, E. (1978). *Orientalism.* London: Routledge.

Selfe, R. J. (2005). *Sustainable computer environments: Cultures of support in English studies and language arts.* Cresskill, NJ: Hampton Press.

Sisk, K. (2001). Assisting the visually impaired in the writing center. *Writing Lab Newsletter, 25*(7), 6–9.

Slatin, J. M. (2006). Becoming an accessibility researcher: A memoir. In J. A. Inman & B. L. Hewett (Eds.), *Technology and English studies: Innovative professional paths* (pp. 143–162). Mahwah, NJ: Erlbaum.

Spivak, G. C. (1999). *A critique of postcolonial reason: Towards a history of the vanishing present.* Cambridge, MA: Harvard University Press.

Sullivan, P., & Porter, J. (1997). *Opening spaces: Writing technologies and critical research practices.* Norwood, NJ: Ablex.

Thaiss, C. (1993). Of havens, nodes, and no-center centers. *Focuses: A Journal Linking Composition Programs and Writing Center Practice, 6*(1), 16–26.

Trimbur, J. (2000). Multiliteracies, social futures, and writing centers. *Writing Center Journal, 20*(2), 29–32.

Welch, G. W. (1974). Organizing a reading and writing lab in which students teach. *College Composition and Communication, 25*(5), 437–439.

White, L. F. (2002). Learning disability, pedagogies, and public discourse. *College Composition and Communication, 53*(4), 705–738.

Whithaus, C. (2006). Contact and interactivity: Social constructionist pedagogy in a video-based, management writing course. *Technical Communication Quarterly, 15*(4), 431–456.

Wilson, J. (2002). Perception is all: Using audio files to reach across the divide. *Kairos: A Journal of Rhetoric, Technology, and Pedagogy, 7*(3). Available at http://english.ttu.edu/kairos/7.3/binder2.html?coverweb/wilson.

Wysocki, A. F. (2003). The multiple media of texts: How onscreen and paper texts incorporate words, images, and other media. In C. Bazerman & P. Prior (Eds.), *What writing does and how it does it: An introduction to analysis of text and textual practices* (pp. 123–163). Mahwah, NJ: Erlbaum.

Zizek, S. (2005). *Interrogating the real.* New York: Continuum.

2

COMPOSING MULTIPLE SPACES

CLEMSON'S CLASS OF '41 ONLINE STUDIO

Morgan Gresham

*University of South Florida
St. Petersburg*

Let me begin by saying that there is a host of scholarship on defining and building Online Writing Labs— ranging back to the early peer tutor encounters on VAX machines that I encountered as an undergraduate in the late 1980s—that has provided a backdrop up against which I tell my story of the Online Studio at Clemson. *Writing Centers in Context* (1993) provides an important view into some of the working spaces that informed the physical and, thus, the Online Studio. Although I am a compositionist, I often view things as a technorhetorician, looking at previous incarnations of writing centers from a progressive standpoint, asking the question "What's next?" In his article "Carnal Conferencing," Janangelo (2000) argues that although "[i]t is a bit late to invent the writing conference or the personal computer" in response to the call to be there "at the genesis of each new technology" (Winner, cited in Janangelo, 2000), it is not too late for us to rearticulate, and re*media*te the technologies involved. Janangelo argues that "human beings can exert a powerful influence on technology either by using it against its primary purposes . . . or by exploiting an alternative power base." That is, we use "new technology to achieve an old end . . . or an older technology . . . to realize a new goal" (p. 101). Ultimately, this is our struggle: to capture the things we do well and move them forward while searching for the new.

Clemson University's Pearce Center for Professional Communication was created in 1989 as a faculty-to-faculty outreach program intended to strengthen undergraduates' communication skills by integrating writing and, as the program evolved, communication across the curriculum. Fostered by strong leadership from Art Young and Carl Lovitt, the Pearce Center was a key component in *TIME* magazine's decision to name Clemson University "Public College of the Year" in 2000: Clemson was spotlighted as "on the cutting edge of the communication-across-the-curriculum movement, in which faculty integrate not only writing, but also oral, visual and electronic communication in all disciplines" (http://www.clemson.edu/clemsonworld/Fall2000/TIME.htm). Kathleen Yancey, then director of the Pearce Center, describes the "What's next?" conversations:

> This [TIME] recognition seemed to signal that we should at least maintain what we had created . . . during the summer of 2000 a new dean joined us, and she too wanted to know what was next for the Pearce Center. Our answer: a new center for communicative arts, a place where students could work individually and collectively on various, often-related, communicative tasks, a space that would become known as the Class of '41 Studio for Student Communication.
>
> This center, now also called the Pearce Studio, is like the "studio" model of composition (Grego) and unlike it, and also like a Writing Center and unlike it. (cited in Gresham & Yancey, 2004, p. 10)

The Class of '41 donated 1 million to develop the Studio, and when I joined the faculty at Clemson in 2002, the process of designing the Studio was underway.[1] Once the physical Studio opened in January 2004, I was tasked by Yancey to develop an Online Studio to accompany the physical Class of '41 Studio for Student Communication. The Pearce Studios grew and developed alongside an existing Writing Center at Clemson. In many aspects, these multiple spaces shared common conceptions and theoretical underpinning. However, we found it important to maintain the distinct missions of the different spaces, and this goal led to several keywords that ultimately drove my design of the Online Studio: *metaphor, play, space, conversation, connect,* and *evolve*. Some are nouns—the things we create—and some are verbs—the actions that create—and some are both—the praxis of creation. What follows, then, is a discussion of how each of these ideas plays out across the virtual, and still unfinished, landscape that would be the Class of '41 Online Studio.[2]

---

[1] Designing the Studio was a wide-ranging team effort. Accounts of the process of designing the physical and curricular visions of the Studio are found in Gresham and Yancey (2004) and Billings et al. (2005). Also, Hart (2007) provides another account.

[2] Yancey left Clemson in 2005; I left Clemson in 2006. At the time of my departure, three functioning prototypes of the Online Studio existed.

In his 2001 book *Experience Design,* Nathan Shedroff provides us with a number of "takeaway" moments, bits and pieces that we are asked to compose into our own experience. Each path is different, and we each take what we need to create understanding and help us visualize design.

In this chapter, I try to recount both the creation itself and the process of the creation. In some ways, it too is a build-it-yourself experience. I narrate, as best I can, the intent and process of the conceptualization and building of the Online Studio iterations while I recognize that at the moment of this writing, some 2 years later, only fragmentary bits and pieces of the Online Studio still exist. As with so many technological experiments, the experiences are ephemeral, existing in a certain space only for as long as the creators and participants are involved. However ephemeral, the process of designing and developing the Online Studio can provide valuable insight for those who find themselves at the beginning of the path.

In recognition of such, I want to highlight the path with breadcrumbs of meaning that our experiences at Clemson reveal. Although negotiating the technologies that house our multimodal approaches to composition can seem daunting, what I take away from my experiences at Clemson is the importance of informed trial and error. As we developed both the physical and online studios, we were attuned to the potential flexibility of the space. Even before the space was realized, we agreed on the multimodality of composition. At Clemson, students were being asked to create powerpoints and videos, embedded charts and graphs, and poetry, much of it visual, across the curriculum. We recognized that our spaces had to reflect the many facets that are composing, and we had to be willing to try out tools, perhaps not as they were intended to be used, so that we could compose and respond to the new kinds of compositions being created.

Every tool is a weapon—if you hold it right.

—Ani Difranco

METAPHOR:
AN OWL IS AN OWL IS NOT AN OWL

For compositionists, metaphor lies at the heart of our work. The conceptual work that we do—creating identities, creating meaning, and creating text—is so unlike everything else that we find it is exactly like everything else: We talk about the process of writing (giving birth, building, creating, digging), the place of writing (at the center, at the margins), the space of writing (online, offline), and the products of writing (softcopy, hardcopy). We construct, we represent, and we compose. We name, we name, and we name.[3] Kastman-Breuch (2004) examines the nature of metaphor in "The Idea(s) of an Online Writing Center," and on the Friends of the Writing Center blog offers helpful tips for exploring and explaining our online writing center metaphors. Because have, by choice and by chance, selected a representative animal, an OWL, for our online writing laboratories, in this chapter, the metaphors I want to name focus on evolution. From early on, when we identify our new pet OWL, we connect it to its evolutionary practices; for it, we highlight the importance of change. In the following fragmentary pieces of quotations, we see this linkage that as writing centers have migrated online, the metaphor evolves—progress, change, evolution, and stasis: "Be *ready to change* what you may consider your final product. After all, there is no final product on the Internet, and web authors must learn that they can neither resist nor control the dynamics of web page" (Langston, 1996; italics added); "In this *rapidly changing sphere of progress*, many challenges exist for writing center thinkers" (Inman & Sewell, 2000; italics added); "The climate in which we work is *complex and ever-changing*" (Jordan-Henley & Maid, 2000; italics added). Lasarenko (1996) most completely creates this perspective in "PR(OWL)ING AROUND: An OWL by Any Other Name" as she names the "critter" and explores its evolutionary processes:

> As in the natural world, *cyberOWLs come in a variety of species*, from completely online, full-service writing centers to those that serve to announce their existence. Rising early enough one day to hunt OWLs, I went searching through the dark, wooded forests of the cyber-jungle and identified the names of some 93 self-styled OWLs! I was astounded by the numbers, amazed that there should be so many of these new "critters," stunned that such a relatively new concept had prolif-

---

[3]See Fisher and Harris (2001) for an insightful discussion of mixed metaphors.

erated so rapidly. Indeed, at the current reproductive rate, traditional writing centers are well on their way to becoming an endangered species.

Such a phenomenon certainly invited greater investigation, and in a truly antiquated, nineteenth-century spirit, I endeavored to gain fame and acclaim as the first cyber OWL taxonomist and un-naturalist. At the bottom rung of the OWL *evolutionary ladder* lie those OWLs that serve as advertisements for a university's already established traditional writing center, listing hours, services offered, and location. I shall leave it to the paleo-cybergeneticists of the future to investigate more thoroughly the complexities of these ancient beginnings. On the next rung of the evolutionary ladder lie those OWLs that offer on-site tutoring services, with specific writing tips, style guides, and other helpful writing instructions online with links to other OWLs and information. At the top of the current evolutionary scale, lie those OWLs that offer a complete set of online services, including online manuscript submission and feedback. I offer the following alphabetic taxonomy and description in an attempt to create some order among the welter and confusion that the current term "OWL" entails. (italics added)

Like most mutations, OWLs have been sites of struggle that accompany the process of evolution as OWL designers Langston, Jordan-Henley and Maid, and Inman and Sewell describe. Yet it is no longer a question of whether writing centers will evolve; rather, the question is *how*—how will they operate and how should we design them? Even as early as 2000, when Trimbur argued that "writing centers will more and more define themselves as multiliteracy centers" (p. 30), a path was set. We now widely accept that students who come to writing centers are not merely writing; rather, they are struggling with multiliteracies, composing in multiple forms, moving from speech to page to PowerPoint to web. They are *remediating*. We who conceptionalize/compose/create writing centers are gradually coming to terms with this multimodality. As the editors of this collection suggest, the time is right for a sustained look at how writing centers should evolve to meet the changing needs of the students we seek to serve. In this chapter, I am going to foreground not the actuality of those changes, although I do discuss in some detail both the physical and virtual spaces we created, but rather the connective processes of creating. Playing in Lasarenkos's metaphor, were I a taxidermist or better yet an anatomist, the cartilage—that which is flexible and connective—is most distinctive.

THE STUDIO

Clemson is a technology-rich campus. When I arrived in 2002, a laptop initiative requiring incoming first-year students to have computers was already significantly changing the kinds of composing students were doing in their classes. Then, in January 2004, Clemson University opened the Class of '41 Studio for Student Communication (see Fig. 2.1). A resource for undergraduate composers, this space—more, a collection of spaces—houses both the Pearce Center for Professional Communication and the Communication Across the Curriculum (CAC) programs while offering students and faculty a shared space for multimodal compositions. As Gresham and Yancey (2004) explained in "New Studio Composition: New Sites for Writing, New Forms of Composition, New Cultures of Learning," Clemson's Class of '41 Studio has a physical presence that invites collaboration and multimodal invention and delivery. It is a 4,000-square-foot space that offers a Class of '41 retrospective, two "studio" spaces for interactive work among teams ranging from 2 to 15, two cloistered areas for multimedia production and editing, and a well-equipped conference room. There are

Figure 2.1 Class of '41 Studio Schematic

Studio Schematic Design

The Class of 1941 Studio for Student Communication is slowly but surely becoming a reality. As you can see from the design schematic below, Pazdan Smith, our architects, are helping us create a terrific set of spaces where students can work on projects ranging from speeches to webpages to lab reports. In January 2003, we will begin hosting a series of sessions to showcase our new Studio, scheduled to open in January 2004.

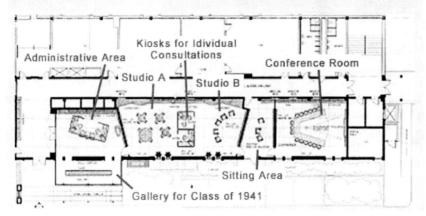

multiple tack boards, white boards, and "SMART" boards throughout the spaces to facilitate interactive conversation and composition. This space is dedicated to the development of communication activities of all kinds across disciplines on the Clemson University campus.

Working with Bolter's concept of remediation—shifting a work from genre to genre, Yancey prepared undergraduate and graduate students to work in the Studio with a course that asked Studio Associates[4] to create text, PowerPoints, posters, and portfolios. The physical space, heralded as "first-in-the-nation kind of center for the teaching and learning of *all* the communicative arts" (Yancey, 2000), provides students with a work environment with skilled advisors in house to provide feedback on works, including digital portfolios, speeches, presentations, and capstone projects. Indeed, before the Studio design process was complete, Kathi asked the members of the Pearce team to imagine, in writing, what a day in the Studio might look like; a segment of her iteration appears in "New Studio Composition." The Studio is designed to be flexible: to house small and large groups, independent writers, and host poetry jams; it has whiteboards for conceptualizing; and it has technologies and tackboards for revising and showcasing. In short, it is a composing space.

SPACE

Since the "invention" of composition in the late 20th century, we have thought of composition studies and the teaching of writing through the metaphor of space. Both intuitively and intentionally, we know that spaces shape what happens in a student text as well as in the composition classroom. We know, for instance, that how (well) writers create a space of the page, and a presence on it, affects their ability to make meaning. Likewise, within the classroom—typically a classroom box, one that often offers only immobile desks—we do our best to *reshape* the given space, moving students to the front of the room, encouraging discussion through the movement of chairs, and helping students through the clustering of desks to become members of a writing team. Now, well into the first decade of the 21st century, as we move into electronic teaching and learning, we recognize that, again, space is the metaphor that bridges the material classroom and virtual learning.

---

[4]Drawn from varying disciplines, Studio Associates are specially trained undergraduate and graduate students who work in the Studio in capacities ranging from technology expert to tutor to sounding board.

Ironically, as important as space is as a trope for writing, we are just beginning to see how we might reconceive this metaphor to make all of our spaces—inside school, outside school, and online—more interactive and more in touch with the multimodal composition that we now find ourselves teaching. Clemson's new physical studio—with its architectures of spaces—and its accompanying online studio offer a reconceptualized teaching space writ plural that allows us to think about the next generation of writing spaces differently. If what we are really about is language engagement, we can use this multiplicity of spaces to foster that language interplay.

The questions as to how to do this are many. What are the key spaces? We think of material, curricular, and virtual spaces as spaces that in the aggregate *create* spaces—spaces for intellectual curiosity, spaces for conversation, and spaces for research—and without pigeonholing students and teachers into reductive roles. Too often writing classrooms, one way or another, are about remediation in the worst sense of the word—you should already know how to do format citations, but because you do not know MLA, here is a worksheet for you. The spaces we are envisioning—and those of the Studio that we are constantly creating—move beyond that to re*media*tion, where students are applauded for what they already know and are supplied the rhetorical tools to move to the next stage of the production. Implicit as well in this conception of writing/space is the idea of circulation of texts among these contexts. How, finally, do we identify these spaces? What is their inter-relationship? How do we organize a curriculum to use them and yet not be bound by them? Perhaps most intriguing: What about language spaces? Those spaces between the speaker and the audience? The word that is said and the yet unsaid word? The space between knowledge and language, if there is one? How have we addressed these spaces in our multiple curricula? Are these spaces too tenuous?

ONLINE STUDIO

When it came time to develop the digital Studio, we thought, the online version of the Class of '41 studio required the same dedication to dynamic remediation and multiliteracies as the physical space. In a later white paper, with input from my Pearce colleagues, I began envisioning the scope of the online studio:

> Jay Bolter describes the ways in which our culture encourages us to revisit and rethink our artifacts in different media as *remediation*—not in its usual sense of being remedial, but rather in the sense of

something old made new again. While we have been blessed with a new physical space what has been more important for us is the ways in which the *idea* of the space and its remediation have offered us space to reconsider and remediate our existing mission. We now have two new spaces—the new physical studio and its online counterpart—that provide us potential to fulfill and enhance the mission of the Pearce Center as it was first conceived. Now, besides working with faculty, the Studio provides a work environment for students as well. And when the online studio matures, we will have a space that simplifies outreach services to K–12 schools and working with the corporate world by limiting the physical space that now separates us. (Gresham, 2004)

Initially, we believed that the Online Studio would be incrementally developed in these three stages:

Stage 1: Electronic Cabinet

- This is a collection of HTML documents (with some PDF counterparts) that are collected, sorted, and displayed electronically. It is to be collected in part by Pearce Team members and added to by students in the initial Studio course.

Stage 2: Asynchronous Communications

- This stage represents the initial foray into two-way communication by offering limited e-mail, e-mail list, and bulletin board capabilities.

Stage 3: Synchronous Communications and Assistance

- In this functionality, we will be able to host synchronous chats with one or more clients. We will be able to provide online feedback on digital media as well as interactive collaborative writing (e.g., Hydra).

> **Technoprovocateurs**
>
> People who, whether loudly and publicly or quietly and subtly, are using technology to get outta the box, so to speak, to do old things new ways or, perhaps, more important, to do new things (in either case disrupting, in the process, the conventional assumptions and ways of doing things).
>
> —Crump

(Gresham, 2004)

Working in these stages helped us plan to modify the design as the physical Studio opened and developed. As The New London Group (1996) argues in "A Pedagogy of Multiliteracies: Designing Social Futures," "when technologies of meaning are changing so rapidly, there cannot be one set of standards or skills that constitute the ends of literacy learning, however taught" (p. 64). We recognized that as students used the physical spaces for production and composition, they would change the processes and products with which they worked, and we expected the usage of the Online Studio to mimic this multiliterate interaction. Just as students were using the physical tack boards in their process of designing technical reports and using the SMART boards to capture drawings embedded in poetry, we believed students would similarly compose animated documents that contained sound and visuals. The Online Studio must provide both the composition space and the space for feedback on that composition.

As The New London Group contends, literacies take place in a range of interactive sites, and students need to be able to move across boundaries to communicate effectively. In attempting to identify the virtual spaces that most closely represent the physical Studio, we concluded that development of the online studio should take place on multiple fronts with various designs.

GO PLAY

> There's usually more than one way to get anywhere.
>
> —Shedroff (2001, p. 84)

What does it take to build an Online Studio?

1. A commitment to conversation;
2. An acceptance of text outside the alphabetic norm;
3. An acceptance of multiple digital tools—no one thing is going to work for all situations;
4. A recognition that the first plan may not always work;
5. An understanding that these things can be cobbled together on a shoestring if folks are willing to put in the time and energy to find the free tools and see what connects them;

6. An acceptance that the studio will always need to be rebuilt. There is little permanence to the digital. What did work does not now, and there is a nifty new tool on the horizon;

7. Composing is a social experience and should take place in a social environment; and

8. We do not know what the next documents will look like, how they will be performed, and how we will be able to provide feedback. What we do know is that there will always be new texts and new means for creating them, and we have to talk back to them.

SITUATED TECHNOLOGY: GETTING A BOX TO GET OUT OF

As a technorhetorigeek, I saw Kathi's request to develop the online version of the Studio as a chance to "go play." But first I needed a playground. It is important, as Selfe (1999) notes, to pay attention to the technological landscape that we inhabit. In planning and developing the Online Studio, what we wanted to do and what we would ultimately be able to do were somewhat at odds. In some cases, the problem was digital access. We needed a literal box—a server—to work with. Despite Clemson's technology focus, we[5] did encounter some difficulties in developing the Studio's online counterpart because we did not own our own server; although we might have been able to budget the initial technology outlay, we would not have been able to afford the expected programming and maintenance fees that the university expected and required. If we were to borrow space on an existing university server, our access would have been heavily moderated, limiting our ability to try out new ideas because of the potential repercussions of mistakes. Ultimately, we needed places to play, to try out our ideas. At least one. We came up with four.

---

[5]The term *we* refers to the Pearce Center research team; although I was doing the technological development of the Online Studio, that development took place in full partnership with the other Pearce team members.

VARIATION 1: STUDIO PARTNERSHIP

The first opportunity developed though a partnership with the Writing Studio at Colorado State University (CSU), directed by Mike Palmquist (see Fig. 2.2). Working within the Course Management System (CMS) that Palmquist developed, we created a working version of our electronic filing cabinet. Pearce team members often offered workshops on CAC topics (e.g., faculty workshops on integrating PowerPoint, assessing electronic writing, and Poetry Across the Curriculum, just to name a few). Handouts from these and other Pearce-related functions were collected and digitized for inclusion in the electronic filing cabinet. As we continued to offer increasingly digitized activities using audio and video, we needed a large digital archive.

In addition to fulfilling our needs for digital storage space, an external partnership allowed us to meet two Pearce Center goals: extending the conversation about composing with others outside our students' own experiences and showcasing the true collaborative nature of many digital compositions. Finally, because this site works on a course management model, we were able to access tools that are already familiar to most students. Site users may create documents and portfolios. They can write and share blogs. They can send off material for feedback from peers and from consultants. In many ways, it digitizes the process of composing, much like a traditional OWL.

Figure 2.2 The Class of '41 Studio on the CSU Writing Studio

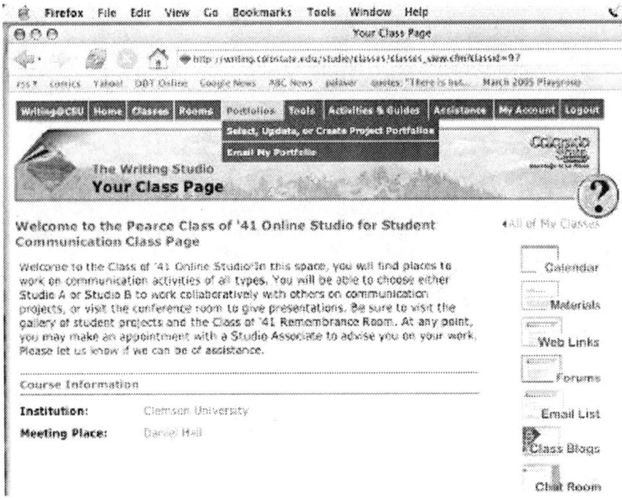

VARIATION 2: THE STUDIO MOO

Issues of access continued to play a role in how the Online Studio would develop. As we were pursuing our partnership with CSU, we learned that a Memo of Understanding needed to exist between the two universities. As we waited for the legal document to wend its ways through the bureaucratic channels, we could not have access to development space on the Writing Studio's server at CSU. Rather than having the Class of '41 Online Studio remain dormant, we began pursuing options for the development of Stages 2 and 3 of the initial plan: asynchronous and synchronous conversation spaces. During the summer of 2004, I received funding to attend Computers in Writing Intensive Classrooms (CIWIC) at Michigan Tech to begin development of the Online Studio as an Independent Project. Over the course of the 2-week sessions working with a programmer to learn MySQL and receiving consultations from Cindy and Dickie Selfe, I developed Variations 2 and 3 of the Online Studio. After hearing a description of the physical Studio, the Selfes recommended developing a MOO space that combines the initial three stages of our model: the Electronic File Cabinet, the Asynchronous Communications, and the Synchronous Communications and Assistance. For this MOO iteration, I quite literally rendered the physical studio. Using text descriptions and static photographic snapshots, I followed the Studio schematic pictured in Fig. 2.1, creating areas for remembrance, reception, small-group work, and presentation space. Crucial to the creation of the Online Studio prototypes were my e-mail conversations with Kathi Yancey, director of the Pearce Center. In these conversations, conceptions of what the spaces should look like[6] and how they should behave became more apparent; this, in turn, allowed me to focus the tools better.

> Because MUDs are simply text, many people are often unimpressed. Indeed, navigating a MUD can be confusing and sparse. What few realize is that they have the ability to create the action and construct the MUD's environment.
>
> —Shedroff (2001, p. 152)

---

[6]I wanted to include screenshots of the MOO Studio, but, despite having developed it on my own private server, the box went down in a move, and I was unable to re-create the MOO Studio with subsequent versions of the MOO software.

Cindy and I talked about the purposes of the Online Studio, and I talked about the collaborative nature of the physical space and how that collaboration really does seem to take place there. Because that is what is so wonderful about the physical studio, she suggested that I focus my energies there rather than the electronic filing cabinet that I had been working on so far. So we were pondering how to mirror that flexible, collaborative space inside the online space. She suggested, and I agree, that a MOO front end is a good possibility. . . . Yesterday afternoon, I used the metaphors that we have been using (revision, remediation, time, space, and place) to help me think through what that MOO space would be like. The technologies in the spaces would mirror that physical studio in a lot of ways: You "walk in" to the reception area to make an appointment to work with a studio associate. There are spaces for studios a and b with recording technology, and white board technology, and filing cabinets. And there's a collaborative writing space (SubEthaEdit has been amazing to work with!). The conference room might have presentation capabilities, and the kiosks would be where folks could work and get feedback on audio and video. And each of these spaces would have a file cabinet to store not only information
that we have collected, but also student docs. And then a gallery area that showcases students' works: portfolios, posters, powerpoints, texts, visuals.

So, at this point, I'm hoping you don't hate the idea :)

VARIATION THREE: MOODLE STUDIO

In a nod to our open source colleagues, the third iteration of the Studio was in Moodle. However, in the Pearce Team's early testing after creation of the Moodle Studio (see Fig. 2.3), we encountered several problems. First, again, the combined lack of our own server and our wary information-technology division meant any Moodle iterations would be hosted offsite, posing difficulties for site maintenance and development. Second, in our initial focus groups with members of the Pearce Research Team and Pearce Corporate Advisory Board, the limitations of the interface as it stood at that time inhibited our group's interactions in the Moodle Studio. Given these difficulties, the Moodle Studio was abandoned shortly after its creation.

Figure 2.3. The Moodle Studio

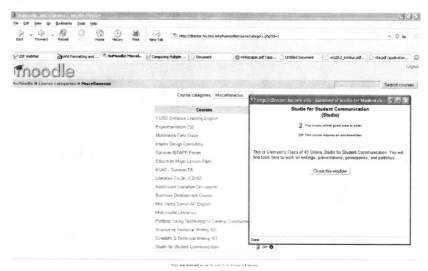

VARIATION FOUR: STUDIO OF COMMON TOOLS

Also at CIWIC, conversations with Anne Wysocki and Erin Smith led to a then-unexpected fourth iteration of the Online Studio: the development of the Online Studio by using tools familiar to students. For example, incorporating an instant-messaging system like IM or Yahoo Chat is less clunky for web-savvy students than having to learn how to chat in a MOOspace with seemingly arcane commands like "emote" and "say." As available technologies continue to change, today those common tools might include multiple blog sites, Google™ Documents, YouTube, and Skype.

> I'm meeting with Erin Smith tomorrow to try out some other ideas; Dickie suggested using moodle, which is another (open-source) course management system, and there's xoops, which is an open-source blog factory. I thought I'd throw some things together there too. And Dickie suggested that the programmer and I try to work on a portal piece that would allow users to log into several pieces of a system at once (for instance, a web login that will allow them to choose options that are housed in the CSU site, the MOO, and in any open-source pieces we have) so that there is a seamless integration of parts.

FOUR DESIGNS, ONE GOAL: EVOLVE

> The mistake that many designers make is in trying
> to design once for all circumstances.
>
> —Shedroff (2001, p. 96)

What is an OWL? It seems that we have long since stopped thinking about OWLs as writing "labs," no longer calling up images of the doctor, the fixer. The online spaces must adapt. In an e-mail to Kathi during that development time, I wrote:

> My plan for what's left of the weekend is to get three options up and running for us to choose among. I think there's good and bad to all the stuff I've got in the works right now, so I think a side-by-side comparison would be really useful, at least to help me think through all the functionalities we want.
> I'm just trying to figure out what the essence of the online space is (or should be) and find the right technology for that.
> 8 July 2004

Ultimately, at the end of 2 weeks at CIWIC, I had four digital creations:

- The Class of '41 Online Studio space on the Writing Studio at CSU

> The writing studio [space] that Mike Palmquist has put together gets at some of what I think we're about, but I don't think that it gets to others (like collaboration and the non-class based nature of things.

- The Class of '41 Online Studio MOO housed on my personal server
- The Class of '41 Online Moodle housed on the Michigan Tech humanities server
- An MySQL database portal that would house usernames and passwords that would provide users access to all these spaces so they could move dynamically from place to place, space to space to find the right tool for the job.

All of the online spaces, as envisioned, would have document storage, asynchronous and synchronous communication spaces, and the capacity to grow. The goals of the conversation, however, remained mostly unchanged: to help students conceive, develop, and revise composed materials. Students' experiences in the physical Studio were far more dynamic and productive than the original conceptions of the Online Studio: the electronic file cabinet, the asynchronous, and the synchronous. Students physically moved from space to space, and, as they did so, their production activities changed as well. Trimbur (2000) describes the quintessential change as:

> I think this is ok, but I wonder about the moo. I'm not a huge fan of them, and the translation of the physical is a bit literal for me. What about a blog? If a blog won't work, then, sure, do the moo for one room and let's see how it goes.
> KYancey@email

> To my mind, the new digital literacies will increasingly be incorporated into writing centers not just as sources of information or delivery systems for tutoring but as productive arts in their own right, and writing center work will, if anything, become more rhetorical in paying attention to the practices and effects of design in written and visual communication—more product oriented and perhaps less like the composing conferences of the process movement. (p. 30)

Shedroff argues that "technologies are not inherently or automatically interactive. They must be made so through careful development process. . . ." (p. 142). Desiring greater interactivity, we must create spaces that account for "a process of continual action and reaction between two parties" (Shedroff, 2001, p. 142). No longer to be a space of tutoring (i.e., of changing, fixing, doctoring, and revising), Clemson's conception of Studio was to be composing (active, doing, etc.). Clearly, this is a complex process of redefinition, transitioning from the media to the message. Studio Associates, especially undergraduates coming from different disciplines, had to be trained to think rhetorically about posters, PowerPoints, and portfolios. My colleague Teddi Fishman addresses some of the issues at stake in training the Studio Associates for such a dynamic space in her chapter in this collection. The physical and online spaces must be able to display and house these multimodal documents. At the core, multimodal documents are continued attempts to communicate a message by any means necessary.

When reading the scholarship surrounding OWLs and other online instruction/communication spaces, I am stuck by the "cautionary tale" aspect of our language. While we try to maintain a sense of hopefulness, it is clear to me that we are often disappointed with what we encounter as digital builders. For example, Jordan-Henley and Maid (2000) write, in their "Advice to the Linelorn: Crossing State Borders and the Politics of Cyberspace," that we can build and plan, but we are always on the verge of drowning or getting stuck or landing in a whirlpool:

> The climate in which we work is complex and ever-changing. Those who work in it constantly fight the danger of drowning in each new wave. So do we, but anyone who regularly uses e-mail recognizes drowning as a distinct possibility. In truth, however, instructors interested in online technology can create their own rafts and life jackets by planning carefully, by anticipating problems, and by gasping for air at the right times. When those fail, as they will, and instructors find themselves snagged on political driftwood, then treading water and allowing the current to change their direction is a viable option. Who knows? Downstream may turn out to be even better. (p. 115)

Their take-away lesson, however, is to go with the flow and see what the next opportunity will bring. Although this approach can be comforting when encountering yet another obstacle in the builder's path, it does give us an overall sense that online spaces are wrought with difficulties. As a group, we design, we build, we encounter troubles, and we move on—to other iterations, other creations, and/or other institutions. Yet despite it all, we keep creating. Indeed, we seem to relish the idea of doing so much with so little.

Another lesson that I have taken away from this process is that, although having a budget does make some of the processes of designing an Online Studio easier, it is not the quintessential component. Rather, I am finding that it is possible to create these kinds of spaces on a shoestring if the vision and flexibility remain. Especially given currently available tools such as Google documents, where co-authors can edit together from a distance, and YouTube, where we can upload, edit, and comment on video, designing multimodal feedback spaces almost means just having access to a web browser.

CONNECT: ONLY CONNECT!

Coogan (1999) closes *Electronic Writing Centers: Computing the Field of Composition* with a plea for a place "to practice a form of reading and writing that strengthens, rather than weakens, connections to each other," and he goes on to suggest that "such an alternative exists, at least potentially, in the idea of the electronic writing center" (p. 119). Coogan's text was a key element of the multiple designs of the Online Studio. Perhaps I should be a quilter; I spend my time cobbling, stretching, and piecing together digital bits into a design experience—the endless search for the right tool for the job. Voloshinov (1986) argues that a word is a bridge between utterer and utterance, a connection point among speakers. In some ways, Forster's narrator is wrong to suggest to "live in fragments no longer" because it is in the fragments that we *do* live; the coherency that we seek comes from a design that we lay on top of the experience. Coherency is an appeal to the seamlessness. For me, composition is the process of seaming, of connecting the various tools and spaces that strengthen our language connections to one another. The goal of the Online Studio, especially in the development of Common Tools, is to provide the most effective tools for the many messages that students create.

> In your life, you probably will never have a more interactive experience than a conversation with someone. . . . Conversations are one of the most important ways we learn. Conversations allow us to be comfortable and conscious of the content, and to forget the form and means of transmission almost entirely.
>
> —Shedroff (2001, p. 180)

Clemson is a technology-rich campus. Moreover, during the creation of Class of '41 Studios, it was a conversation-rich[7] campus. A colleague from chemistry once called the physical Class of '41 Studio "the intellectual center of campus" because of its—or our—ability to bring together faculty, students, and staff into contiguous spaces that called for, urged, created, and composed conversations. The physical Class of '41 Studio is a distinctive space. It has a carefully composed series of design elements that function as rhetorical tools. Users come to the space, see what is available, and use and modify the space according to their goals. For many, those goals are compositions; for some, conversations; for still others, a combination of the two. When we set out to design the Class of '41 Online Studio, we wanted to use the same care to approach and appeal to the multiple stakeholders who had been crucial to the final shape of the physical studio.

---

[7]I must thank my colleagues from the Pearce Team at Clemson, Teddi Fishman, Michael Neal, Barbara Ramirez, Summer Taylor, Kathleen Yancey, and Art Young, for continuing our conversations about the shape of the spaces in which we compose. I could not have composed without them.

> And these fragments I have shored against my ruins.
>
> —T. S. Eliot, *The Waste Land*

But we also design that with which we are already familiar. Sometimes it is difficult to move away from the stories, the designs that already exist. OWLs are familiar; the writing process is known. How do we create a space for the unknown text? The anticipated text? The yet unspoken? We cannot design *that* space; rather the users/the speakers/the composers must, in anticipation of the conversation yet to come. Like an electronic conversation, we have remnants and artifacts to witness its existence. This is the true language interplay: the play of context upon space, the play of space upon text, and the play of word upon word upon word. It is building and rebuilding. Multimodal. Modes upon modes upon modes. Building blocks. In anticipation of what will come next. We experience, we design, we compose.

FAQ

- What was the hardest part about creating the Online Studio?

   ◊ Gaining server access. Wherever possible, use a server dedicated to the project. If that is not possible, strongly consider using common tools to create access to the kinds of documents you would like to see produced.

- Who used the Online Studio? What parts, if any, of the Online Studio were used by students?

   ◊ Students would have had access to all parts of the Online Studio, including the electronic file cabinet where we hoped to store handouts, tutorials, videos, and other materials. Unfortunately, the Online Studios never made it past the prototype state of development. Although we collected artifacts for the electronic file cabinet, only a few test documents (PowerPoints, videos, and handouts from presentations) were uploaded.

- What role did Studio Associates play?

   ◊ Studio Associates served as guides and, in a sense, as tutors. Studio Associates were not necessarily trained in the technology—How do you make a web page?—but were trained to identify the rhetorical concepts that would push them to ask students—Would this message work better in a web page or in a poster? This would be true regardless of whether they were working in the physical or Online Studio.

- What iteration did you like best?

  ◊ If it's not clear from the text, the MOO Studio was my favorite. As I said in an e-mail message, I was surprised by how much I liked the MOO: **I understand your concern about the MOO; I was never a big proponent of them because I couldn't "get" the object-oriented thing, and as many folks keep telling us, MOOs are dead ☺ but for this application, I think I do "get it" and the technology seems right for part of the collaborative environment we're trying to achieve.** Ultimately, however, I believe that the Studio of common tools would be the most workable solution. It is difficult enough to find the resources to initiate an online writing space that enables development and feedback on multimodal compositions. If we have to teach the tools, we risk two problems: (a) that the technology we choose will have rapid obsolescence and (b) that students who might benefit from the spaces won't have the time or patience to learn "our" technologies to suit their purposes. It is easier to meet them where they are.

- How can we foster greater collaboration among writing centers/writing studios?

  ◊ I found working with the Studio at CSU invigorating, and seeking partnerships across institutions is a goal I continue to have. I'm currently at an institution that doesn't have the budget to create the kind of Studio I would like to develop, but I believe through partnerships with other institutions we can establish a good working model.

REFERENCES

Billings, Andy, Fishman, Teddi, Gresham, Morgan, Justice, Angie, Neal, Michael, Ramirez, Barbara, Taylor, Summer Smith, Powell, Melissa Tidwell, Winchell, Donna, Yancey, Kathleen B., and Young, Art. (2005). New designs for communication across the curriculum. In Sharon James McGee & Carolyn Handa (Eds.), *Postmodernity and writing programs* (pp. 158–180). Logan: Utah State University Press.

Bolter, Jay David, & Grusin, Richard. (2000). *Remediation: Understanding new media.* Cambridge, MA: MIT Press.

Clemson World. Clemson Hits the Big TIME. Retrieved January 2, 2008, from http://www.clemson.edu/clemsonworld/Fall2000/TIME.htm.

Coogan, David. (1999). *Electronic writing centers: Computing the field of composition.* Stamford, CT: Ablex Publishing.

Crump, Eric. (February 23, 1998). *Re: technoprovocateurs.* Post on WPA-L. Retrieved June 14, 2007, from http://lists.asu.edu/cgi-bin/wa?A2 = ind9802&L = wpa-l&P = 35889

Difranco, Ani. (1993). My I.Q. *puddle dive.* Righteous Babe Records.

Eliot, T. S. (1922). *The waste land.* New York: Boni and Liveright.

Fischer, Katherine, & Harris, Muriel. (2001). Fill 'er up, pass the band-aids, center the margin, and praise the lord: Mixing metaphors in the writing lab. In Jane Nelson & Kathy Evertz (Eds.), *The politics of writing centers* (pp. 23-36). Portsmouth, NH: Heinemann Boynton-Cook.

Forster, E. M. (1910) *Howard's end.* Retrieved January 2, 2008, from http://www.doc.ic.ac.uk/ ~ rac101/concord/texts/howards_end/howards_end3.html#8176.

Gresham, Morgan. (2004). *The studio and the online studio.* Unpublished proposal.

Gresham, Morgan, & Yancey, Kathleen Blake. (2004). New studio composition: New sites for writing, new forms of composition, new cultures of learning. *Writing Program Administration: Journal of the Council of Writing Program Administrators, 28*(1), 2.

Hart, D. Alexis. (2007). Textured literacy: An interview with Kathleen Blake Yancey. *Kairos, 11*(2). Retrieved June 15, 2007, from http://kairos.technorhetoric.net/11.2/binder.html?interviews/yancey/TexturedLiteracy.html

Inman, James A., & Sewell, Donna N. (2000). Reeling in the horizon: OWLs and perspective in writing center work. In James A. Inman and Donna N. Sewell (Eds.), *Taking flight with OWLs: Examining electronic writing center work* (pp. xxv–xxx). Mahwah, NJ: Erlbaum.

Janangelo, Joseph. (2000). Carnal conferencing: Personal computing and the ideation of a writing center. In Lynn Craigue Briggs & Meg Woolbright (Eds.), *Stories from the center: Connecting narrative and theory in the writing center.* Urbana, IL: NCTE Press.

Jordan-Henley, Jennifer, & Maid, Barry. (2000). Advice to Linelorn: Crossing state borders. In J. A. Inman & D. N. Sewell (Eds.), *Taking flight with OWLs: Examining electronic writing center work* (pp. 105-115). Mahwah, NJ: Erlbaum.

Kastman-Breuch, Lee-Ann. (2004). The idea(s) of an online writing center: In search of a conceptual model. *The Writing Center Journal, 25*(2).

Kastman-Breuch, Lee-Ann. (2005). *Closing thoughts about OWC. Friends of the Writing Center Journal Thursday, November 17, 2005.* Retrieved April 29, 2008, from < http://writingcenterjournal.blogspot.com/ >

Kinkead, Joyce A., & Harris, Jeannette. (1993). *Writing centers in context: Twelve case studies.* Urbana, IL: National Council of Teachers of English.

Langston, Camille. (1996). Resistance and control: The complex process of creating an OWL. *Kairos, 1*(1). Retrieved December 31, 2007, from http://english.ttu. edu/kairos/1.1/binder2.html?owls/langston/langston1.html

Lasarenko, Jane. (1996). PR(OWL)ING AROUND: An OWL by any other name. *Kairos, 1*(1). Retrieved December 31, 2007, from http://english.ttu.edu/kairos /1.1/binder2.html?owls/lasarenko/prowl.html

The New London Group. (1996). A pedagogy of multiliteracies: Designing social futures. *Harvard Educational Review, 66*(1), 60–92.

Selfe, Cynthia. (1999). *Technology and literacy in the twenty-first century: A story about the perils of not paying attention.* Carbondale, IL: Southern Illinois University Press.

Shedroff, Nathan. (2001). *Experience design.* Indianapolis, IN: New Riders.

Trimbur, John. (2000). Multiliteracies, social futures, and writing centers. *The Writing Center Journal, 20*(2), 29–32.

Voloshinov, V. N. (1986). *Marxism and the philosophy of language.* (Ladislav Matejka and I. R. Titunik, Trans.). Cambridge, MA: Harvard University Press.

Yancey, Kathleen Blake. (2000). The Pearce Center for Communicative Arts: A Concept and Space Proposal. Retrieved 14 June 2007 from http://www.clemson.edu/1941 studio/images/proj&plan/whitepaper.pdf

Operation
and Practice

3

WHEN IT ISN'T EVEN ON THE PAGE

PEER CONSULTING IN MULTIMEDIA ENVIRONMENTS

Teddi Fishman

Clemson University

[W]riting gains its power—as a cognitive process, as a cultural practice, and even as a metaphor—by linking these two powerful systems: the material realm of time and space with the quintessentially human act of language.

—Christina Haas (1996, p. 3)

Technological creativity is a form of imaginative play with alternate worlds and ways of being.

—Andrew Feenberg (1996)

I just need someone who can make my pictures show up on my web page. Please! This is due in ten minutes!

—Student seeking help in the studio

WELCOME TO THE STUDIO

On an average day in early November, the newest student tutors in our multimedia literacy center have completed nearly all of the preparation they receive to work in our center. They have been through most of their semester-long pedagogy course and are now engaged in *shadowing*, a term we use for their apprentice period. For all intents and purposes, they are now tutors in the center. They help students work on projects and digital portfolios, but they are still in the process of becoming tutors. By this time, they have worked through most of their uncertainties about tutoring, from negotiating the technology to becoming comfortable looking up the finer points of grammar, and they are ready, willing, and even eager to share what they know with the wide range of students who come into the collaborative, student-driven, multiliteracy center seeking help.

To get to this point, the associates had to complete a 3-hour, for-credit course during which they were introduced to writing center theory and practices, the practical and scholarly aspects of technology, and a smattering of both rhetoric and aesthetic principles. They have engaged in role-playing exercises in which they attempted to engage reluctant "tutees." They have practiced walking them through complex technological machinations and gently correcting grammar mistakes. They have been primed to let the students who come in set their own agendas, ask questions instead of directing the sessions, and concentrate on facilitating the development of sound communication practices, rather than simple mechanical proficiencies or, as Stephen North (1984) puts it, focus on developing "better writers, not better writing" (p. 438). Now, students are coming in, seeking their help with projects that range from traditional papers to film projects to multimedia work and e-portfolios that may contain all of these things and more. There is just one problem: When you ask students, or even require them to set their own agendas, you quickly find that students have their own ideas about what happens (or what *should* happen) in a studio that provides multiliteracy support. Theirs does not necessarily align itself with ours.

To prepare studio associates to work with the students who come in seeking their help, the associates are required to take a semester-long course during which they read about the history and theoretical positioning of literacy centers, role-play various scenarios in which they help (each other) with real writing and technology issues, and engage in research related to the studio. The goals of the course are threefold: to familiarize them with literacy center theory and practices, to ease them into their new roles as student tutors, and to make sure they have all the necessary technical skills to help students solve their problems. In reference to the last item, it is important to note that, although the course aims to help the tutors learn to solve technology problems, it can in no way equip them with all the specialized knowledge they need. Rather than learning specific information, they practice technology problem solving so that, regardless of the situation, they are adept at identifying the problem's origin and locating the proper resources to address it.

A typical exercise to promote this kind of familiarity takes place when the tutors are introduced to Mind Manager—a tool for graphically composing and displaying mind maps (see Fig. 3.1). Most tutors have never encountered this software before, so it provides ideal opportunities for both modeling the type of dialogic "instruction" that they will later engage in, and developing the critical skills and confidence needed to assist other students with technology with which they are not yet familiar. The exercise begins with a task—typically something like developing a mind map for the class research project. It is important that the need for the technology is indicated or dictated by the task because this is one of the recurring themes of the course.

After the task has been explained, the software—in this case, Mind Manager—is introduced as a potential tool to accomplish the task. It bears mentioning that if, at this stage of the exercise, a student proposes using another software program instead, it would be inconsistent with the tenets of the course not to explore both and select the most promising solution to

Figure 3.1. Example of a Mind Manager map made by a Studio Associate

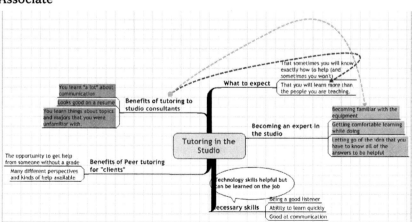

the task at hand. Tutors are encouraged to view the various technological resources as means to ends rather than the *telos* of any activity, and to model that approach to the students that they work with.

Next comes the exploratory phase, during which the tutors work together to figure out how to utilize the software to complete the task. As in the first phase, they work with minimal input from the instructor but in collaborative mode with each other. When there is a question, they are prompted to propose possible solutions and to weigh the pros and cons, rather than finding a single right answer. When they ask questions, the job of the instructor is—as their job as tutors will be—to ask questions and make suggestions rather than simply providing the answers. In both cases, the primary benefit to be derived from the activity is the "solving," rather than the solution.

By the end of the activity, the tutors will not only have accomplished their task and become more familiar with a new software program, but they have evaluated a technology for its usefulness to a particular task, participated in collaborative problem solving, engaged in systematic, goal-driven mastery of a technology, and, perhaps most significantly (to their development as tutors), engaged in the practice and teaching of a *techne*— a learnable art—when they had not yet mastered it. All of these skills (and more) will be critical to their development and success as tutors.

Although the associates are prepared to help them identify issues, select appropriate technologies, remediate information, and negotiate genre constraints, it is often the case that the students who come in neither expect nor want any of those things. They do not necessarily see the work of a multiliteracy center as being about writing; instead, they come in seeking help fixing problems—preferably in the most expedient way. They want technical assistance and efficiency—something along the lines of what they would get at a Kinkos. In fact, often what they specifically do not want is another teacherly figure prompting them to suss out the motivations behind an assignment, identify the metaphors that inform various modes of communication, or critique the roles that technology can play in creating meaning. They do not want us to teach them to "question expectations, goals and motivations of the power structures" (Decker, 2005, p. 22). They do not want lessons in rhetoric or communication. They have not yet come to the previously mentioned position that the benefit is in the doing. They want solutions to their problems, and their understanding of exactly what those problems are often differ considerably from the perspective of the tutors.

As Sheridan notes (chap. 9, this volume) typical visitors to a multiliteracy center come in and ask for help fixing problems that they identify as technological or even mechanical. The associates attempt to ask them questions like "Why did you choose this application?" (Are you sure PowerPoint is the most appropriate choice to make a poster?) and "How does the multimedia aspect of your project enhance your message?" (Do those blinking images and sound effects help your presentation?), but those are not the questions students see as central. Their exasperated expressions say clearly, "If I knew enough about what I'm doing to know the answers to those questions, I wouldn't need your help" or "Can you please just help me fix my problem?"

It should come as no surprise that we are no closer to identifying or agreeing on what exactly a multiliteracy center should do than we were to agreeing on a definition of a writing center two decades ago. At that time, North (1984) pointed out that although they are generally known to exist, no one understands exactly what happens or what *can* happen in a writing center. Multiple, contradictory expectations regarding multiliteracy, complicated by questions about the role that student tutors should or can play in providing assistance with multimedia assignments leave little hope at arriving at a universal definition. Perhaps that should not even be our goal. From their inception, the roles and functions of multiliteracy centers have been actively negotiated, each within its unique institutional context, with each specific instance of a multiliteracy center ultimately defining itself in a way that makes sense within its specific institution.

In our case, the multiliteracy center came into being when an alumni class made a gift to the university for a center that would be used to enhance undergraduate communication skills. Oversight of the project was given to a group on campus that had a longstanding relationship with the class as well as a mission to support and promote communication. Thus, this center, unlike most institutional spaces, was planned by academics with interaction, communication, and multimedia literacy support in mind from the outset. Throughout the design process, no fewer than 75 people either directly or indirectly associated with the university were consulted (Billings et al., 2005) just to decide on a configuration for the physical space.

The configuration that resulted has three distinct and distinctly purposed areas—the main studio area was designed as flexible space for collaborative work in progress. It was furnished with an eye toward maximum flexibility and features two infinitely reconfigurable studio spaces along with two multimedia work stations in glassed-in kiosks. The conference room was envisioned as a presentation space with reconfigurable conference tables, rolling executive chairs, and state-of-the-art remote-controlled multimedia projection. The third area is the most difficult to define: a transitional, multipurpose space between the two larger areas, featuring whiteboards and tackboards, as well as a counter and sink area. This third space serves as a staging area for presentations in the conference room, as well as a space for smaller groups to meet. A reception area and a small glassed-in display area that also serve as "overflow" spaces when needed complete the studio.

The space that is now the studio was originally a row of classrooms, but was repurposed using an alumni gift from the class of 1941. The people who teach the studio course have been, up to this point, part of the same people who designed the studio and envisioned how it would function in relationship to the university (see Fig. 3.2).

Throughout the design process, the design team kept a core set of goals in mind. Because the only confident prediction we could make about how the studio would be used was that the technology it would utilize and the purposes to which it would be put would change more quickly than we would be able to remodel, our first principle was that we should maximize, whenever possible, the flexibility of the space. Toward this end, every single piece of furniture in the studio was chosen for its ability to be reconfigured as necessary. The small tables have wheels. The larger ones are built in sections so they can be reshaped. Everything was chosen from the same color palette so that pieces could be moved from one room to another as needed. Even the kiosks are reconfigurable. In addition to the screens for the smartboard displays, the walls are covered with a mixture of whiteboards and tackboards so that they can be used for active construction of texts rather than the more typical (and more passive) display.

To everyone but the most casual observer, it is clear that the reconfigurable design of our multiliteracy center was designed to meet a diverse array of needs—some of which we could not anticipate or plan for specifically. Knowing that the space would outlast the purposes we could predict,

Figure 3.2. Floor Plan for Clemson's Class of '41 Studio

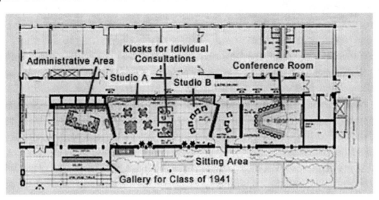

its design not only needed to signal our vision of the studio as having a unique role and purpose, it also had to enact the flexibility that would allow it to perform in ways we could not foresee. Like the preparation of the tutors, the challenge in designing the physical space was to prepare for a wider variety of needs than could be identified—knowing that the ability to adapt was more critical than any particular or specific accommodation, and like multiliteracy centers themselves, the space had to be ready to meet a variety of ever-changing needs.

The rationales and purposes for multiliteracy centers appear, at first glance, to be practical, necessary, straightforward, and commendable: to provide a place where both the principles and practices of multimedia literacy can be explored; a nonevaluative setting where students can get help with a wide range of communicative endeavors; a resource to use while developing and working on the content, format, and technological aspects of multimodal projects; and a place to collaborate or even just investigate the many technologically infused and/or determined mechanisms for making meaning. In practice, however, these contemplative, scholarly ideals give way to "messier" applications and unending questions. What kinds of help are acceptable for studio associates to offer to students? How much of the work has to be exclusively that of the student? Who decides what to work on first? What is the best technology for an assignment? Who should provide access to the technology? How much time should be spent on content as opposed to presentation? In practice, none of those questions has an answer that can be agreed on, which both enriches and complicates the process of learning how to work in a multiliteracy center.

PREPARING TO WORK IN THE STUDIO

Preparing Student Associates to negotiate that tricky intersection of theory and practice is, itself, a negotiation. They are, after all, immersed in the same culture that leads students not just to expect efficiency, but to value it more highly than a more lengthy, process-based approach. Coming to see the value in understanding when and why to employ a particular multimedia technology, as opposed to simply learning *how* to use it, requires a shift in perspective as well as priorities. Adhering to that ideal while frantic students beg to have their projects "fixed" requires not only commitment and resolve—it requires "buy-in." The development of that perspective, that appreciation, along with imparting the technological and pedagogical "how-tos" of the studio, are the goals of the studio course and orientation process.

ORIENTATION PRACTICES

The first steps in the Studio Associate course are concerned with orientation—theoretical orientation, technological orientation, and orientation to the specific resources of our multimedia studio. For theoretical orientation, we rely most heavily on writing center and writing across the curriculum (WAC) principles for their student-centered, epistemic, process-based, and nonevaluative principles. But as denizens of a center—a physical place—and also a technological resource, our orientation must also include readings on ideologies of space and technology. The initial readings serve as background and introduction to the goals of the studio which are to:

- foster the development of multimedia literacy (and only secondarily the development of multimedia texts);
- provide feedback and support via student-driven interaction (rather than evaluation, direction, or tutor-led interaction);
- facilitate informed, selective, and tactical implementation of technologies to meet rhetorical goals; and
- maintain a student-centered atmosphere that supports collaboration, creativity, interaction, interdisciplinarity, and reflective practices.

THEORETICAL PRACTICES

Readings that are used to support and inform the tutors' development and professionalization include texts dealing with media, design, and remediation processes in concrete ways—such as Robin Williams' (1994) *Non-Designer's Design* book and Donald Norman's (2002) *The Design of Everyday Things,* as well as more abstract theoretical texts including selections from Terry Winograd and Fernando Flores' (1986) *Understanding Computers and Cognition* and Michael Joyce's (1995) "Siren Shapes." Additionally, there are texts that speak directly to their development as tutors, such as Michael Pemberton and Joyce A. Kinkead's (2003) *The Center Will Hold* and Gillespie and Learner's (2000) *The Allyn and Bacon Guide to Peer Tutoring.* These texts, like the exercises described earlier, serve the twin purposes of educating in and of themselves while helping to professionalize the tutors as they not only learn, but also utilize the information from the texts.

Perhaps the most critical aspect of the associates' orientation, however, is that which deals with real practice. Even more than their initial reading and classroom exercises, practice is what allows the new associates to become comfortable in their new roles as tutors. There are three distinct sets of practices that the new associates must master. First, the administrative practices of the studio must be mastered. Although each multiliteracy center will necessarily have its own specific practices, there are necessary functions that most will have in common. Time for consultations/appointments must be scheduled and managed. Technology resources must be checked out and maintained. The facility and technology must be monitored and secured. Most important, tutoring sessions must be conducted.

TECHNOLOGY PRACTICES

The second set of practices that the associates must learn has to do with the technology. All the high-tech equipment from the remote control that operates the drop-down screen and lighting in the conference room to the image and video editing software in the kiosks must be tried, explored, and figured out. There are no short cuts or substitutes for simply using the technology, so part of the job of the faculty member teaching the studio course involves designing tasks and sometimes even games that require utilization of the technology so that the associates' practice is goal-driven.

As the associates become familiar with the studio-specific technology, they must also begin developing awareness or metacognition of the ways that people learn technology. This is necessary for two reasons. First, it is essential as they work with students who need to learn the various applications. Second, they need strategies that they can employ on the occasions when they do not know the answer to a student's technology question and must puzzle it out with them, on the spot. Knowing how to figure out systematically a new piece of software is as important to developing confidence as it is to becoming competent, so it is essential not only that the new associates practice, but also that they become aware of how they are "learning to learn" as they master the various hardware and software. By becoming aware of how much they already know about figuring out software, as well as how many strategies they have at their disposal for figuring things out, they become more confident of their own abilities and better able to help others become similarly self-sufficient.

TUTORING PRACTICES

The final set of practices that are addressed in the course have to do with the actual methods of tutoring. In our studio, we made the conscious choice to call our tutors *associates* both to avoid the remedial connotations of the term *tutoring* and to tap into the more professional *ethos* of *associate*. Nevertheless, the instruction that associates receive regarding their interactions with students springs directly from the traditions of writing center tutors and follows the familiar cardinal rules of tutoring:

> *The focus of any session should be on the development of understanding and skills, rather than the development of a particular text.* The goal of the tutor should be to shed enough light on the rationale and process so that the next time students encounter the same situation, they will be able to address it themselves or at least bring a greater understanding to it.
>
> *Whatever the work is, it is the student's work.* Therefore, the work, whether it exists on a video screen, on paper, on posterboard, or any other format, must be worked on by the student, exclusively. The keyboard, the tablet, the paper, the screen, the mouse, and any writing instrument or inputting instruments should stay in the student's hands and never in the hands of the tutor. This rule is important not just as a boundary-setting mechanism in the studio, but also as a way of maintaining the reputation of the studio externally. It also sends an important signal to students about the role and function of the associates. Just as writing centers have to guard against the perception that they finish or edit students' work for them, multi-literacy centers must guard against the perception that the studio associates do work that is integral to graded assignments.
>
> *The student should set the agenda.* Although it is permissible for the tutor to ask questions and encourage students to consider their priorities, the decision about what to work on and what approach to take belongs to the student. This is a tricky rule to negotiate because often students may not be aware of some of the most serious issues with their projects.
>
> *Associates are not permitted to offer opinions about or assessments of grades.* Under no circumstances should associates

answer questions about what grade a project would be likely to earn.

Associates can neither interpret nor critique assignments. Although it can be helpful (and is permissible) for associates to point out aspects of an assignment that students appear to have overlooked (when reading from an assignment sheet or course web page) the interpretation has to be that of the student.

Although these rules have much in common with guidelines for writing center tutors, there are some issues that are particular to multimedia literacy centers. Because most students do not perceive technological skills as being integral to their work, but rather as tools for getting it done, they often do not see a problem with asking an associate to do the technical part of an assignment. Ironically, the more central the technology is to the task, the more likely students may be to ask for an associate to do it for them. When constructing a website, for instance, students may ask an associate to set up a page or publish it online. Because it is not possible for studio associates to know the goals of all of the assignments, our rule of thumb is that if a task could affect evaluation in any way, the student must do it themselves. This does not mean that an associate is enjoined from offering help. It does mean, however, that the work must be done by the student.

This rule is more difficult to follow than it would seem. Depending on the level of familiarity that students have with the technology, it is entirely possible for them to lack even the necessary vocabulary to understand the instructions. It is common for students with no previous web experience to need a brief primer on file types, directories, and folder organization before they can successfully set up and set permissions for their first web page. During high-traffic times, it is tempting for the associates to assume control of the mouse, quickly click a few buttons, and complete the setup process for them. The hazards of that approach, however, become evident the next time the student has to locate or change the files or directory structure and is not able.

Studio associates also learn some of the theory that informs multiliteracy center practices. Those theories can be divided roughly into two primary theoretical frameworks—those that describe and inform the kind of academic work in which the students are engaged (rhetorical and visual theory, technology and media theory) and those that describe and inform the tutoring work in which the associates are engaged (WAC theory, student-centered pedagogy). Naturally, there are overlaps in those two groups.

In our center, associates are encouraged to think about and employ theories in practical ways. Specifically, we encourage them to think of theoretical approaches as tools that they can bring with them to the tutoring sessions and take out to use as necessary rather than starting from a particular theory or pedagogy as a basis for a tutoring session. This "tools" approach is essential in the multimedia center where it is often necessary to work through numerous related decisions (which genre to work in, which medium to use, which application to work with) that each have technological, rhetorical, and visual dimensions. As Sheridan (2006) has pointed out, this means that tutors in multiliteracy centers must draw on not just pedagogical and technological skills, but also their rhetorical expertise, which will often dictate how the other skills will be employed. Thus, when helping a student choose an appropriate technology for an assignment, the rhetorical considerations of audience, context, and purpose might be invoked as a way to make technological choices. When student asks for help selecting and arranging images to appeal to a particular audience, visual rhetoric and technical considerations might be the two primary factors in making an appropriate selection regarding pedagogy. In each situation, the tutors must draw on multiple skill sets to address the various facets of the increasingly complex assignments and tasks.

CHANGING VALUES

The final step in preparing students to assume the role of tutor/associate is not one of theory or practice, yet it is perhaps the most tricky to negotiate: the question of values. In our setting, as in most universities, there are stated and unstated values that conflict, sending students (and faculty) mixed messages about the goals and purposes of their work. Nowhere are these conflicts more significant than in the multiliteracy center, where the values of process, growth, and reflection are at odds with the demands for speed, efficiency, and performance. To adhere to our prior goals, it is necessary not just to put processes into place, but to change the way both the associates and the students think about the work that we do.

Although the questions that students bring to the studio vary in their subject matter, scope, and complexity, they nearly always concern the "how" or the "what": How do I start? What is a good subject? How do I arrange my information? What software do I use? What is the right image format? How do I link my pages? What is an executive summary? How do I finish? To effect the values change, it is necessary to change those questions from "what" and "how" to questions like "why" and "when" and "to what purpose." To bring about that change in thinking, the new associates are encouraged to think about the students who come in (rather than the texts they bring with them) as the focus for their improvement efforts. In other words, as tempting as it is to pay attention to the screen, the page, the images, or the technology, multiliteracy—the aim of the center—is a quality that resides within the associates, and within the students with whom they work. The real work of associates is to work with *students* and to help them develop themselves.

Preferably, an associate works with a student to develop not just a specific project, but to amass a set of approaches and skills that will allow the student to approach his or her next task with a higher degree of autonomy and a greater critical awareness. Better still, during the process of making choices about a project or text, students becomes aware that the choices belong to them; that they can make their work meet their own needs, as well as the needs of the institution, and, as Marilyn Cooper (1994) has written, learn to "negotiate between institutional demands and individual needs" (p. 140).

To reinforce that message, new associates role-play tutoring sessions in the studio associate class. With one student playing the role of a tutor, one playing a student, and a third taking notes, associates practice shifting the conversations from strictly instructional to critical and reflective. A session that begins with questions about how to link pages becomes a conversation about the reader's role in the text. Questions about how to change the default background in PowerPoint evolves into a discussion of the role of color in establishing *ethos*. A request for help with the scanner morphs into a brief exchange about fair use and copyright. As the process of role-playing is repeated, the associates present greater challenges to their "tutors" while the tutors begin to internalize the values that inform the exchanges. By the end of the semester, the new associates have become our ambassadors, spreading the message that what happens in the studio can be more than the quick fix that most students are seeking when they come in for the first time.

WELCOME TO THE STUDIO

It is 9:00 a.m. on a chilly morning in December. Today, as is usual this time in the semester, students are waiting when the associates arrive, explaining what they need as the associates unlock the studio doors. They have become accustomed to the kinds of problems students have, even if the specific requests are unique: "When I finished this last night, all the images worked, and now they just aren't there!" "I have one week to do an e-port-folio and I don't know how to link!" or "I have to do a storyboard, and I don't even know what that is!"

The associates are increasingly skillful and sophisticated in handling the panicky students. They usher them into the studio, pull chairs up next to them, and start to work. They get at rhetorical and communication theory obliquely, couching their questions about goals and audience in terms of grading criteria and what the teacher wants. They elicit some consideration of "why" even as they succumb to consistent requests to explain "how" and simply give them "the practical knowledge they need" (Harris, 1995, p. 34). Students rush in and out without understanding why all the questions that the studio associates ask are important, but grateful for the help that comes along with them. The students feel harried and pressured to perform and are driven more by grades than their own intellectual needs. The associates do their best to pass on the lessons about multimedia literacy that they are still learning themselves and are conflicted as to their roles as tutors *cum* students. No one ever knows all the right answers, and sometimes they do not even know the right questions. This is life in the new multiliteracy center, where although we cannot predict what we will be doing next year or even tomorrow, evolving technologies and competing demands ensure that the work that we do will continue to be necessary for the foreseeable future. Welcome to the studio.

REFERENCES

Billings, Andy, Fishman, Teddi, Gresham, Morgan, Justice, Angie, Neal, Michael, Ramirez, Barbara, Taylor, Summer Smith, Powell, Melissa Tidwell, Winchell, Donna, Yancey, Kathleen B., & Young, Art. (2005). New designs for communication across the curriculum. In Sharon James McGee & Carolyn Handa (Eds.), *Postmodernity and writing programs* (pp. 158–180), Logan: Utah State University Press.

Cooper, Marilyn. (1994). Really useful knowledge: A cultural studies agenda for writing centers. *The Writing Center Journal, 14*, 97–111.

Decker, Teagan. (2005). Diplomatic relations: Peer tutors in the writing classroom. In Candace Spigelman & Laurie Grobman (Eds.), *On location: Theory and practice in classroom-based writing tutoring* (pp. 17–30). Logan: Utah State University Press.

Feenberg, Andrew Heidegger. (1996). *Heidegger, Habermas, and the essence of technology. Talk at the International Institute for Advanced Study, Kyoto.* Retrieved May 16, 2008, from http://www-rohan.sdsu.edu/faculty/feenberg/ kyoto.html

Gillespie, Paula, & Lerner, Neal. (2000). *The Allyn and Bacon guide to peer tutoring.* Boston: Allyn & Bacon.

Haas, Christina. (1996). *Writing technology: Studies on the materiality of literacy.* Mahwah, NJ, Erlbaum.

Harris, Muriel. (1995). Talking in the middle: Why writers need writing tutors. *College English, 57*(1), 27–42.

Joyce, Michael. (1995). *Of two minds: Hypertext pedagogy and poetics.* Ann Arbor: University of Michigan Press.

Norman, Donald A. (2002). *The design of everyday things.* New York: Basic Books.

North, Stephen. (1984). The idea of a writing center. *College English, 46*(5), 433–446.

North, Stephen. (2001). Revisiting the idea of a writing center. In Robert W. Barnett and Jacob S. Blumner (Eds.), *The Allyn and Bacon guide to writing center theory and practice,* (pp. 79–91). Needham Heights, MA: Allyn and Bacon.

Pemberton, Michael A. and Kinkead, Joyce A. (2003). *The center will hold: Critical perspectives on writing center scholarship.* Logan: Utah State University Press.

Sheridan, David. (2006). Words, images, sounds: Writing centers as multiliteracy centers. In Christina Murphy & Byron Stay (Eds.), *Writing center director's resource book* (339–350). Mahwah, NJ: Erlbaum.

Williams, Robin. (1994). *The non-designer's design book.* Berkeley, CA: Peachpit Press.

Winograd, Terry, & Flores, Fernando. (1986). *Understanding computers and cognition: A new foundation for design.* Norwood, NJ: Ablex.

MAPS

4

ALL THINGS TO ALL PEOPLE

MULTILITERACY CONSULTING
AND THE MATERIALITY OF RHETORIC

David M. Sheridan

Michigan State University

Although it would be easy to pursue this trail of possible resources further, identifying an assortment of sites and texts that could be used to teach tutors HTML and JavaScript, or how to use Microsoft FrontPage or Netscape Composer, we should stop and think carefully about how far we are really willing to go down this path in our quest to create "better" writing tutors. Ultimately, we have to ask ourselves whether it is really the writing center's responsibility to be all things to all people.

—(Pemberton, 2003, p. 21)

I JUST WANT TO SCAN!

At the MSU Writing Center, we have been, at various times, plagued by a recurring nightmare. The details change, but the basic narrative remains the same. It goes something like this. A client makes an appointment with one of our Digital Writing Consultants (DWCs). When the client arrives, the DWC leads with our usual set of questions meant to generate a rich profile of the rhetorical situation: Tell me a little bit about your project? Who is your audience? What is your purpose? What opportunities are there for using images, sounds, and words to reach your audience and achieve your purpose more effectively? But the client waves his or her hand through the air impatiently, cutting these questions short. He or she pulls out a photograph and hands it to the DWC, saying, "I just need to scan this."[1]

This scenario is scary because it seems to suggest a reductive model for our Writing Center that we daily labor against, a model that reduces us to something even worse than a grammar lab: a tech lab where students come not to engage in critical conversations about communication, but to perform mindless technical procedures. Our skills-drills nightmare has been replaced by a point-and-click one.

There are institutional dimensions of this nightmare as well. If we offer basic how-to technical instruction, we are potentially encroaching on turf staked out by other units on campus. Our claim that tech work is within our mission rests on our belief that technology is inextricably linked to communication. We point out that communication increasingly occurs in spaces different from the 8.5" X 11" sheets of paper used for traditional essays. Increasingly, communication is accomplished through websites, digital slide presentations, digital videos, and desktop-published documents. Communicators are asked to avail themselves of the affordances associated with these media and modes, which means that communication is not limited to written words, but is the result of the "interanimation" (Blakesley, 2004, p. 112) of semiotic elements: written and spoken words, moving and still images, graphs, diagrams, illustrations, animations, layout elements, and music and other sounds. Even composing in print media increasingly means using sophisticated desktop-publishing applications to create intensely designed, multimodal documents. The sociocognitive processes of composing in and for these "new media" are inextricably linked to technical processes. Supporting the one without the other makes no sense (see Appendix A for an example of how we represent our Composing and Teaching in Digital Environments program to the university).

But what happens when student composers want to separate out their technical concerns and anxieties? What happens when—impatient with our questions about their rhetorical situations and the messages they hope to communicate—they try to pressure us into providing basic technical tutorials? Surely something is wrong.

Or is it? The field of composition and rhetoric is currently reconfiguring itself in ways that make this "I just want to scan" nightmare less scary.

---

[1] The earliest documentation of this problem at MSU that I can find is in an unpublished paper that Mark Hara wrote as an Undergraduate Writing Consultant in MSU's Writing Center in 1997 (see Thomas, Hara, & DeVoss, 2000).

In this chapter, I would like to locate the preparation and practice of multi-literacy (ML) consultants within the field's newly reinvigorated concern for rhetoric as a material practice. It should be noted from the start, however, that an emphasis on the material and the corporeal is a retreat from neither the cultural nor the symbolic. As John Fiske (1992) observes, "the material, the symbolic, and the historical are not separate categories but interactive lines of force" (p. 155).

In focusing on rhetoric's materiality, I mean to emphasize two fundamental and related considerations. First, I mean to focus on the specific material forms that rhetorical compositions take: black words on a white sheet of paper, black words and color photographs on a glossy sheet of cardstock, a PDF document posted on a website, and so on. The message "Stop the war" can be communicated through a photograph depicting the horrors of war, through a set of bullet points on a PowerPoint slide, or through a research-intensive essay. These differences in material form are not incidental (see e.g., Blair, 1999; Kress & Van Leeuwen, 2001).

Second, I wish to emphasize the material processes involved in rhetorical production, reproduction, and distribution. We are used to treating the "composing process" as a sociocognitive activity, but until recently, we have not paid much attention to it as a process that involves technologies, media, and other material resources. Still less have we thought about what happens after the composition is complete. The question of how a given composition will get to its audience is often elided (see Trimbur, 2000; Yancey, 2004).

MULTILITERACY CONSULTING AT MSU

Before I begin my proposal for materializing consulting practices, I want to briefly describe the context that facilitated my thinking about these issues. My views have been shaped primarily by my experience at MSU's Writing Center, where I worked as a graduate student (1998–2000) and then as associate director (summer 2003–summer 2006), codirector (fall 2006), and director (spring and summer 2007).[2] MSU's Center has a long history of experimenting with emergent technologies and media (DeVoss, 2002; Thomas, Hara, & DeVoss, 2000). The Center supports a wide range of practices related to technology, new media, and multimodal communication. DWCs provide one-on-one support for composers working on multimodal

---

[2]The current director of the MSU Writing Center is Trixie G. Smith.

compositions, including webpages, desktop-published documents, digital animations, and digital videos. We also offer a series of "Communicating Effectively with . . ." classroom presentations ("Communicating Effectively with Poster Displays," ". . . with the Web," ". . . with Designed Print Documents," ". . . with PowerPoint," ". . . with Digital Video"; see Appendix D). In addition to working with students, we contribute to faculty development through workshops on integrating new media into the writing-intensive classroom and through one-on-one support. Faculty make appointments with DWCs to work on their own websites or PowerPoint presentations, and they meet with administrators to plan assignments and syllabi. To support all of this work, the MSU Writing Center provides a technology-rich space for composers, investing not only in computers, but also scanners, cameras, microphones, and other media-production tools. As laptops have become increasingly powerful, the Center has successfully applied for funding for laptop carts, which has increased our capacity in numerous ways. The perspectives I articulate in this chapter have been thoroughly shaped by this environment.

MATERIALITY AND THE LABOR
OF RHETORICAL PRODUCTION

When I said a moment ago that the message "Stop the war" can be communicated through a variety of modes and media, I was engaging in a bit of sleight of hand. These various semiotic options have not all historically been treated under the domain of rhetoric, and they have not all been available to nonspecialist composers. Writing and speaking have been considered "general skills," but producing video content or complex print documents have long been relegated to highly trained specialists: cinematographers, photographers, audio engineers, graphic designers, illustrators, typesetters, lithographers, and so on. The "writer," in this system, is only contributing a fraction of the labor that results in effective communication.

But systems for dividing labor are always in a state of flux. This division of labor is not inevitable, but rather the result of complex cultural and technological realities. At one time, those who could afford to do so might have written documents longhand and paid someone else to type them. The ease of word processing, however, has altered this practice. Digital technologies are bringing about radical changes in the way we think about and practice the labor or rhetorical production. As John Trimbur (2004) points out, "distinctions between author, designer, and printer are starting to collapse" (p. 269). Likewise, Kress and Van Leeuwen (2001) observe that, although multimodal texts may have previously required multiple composers with different specialties,

> in the age of digitization, the different modes have technically become the same at some level of representation, and they can be operated by one multi-skilled person, using one interface, one mode of physical manipulation, so that he or she can ask, at every point: "Shall I express this with sound or music?", "Shall I say this visually or verbally?", and so on. (p. 2)

The ensemble of specialists who have historically divided up the tasks of media production in previous eras is converging into a new kind of rhetor, a nonspecialist who controls a dizzying variety of semiotic resources (words, graphs, music, photographs, video clips, colors, interactive components) and who is not just responsible for the production of rhetorical compositions, but who is also responsible for overseeing their circulation, including their *reproduction* and *distribution*.

This reconception of the rhetor, however, runs counter to some of our more entrenched constructions of the academy and the work that goes on there. The academy is populated by scholars and researchers whose job it is to have ideas and write about them. The labor of giving that writing material form, of typesetting and design, as well as the labor of delivering that writing to an audience has historically been viewed as nonacademic labor. Not only does this reconception of the rhetor involve a "collapse" in the division of labor associated with rhetorical production, it also involves a critique of traditional hierarchies that privilege the symbolic expression of ideas in words over the material labor of production. Writing has always had what John Trimbur (2000) calls its "blue-collar side" (p. 189); we have all experienced the work of photocopying, collating, and binding a complicated report for a large group of people; we have all had to deal with paper jams and misfeeds. New media production, however, can involve rather more work of this sort: digitizing video, burning DVDs, managing files on a networked drive—and, yes, scanning photographs.

"For post-process theorizing to rematerialize writing," John Trimbur (2004) writes, "we need to recast the figure of the composer and its essayist legacy—to see writers not just as makers of meaning but as makers of the means of producing meaning out of the available resources of representation" (p. 262). Trimbur cites Walter Benjamin's conception of the "author as producer." Benjamin rejects the reliance on academically privileged forms, claiming that

[margin handwritten note: material production]

> Significant literary work can only come into being in a strict alternation
> between action and writing; it must nurture the inconspicuous forms
> that better fit its influence in active communities than does the preten-
> tious, universal gesture of the book—in leaflets, brochures, articles, and
> posters. Only this prompt language shows itself actively equal to the
> moment. (cited in Trimbur, 2004, pp. 265-266)

Given this embrace of multiple material forms, one suspects that Benjamin
would have loved the idea of multiliteracy centers.

Stuart Selber helps us confront the transformation from composer to
producer that Trimbur describes. Selber (2004) argues for a "professionally responsible" approach to computer literacy. Conceding that "most
approaches to functional literacy are utterly impoverished," Selber sets
forth "parameters" that "position functional literacy as essentially a social
problem, one that involves values, interpretation, contingency, communication, deliberation, and more" (p. 498). Within this more sophisticated
framework, Selber argues that the writing classroom should include opportunities to learn the technical quotidian that many writing instructors—
adopting what Haas and Neuwirth (1994) have called a "computers are not
our job" attitude (p. 325)—would rather ignore. Noting that "students reach
technological impasses when they lack the computer-based expertise
needed to solve a writing or communication problem," Selber suggests that
"a functionally literate student resolves technological impasses confidently
and strategically" (p. 493).

Likewise, DeVoss, Cushman, and Grabill (2005) explore the notion of
author as producer in their recent discussion of the relationship between
infrastructure and communication. Claiming that "infrastructures are
absolutely necessary for writing teachers and their students to understand
if we hope to enact the possibilities offered by new-media composing" (p.
16), they offer the following list of infrastructural components:

- computer networks
- network configurations
- operating systems, computer programs, interfaces, and their
  interrelatedness
- network, server, and storage access rights and privileges
- courses and curricula
- the existence and availability of computer classrooms
- decision-making processes and procedures for who gets
  access to computer classrooms

- the design and arrangement of computer classrooms
- time periods of classes
- availability of faculty, students, and spaces outside of set and scheduled class times
- writing classifications and standards (e.g., what is writing; what is good writing)
- metaphors of computer programs; metaphors people use to describe programs; metaphors people use to describe their composing processes
- purposes and uses of new-media work
- audiences for new-media work, both inside and outside the university. (pp. 21–22)

Embodying the interrelatedness of the material, the cultural, and the historical that Fiske references in the passage quoted earlier, in this list, the technical intermingles with the human, the material with the social and symbolic.

DeVoss, Cushman, and Grabill (2005) observe that new-media composers are asked to make "a number of 'nonwriting' decisions related to audience and the technological and rhetorical needs of that audience (e.g., bandwidth, screen size, media form and function)" (p. 30). Noting that "few scholars offer frameworks for understanding the spaces within which such compositions are produced" (p. 37), they provide an "infrastructural framework," which

> creates a tool for composers to navigate the systems within and across which they work, creates a moment for reflection and change within institutional structures and networks, and creates a framework for understanding writing that moves forward our understandings of how composing and compositions change shape within the complex dynamics of networks. (p. 37)

A multiliteracy center can be both a part of the infrastructure that supports new media composing and a space where students critically reflect on and learn to exploit the infrastructural resources available to them. It can facilitate a professionally responsible approach to functional computer literacy. In short, it can be a site that welcomes the author as producer. From this perspective, the nightmare of the student who comes to the multiliteracy center to scan is no longer scary. Trimbur (2000, 2004), Selber (2004), and DeVoss, Cushman, and Grabill (2005)

recover the importance of supporting the material dimensions of composing as both crucial to the concerns of communicators in a digital age
and as legitimate points of focus for those charged with the teaching of
writing.

Of course, while the scanner's lamp slides across the photograph, an
ML consultant might happen to ask the student composer a few questions,
such as, "How do you plan to use this image in your project?" and "What
does this image mean to you?" <u>ML consultants know how to be sneaky.</u>
More important, as the student looks around the Center and meets consultants, she or he will hopefully see the value of returning for additional support and may be more receptive to these richer conversations (see chaps.
3 and 6, this volume).

MULTILITERACY CONSULTING
AND EXPERTISE

With this orientation toward materiality, we are better able to confront the
question of how to prepare ML consultants for their daily work. What do
ML consultants need to know if they are to support the material processes
of production, reproduction, and distribution that new media rhetors must
engage in? What kinds of expertise and skill sets should they possess? How
does materiality ask us to transform our models of consulting?

These questions raise the vexed issue of expertise as it relates to the
collapse in the division of rhetorical labor. Communicators in the age of
new media are able to choose from a broader range of semiotic assets, and
they are asked to control a broader range of material processes, including
processes of reproduction and distribution. This convergence, however,
does not imply that communicating with words is the same as communicating with photographs or that a paper-based essay is no different from a
digital video. Different materials require different literacies and different
competencies. On any given day, ML consultants might find themselves
helping clients lighten and color-correct digital photographs, offering "readings" of video clips that clients have embedded in their websites and
manipulating type in complex and precise ways to accommodate a graphical element in a poster. Here is the hard truth of the matter: ML consultants *are* asked to be "all things to all people." They are asked to be photographers, graphic designers, illustrators, web coders, technicians, program-
mers, as well as teachers and meaning makers.

To confront rhetoric as a material practice, ML consultants need three fundamental literacies: (a) ML consultants need to understand the particular material forms that rhetorical compositions can take, as well as the material contexts in which they circulate: a web page that combines photographs, words, and design elements or a chapbook that combines charts, graphs, and illustrations. ML consultants need to be sensitized to the affordances and constraints of these material forms. This set of literacies allows ML consultants to engage clients in generative conversations about their work, suggesting at times that it might be useful to offer an interpretation of a photograph, while at other times it might be more productive to explore the placement of the photograph within the larger composition. But the clients with whom ML consultants work want to do more than just talk and plan. They will want to produce and publish their compositions. Therefore, (b) ML consultants will need to understand the material processes of production and distribution, which means (in part) helping clients negotiate the technical processes demanded by the specific material forms within which they are working. But a brilliant rhetorician who is also an expert technician will not necessarily be able to create rich learning environments for the clients with whom she or he works. For that, (c) ML consultants will need pedagogical literacies. This means knowing when to offer an interpretation of a video clip or illustration and when to invite clients to articulate for themselves the messages they are hoping to communicate. It means knowing when to ask a question ("Can you remember the protocol for naming an HTML file?") and when to provide direction ("HTML file names should not contain space characters"). It means knowing when to impose a firm structure on a session and when to invite the client to play freely with the available technologies.

As I describe them here, multiliteracy center workers sound like super-consultants. They possess an amazing array of literacies and capacities related to everything from desktop publishing to video editing. They can provide a sophisticated rhetorical analysis of a photograph or poster as easily as of an academic essay. They know just how to use their knowledge and skills to create the richest possible learning environment for the student composers they serve. Asking for such consultants might seem like asking for the sun, moon, and stars if it were not for the fact that we are all increasingly asked to have these skills in our public, professional, and personal lives—and if it were not for the fact that I have been fortunate enough to have worked at writing centers over the past 10 years alongside many ML consultants who have more than met these expectations and have collectively provided effective support for thousands of clients working on new media projects.

PREPARING ML CONSULTANTS:
THE PROBLEM OF REDUCTIONISM

If I am right, and to some extent ML consultants need to be all things to all people, how does a multiliteracy center develop a cohort of these superconsultants? Clearly, the answer calls for a multifaceted approach. Recruitment strategies are an important piece of the puzzle. In addition to recruiting through long-cultivated connections with language-centered units, we need to develop relationships with folks in graphic design, film and video production, and related units. We need to pay more attention to sections of resumes—like "Technical Skills" or "Computer Experience"—that previously seemed peripheral. Certain experiences that consultants bring to the center—past employment as webmaster, for instance, or serving as layout editor of the high school newspaper—will take on new relevance. Elective classes in web design or video production will become noteworthy (for discussions of recruitment, see Selfe, 2005; Sheridan, 2006).

Most ML consultants I have worked with have entered the writing center with a foundation of relevant literacies developed through professional, academic, and personal experiences. They might be amateur film-makers, for instance, or might have served as web designers for a local nonprofit organization. At MSU, except for a few special cases, our DWCs are generalist consultants as well. They have been prepared alongside their "analog" peers and have extensive experience creating rich learning opportunities for students working on traditional academic writing. They have a deep understanding of the fundamental philosophy of the writing center, including our desire to "produce better writers, not [just] better writing" (North, 1984, p. 438). Preparing DWCs, then, rarely means starting from ground zero. Instead, the challenge is to supplement the existing experiences and competencies that consultants bring to the project of multiliteracy consulting by creating additional opportunities for guided observation, practice, reading, and dialogue.

Having said this, I want to turn to what I perceive to be one of the key challenges of preparing ML consultants. Faced with the overwhelming task of having to be all things to all people, it is easy to become reductive. Most of us who consider ourselves amateur web designers, for instance, are familiar with the various "rules" or "tips" that proliferate on the web: "avoid clutter," "use a consistent color scheme," and "never use popup windows." I would argue that such tips serve an important function. To find our way in territories of communication that are new to us, we need concrete help that guides us through decisions, especially when those decisions need to be made quickly and expediently.

But there are risks involved here as well. Relying on easy formulas risks communicating to learners an impoverished understanding of multimodal rhetoric. Writing centers and the field of composition have had to fight against a rule-based approach to the teaching of writing. We have labored to help students and the broader public see that writing cannot be distilled into simple forms and formulas or rules for "correctness," but is a complex set of social, cultural, and cognitive practices learned over time through embedded experience. Expanding our work to include multimodality should not be an occasion to reintroduce a skills-drills approach.

Designer Nick Ragouzis (1997) addresses this issue, noting that, "in our concern to help amateur designers to avoid making the worst web design mistakes, we forge and promulgate a body of rules—those familiar lists of Dos and Don'ts that we find in countless texts on 'good' web design." But this "rule-making . . . is insidious" because "it encourages the notion that one can do an acceptable design without wrestling with the difficult questions raised by the total context in which a site exists." If we "are really concerned with educating amateur designers to do good design on the web, then we should teach them design . . . not give them lists of silly rules." I do not know whether Ragouzis has ever taught writing, but I find the goal of getting communicators to "wrestle with the difficult questions raised by the total context" a nice encapsulation of what I try to do in the writing classroom and what I try to prepare my writing consultants to help their clients do in the Writing Center. The question, then, is how do we preserve the richness and complexity of wrestling with multimodal rhetoric as an embedded practice (as Ragouzis suggests, we should be wary of shortcuts).

I offer four answers to this question: (a) make a point of mapping out the knowledge domains that relate to multimodal rhetoric, (b) seek out heuristic rules rather than algorithmic ones, (c) have conversations about lots of examples of multimodal compositions, and (d) adopt a project-based approach.

> 1. *Map the Terrain.* Rather than turning hastily to a reductive set of rules and formulas, we might ask ML consultants to be strategic surveyors of relevant knowledge domains and paradigms. They might not have time to add a second major in video production, for instance, but they can map out the broad contours of this field, gaining a broader sense of the possibilities and options available to them and the clients they serve.

This became clear to me at a recent presentation by Susan Hilligoss. In her talk at the 2004 CCCC, Hilligoss (2004) handed out a map of visual rhetoric that consists of useful categories, each illustrated by key works. Hilligoss' categories include "Vision research," "Visual culture," "Information graphics and visualization," "Visual rhetoric and visual argument," and "Formalist theory." Although some might find this gesture unremarkable, I would argue that, for those of us new to visual rhetoric, important learning happens as we interrogate this map. We learn, for instance, that visual studies is not just another word for graphic design. We are introduced to different paradigms that approach the problem of visuality from different directions. Hilligoss offers us a taxonomy of possibilities. Without this broader sense of the range of possibilities, we cannot make informed choices about what to focus on at any given moment as we work on our own professional development or as we work with other composers. Our choices will be capricious rather than strategic.

2. *Seek out heuristic rules instead of algorithmic ones.* Mike Rose (1980) makes a distinction between an "algorithmic" rule (which tends to be rigid, authoritative, and limiting) and a "heuristic" rule (which tends to be flexible, open ended, and generative). We should seek out heuristic rules as we confront multimodality. Many of us, for instance, have found Robin Williams' *Non-Designer's Design Book* useful. Rather than offering a series of tips or formulas, Williams presents four principles of design: contrast, repetition, alignment, and proximity (CRAP). Using simple examples, Williams demonstrates the power and elasticity of these principles, which can be applied to a variety of modes and media: from brochures to web pages. I am sure some professional graphic designers would object to the simplicity of Williams' presentation, but her principles have a greater heuristic value than the "avoid clutter" variety that composers new to multimodality often turn to in desperation.

3. *Have conversations about lots of examples.* Discussing examples of multimodal rhetoric allows ML consultants to apply diverse approaches to multimodality. For instance, one of my favorite texts to use in ML consultant preparation is the famous *We Can Do It!* poster that depicts Rosie the Riveter. The goal is to

inquire not just into our interpretation of this text, but into the various frameworks that enable the interpretive process. We systematically rotate through different approaches, interrogating what each one reveals and hides.

Rhetoric

What was the rhetorical context that gave rise to this text?
What exigencies was it meant to address?
Who was its intended audience?
What strategies of persuasion are employed?
What considerations of the ethics of persuasion need to be considered?
Is this propaganda?

Graphic Design and Illustration

How are space, typography, and color used in this composition?
What visual style does this depiction take (e.g., photoistic, pen and ink, watercolor)?
What tools were used to produce this composition?

Cultural Studies

What do we need to know about the cultural and historical context for this composition in order to approach it productively?
How are gender, class, race, and national identity evoked?
What considerations of the ethics of representation need to be accounted for?

We take a similar approach with a wide range of multimodal artifacts: photographs, video clips, websites, and desktop-published documents (see Appendix B for a list of examples).

To foreground the challenges that multimodal rhetoric as a set of rhetorical practices introduces into writing center practice, I have developed a set of "thought puzzles" like the following:

Max is working on a brochure for a student organization and comes to the writing center for help. The organization values diversity and Max is determined to select a photograph for the cover of the brochure that visually communicates this. But he's been unable to find a suitable photograph and asks his consultant to show him how to make a composite photo. He hopes to insert a student of color from one photo into another photo that includes only white students. What kind of conversation should the digital writing consultant have with Max? Would it change things if Max possessed a photo similar to the proposed composite, but couldn't use it because it was technically deficient (dark, blurry, small, etc.)?[3]

Narratives like this one help us go beyond issues of design and communication to discuss pedagogical options, providing a chance for ML consultants to generate ideas for shaping the conversation in productive ways.

4. *Take a project-based approach.* The most important learning occurs as ML consultants work individually and collaboratively on their own multimodal projects. Depending on the situation, they identify projects that are relevant to their personal or professional goals, such as a digital portfolio, or identify projects that will contribute to the mission of the Writing Center, such as a new brochure or a new resource for our website (see chaps. 8 and 9, this volume). Projects are selected so that consultants can experience and reflect on a wide range of practices related to multimodal rhetoric within an authentic rhetorical context that includes an exigency, purpose, and audience. Again, we systematically name for each other the different frameworks that can be applied to our projects, asking how a graphic designer might critique our layout, how a cultural studies critic might analyze a photograph that we have chosen, or how a usability specialist might test the site's architecture.

As we go about this project-based work in the technology-rich space of the Writing Center, we are working to establish a professional community of collaboration and inquiry. We rely on each other as resources for solving technical and rhetorical problems. We critique each other's compositions and share examples of compositions that make productive comparisons

---

[3]This scenario was inspired by an actual case in which an African-American student was inserted into a photograph being used for a college recruitment brochure (see Durhams, 2000). For other scenarios, see Appendix C (see also Dragga, 1993, pp. 83–84).

with our own. This working community of what Richard Selfe (chap. 5, this volume) calls "advanced literacy practitioners," I would argue, more than a set of skills or a body of knowledge, is the basis for our practice.

MULTILITERACY CONSULTING

If kairos refers, as James Kinneavy (1986) says, to "the appropriateness of the discourse to the particular circumstances of the time, place, speaker, and audience involved" (p. 84), our approach to consulting at the Writing Center is fundamentally kairotic. As writing consultants, our job is to facilitate conversations in which students explore the possibilities for rhetorical success that can be realized through a negotiation between themselves as rhetorical agents and the context in which they are writing. This means, among other things, that we do not adopt simplistic notions of "good" writing or "bad" writing. A poem might be wildly successful within the context of a literary journal and its readers, but completely useless as a memo. To make the concept of kairos accessible to writers, we use the acronym Mode/medium/genre, Audience, Purpose, Situation (MAPS). MAPS is an easy way to remind ourselves and our clients of fundamental contextual variables that converge into an opportunity for rhetorical intervention at any given moment in time.[4]

As several writers have observed, a kairotic approach can be productively extended to include not just traditional rhetorical choices about diction, style, and argumentative strategy, but also choices about mode and medium and the technologies associated with them (see Sheridan, Ridolfo, & Michel, 2005; Shipka, 2005; Yancey, 2004). For instance, a composer who hopes to communicate a message to a particular neighborhood might decide that a more traditional paper-based newsletter hand-delivered to residents would be more effective than a beautiful web page in a neighborhood whose residents lacked access to the Internet. Even a client who has been assigned a particular medium (e.g., a PowerPoint to accompany an oral presentation) typically has a number of choices to make about material issues, such as mode: Should the composition include photos, charts, illustrations, music? What color schemes, layout schemes, and fonts should be used? Like choices about diction and argumentative strategy, we feel

---

[4]Patricia Stock, founding director of the MSU Writing Center, introduced the use of MAPS to our practice. She was introduced to this approach by Bernard Van't Hul, former director of composition at the University of Michigan (Stock, 2001).

that such choices should be informed by the audience of and purpose for the rhetorical intervention. One audience might find that strategic integration of music would be engaging, whereas another might feel it distracting (for related discussions, see Fishman, chap. 3, this volume, Griffin, 2007; Thomas, Hara, & DeVoss, 2000).

When clients come to the Writing Center seeking help with a web page, digital video, or other multimodal project, we typically begin by developing a rich profile of their rhetorical situations. We initiate conversations away from the computer, which allows us to have a generative discussion without the distraction of keyboards, mice, and urgently flashing cursors (Thomas, Hara, & DeVoss, 2000). We tell clients that we will be able to serve them more effectively if we begin by gathering important information about their assignment, their project, and the context in which they are working. We ask to see assignment sheets; we ask clients to identify their target audience and rhetorical purpose.

But with a material understanding of kairos operating, new issues arise. To this end, I have adapted MAPS so that it focuses attention on materiality, expanding the contextual variables to include, for instance, media of delivery and media of distribution (see Table 4.1). Moreover, listing these factors along both X and Y axes helps to establish relationships between factors, reminding us that these variables are not isolated and independent, but instead form a network of interconnected concerns. At the intersection of mode and purpose, for instance, we are reminded of concerns about which modes will best address the rhetorical purpose of the project. A student exploring the way the dominant culture reinforces gender stereotypes, for instance, might decide that a visual mode is important because it will allow the student to directly address images found in print and TV advertisements. Looking at the intersection of mode and media of delivery would help remind us to select media that are appropriate for visual modes; for instance, a digital slide presentation might be more effective than paper because it negates the need for color printers. But how will this slide show get to its intended audience? We are reminded of this question at the intersection of audience and media of distribution, which forces us to inquire into whether it is practical to distribute a digital slide show to our intended readers. If our only audience is the teacher, we can burn the slide show on a disk and hand it to him or her during class. But if we need to get the show to 100 end users who are dispersed in space, CDs might not be practical. We might turn to e-mail, but that decision will lead to other decisions about keeping the file size of the presentation small enough. I designed this table not for clients, but for ML consultants, wanting to provide them with a tool for keeping track of the web of relationships that can inform their conversations with the student composers who come to them for support.

In the initial stages of our session, we often ask clients to sketch the layout of their website. We have photocopied on oversized paper the image of an empty web browser—scaled to 800 X 600 pixels (a common monitor resolution)—so that clients can create quick mock-ups of their sites. For digital video projects, we might suggest that clients storyboard their projects. Although analogous to outlining in the sense that it involves the representation of ideas through time, storyboarding is different in the way that it maps out the sequence and simultaneity of multiple semiotic resources (visual and aural elements) in a way that does not have a ready analogue in traditional academic essays.

If clients are at the beginning of their composing process when we meet with them, some of the decisions they make during this session will dictate possibilities and limitations that they will have to live with for the remainder of their projects. For instance, most clients, as experienced consumers of web content, can describe the layout and semiotic elements of a website, but many cannot guess the constellation of software applications that might be used to produce such a composition. They see the use of specialized fonts, graphical elements, and animations configured in a precise spatial relationship, but they do not understand the amount of time and the level of expertise that went into creating the page. They rely on us to guide them through this planning process. If, for instance, they follow our recommendation to begin by mocking up their site in Photoshop, they will have to live with the consequences of that decision. One set of the consequences arises from the fact that, although Photoshop can create the graphical elements of a website and is often used as a tool for mocking up a layout, it is not the best application for producing the working HTML version of the page. This means that clients will have to plan for the extra step of converting their mockup to an HTML format in order to complete their project. My point here is not to rehearse the technical details of Photoshop and HTML, but to give a sense of the literacies that ML consultants rely on as they help clients negotiate the material processes of production.

[handwritten marginal note: Storyboarding]

TABLE 4.1.
MAPS HEURISTIC, RECONFIGURED TO REFLECT MATERIALITY.

	PURPOSE & EXIGENCY	AUDIENCE	GENRE	MODES
GENERAL	What is this rhetorical intervention meant to accomplish? What problems is this composition meant to address?	Who is (are) the target audience(s) for this composition? What values, attitudes, behaviors and beliefs do I need to take into account as I plan for this rhetorical intervention?	What are the constraints and affordances of available genres? (e.g., argumentative essay, memo, poem, letter, jeremiad, etc.)	What are the constraints and affordances of available modes? (e.g., aural, visual, kinesthetic, multimodal.)
PURPOSE & EXIGENCY	—	What is the relationship between my target audience and my purpose? What role does my audience play in addressing my exigency? What beliefs, dispositions, and actions should my rhetorical intervention facilitate in order to address my exigency? What audiences does my purpose suggest that I address?	What genres will best address my exigency? (e.g., a personal narrative might be suited to establishing an emotional connection with an audience, but might not be suited to communicating more general information necessary for informed action.)	What modes will best address my exigency? (e.g., if I'm trying to address the negative images people associate with the city of Detroit, perhaps a visual mode is appropriate.)
AUDIENCE	See Audience > Purpose	—	What genres will be most effective with my target audience? What genres do they value? Are they familiar with? (e.g., if I try to introduce a neighborhood group I'm helping to start through an academic essay, I might alienate my non-academic audience.)	What modes will be most effective with my target audience? Do they value? (e.g., some audiences might be pre-disposed to appreciate multimodal rhetoric while others might privilege the written word.)
GENRE	See Genre > Purpose	See Genre > Audience	—	What confluence of genre and mode will be most effective in my rhetorical situation? (e.g., if my goal is a detailed

MEDIA OF DELIVERY	MEDIA OF DISTRIBUTION	INFRASTRUCTURAL RESOURCES	RELATION TO OTHER TEXTS
What are the constraints and affordances of available media of delivery? (e.g., website, DVD, paper, etc.)	What are the constraints and affordances of available media of distribution? (e.g., e-mail, WWW, telephone, radio, TV, direct mail, community bulletin boards, etc.)	What infrastructural resources are available to me? What technologies, raw materials? How much time? What knowledge and competencies do I possess? What knowledge and competencies do potential collaborators possess?	How does this composition relate to other texts that I have created or might create? That others have created or might create?
What MoDe of delivery will best address the problem that I'm hoping to address? (e.g., if I'm trying to raise initial interest in a neighborhood group, perhaps a tri-fold brochure is appropriate.)	What MoDi will best address my exigency? (e.g., if I want to raise initial interest in a neighborhood group, perhaps walking door-to-door with my brochure is an effective way of getting my message to my audience.)	What do I discover when I assess my infrastructural resources from the perspective of purpose and exigency? (e.g., to produce a photo-intensive website, I might need a camera, computer, web editing application, etc.)	How can an orchestrated use of multiple texts (written by me or by others) help me achieve my purpose? (e.g., my brochure might include a URL to a website that contains more detailed information.)
What MoDe will be most effective with my target audience? What MoDe do they value? What attitudes and dispositions do I need to consider? (e.g., some audiences might value a video while other audiences might privilege the book as a form.)	What MoDi will be most effective with my target audience? What MoDi do they value? (e.g., if the most salient fact about my audience is that they are intensive web users, web-based distribution might be appropriate.)	What infrastructural resources does my audience have access to? (e.g., if my audience doesn't have access to the Internet, a webpage isn't going to be an effective medium.)	What relationship does my audience have with other texts that I and others might create? (e.g., if I put the URL to a website on a brochure, will my audience visit it?)
What confluence of MoDe and genre will be most effective in my rhetorical situation? (e.g., A long analytical	What confluence of MoDe and genre will be most effective in my rhetorical situation?, (e.g., if my goal is to	How do infrastructural resources available to me and my audience support my choice of genre?	What other genres might be placed into service to complement the affordances of my chosen genre?

	PURPOSE & EXIGENCY	AUDIENCE	GENRE	MODES
				deconstruction of negative images associated with the city of Detroit, perhaps an analytical essay combined with visuals like photographs would be appropriate.)
MODE	See Mode > Purpose	See Mode > Audience	See Mode > Genre	—
MEDIUM OF DELIVERY	See MoDe > Purpose	See MoDe > Audience	See MoDe > Genre	See MoDe > Modes
MEDIUM OF DISTRI-BUTION	See MoDe > Purpose	See MoDi > Audience	See MoDi >Genre	See MoDi > Modes
INFRA-STRUC-TURAL RESOURCES	See IR > Purpose	See IR > Audience	See IR > Genre	See IR > Modes
RELATION TO OTHER TEXTS	See Texts > Purpose	See Texts > Audience	See Texts > Genre	See Texts > Modes

Note: For the purposes of this table, *Media of Delivery* refers to the end experience of the reader, whereas *Media of Distribution* refers to the way a composition gets to a reader. I might, for instance, know that my target audience is mostly faculty at research universities who have

MEDIA OF DELIVERY	MEDIA OF DISTRIBUTION	INFRASTRUCTURAL RESOURCES	RELATION TO OTHER TEXTS
essay is appropriate might be easier to read on paper than on a computer monitor.)	distribute a detailed written analysis printed on paper, perhaps emailing a PDF or mailing a hardcopy would be best.)		(e.g., a website might have links to both a white paper and a fact sheet.)
What medium will support the modes that you have identified as appropriate? What modes does your chosen medium lend itself to? (e.g., the Web can support visual and aural modes; at the same time, the Web demands certain attention to the visual in ways that other media might not.)	What medium of distribution will support your preferred modes? What modes does your preferred medium lend itself to? (e.g., a brochure might accommodate photographs and design elements—visual modes —but it might be more difficult to distribute than a website.)	What kinds of modes do the available raw materials, technologies, and skills enable? What kinds of resources do your chosen modes require?	What modes might be enabled by past or future texts that I or others might create? (e.g., a white paper with lots of written information might be coupled with a website that contains more iconic information.)
—	What media of distribution will enable my chosen media of delivery (and vice versa)?	What infrastructural resources are needed to enable my chosen modes? What modes to available resources suggest?	How can other texts that I or others might create complement my chosen mode?
See MoDi > MoDe	—	What MoDi are enabled by available resources? What resources are needed to enable the MoDi I've chosen?	How can various media enable the distribution of other texts that I or others might create?
See IR > MoDe	See IR > MoDi	—	What other texts might available resources enable?
See Texts > MoDe	See Texts > MoDi	See Texts > IR	—

access to free laser printing and high-speed Internet connections. I might distribute an article to them by e-mailing a PDF. The medium of distribution is the Internet and computer, but (if my readers print the PDF and read from hardcopy) the medium of delivery is a paper.

CONCLUSION

My goal in this chapter has been to locate multiliteracy consulting within the field's evolving understanding of rhetoric as a material practice. This understanding can provide a coherent basis for a set of practices that at other moments in history writing centers might not have viewed as "writing." To many, it may still feel strange that writing centers, even if they are reconceived as multiliteracy centers, should take on the mission of supporting communication that happens through photographs, music clips, and other media elements, in addition to the written word. It may feel even stranger to assume responsibility for providing technical support: scanning photographs, digitizing video, recording voiceovers, and coding CSS style sheets for web pages. If we accept, however, that rhetoric is a material practice as well as a sociosymbolic one, these extensions of our work may seem less strange. Indeed, they may seem essential.

APPENDIX A
Flyers Summarizing the MSU Writing Center's
Composing and Teaching in Digital Environments Program

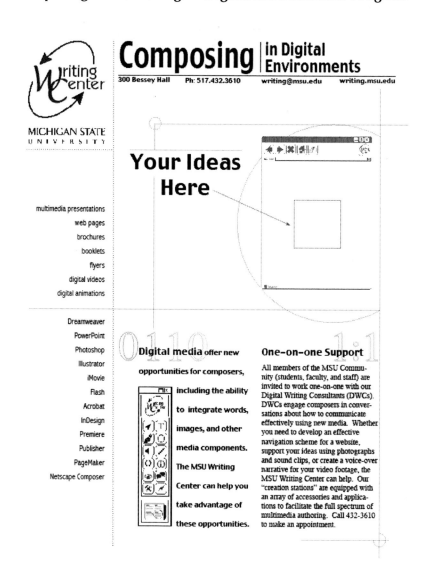

Teaching | in Digital Environments

300 Bessey Hall   Ph: 517.432.3610   writing@msu.edu   writing.msu.edu

MICHIGAN STATE
U N I V E R S I T Y

multiple literacies

visual rhetoric

presentational skills

public speaking

document design

digital communication

color schemes

non-linear structure

audience awareness

chat discussions

threaded discussions

document markup tools

digital collaboration

> [C]omputers are altering the way many of us read, write, and even think. It is not simply that the tools of literacy have changed; the nature of texts, of language, of literacy itself is undergoing crucial transformation.
>
> —William Costanzo[*]

Support for Instructors

The Writing Center can help instructors integrate new technologies into their courses in a variety of ways. Digital Writing Consultants (DWCs) work with instructors who are developing websites, PowerPoints, and other digital materials related to their teaching or research projects. Additionally, we offer a variety of **classroom presentations** focusing on specific aspects of digital composing.

Instructors are also invited to meet with Writing Center faculty to plan pedagogically effective assignments that involve digital communication. Faculty consultants can help instructors frame assignments so key rhetorical concepts, such as mode, audience, and purpose, are foregrounded. We can discuss rubrics for assessing multimedia projects effectively, and can help instructors determine hardware and software needs.

Examples of recent projects include:

- student-produced webzines
- electronic portfolios
- chapbooks of student writing
- digital video essays
- websites for non-profit organizations
- digital storytelling projects
- poster design
- electronic family histories

For more information, please contact David Sheridan (sherid16@msu.edu).

[*]Costanzo, William. "Reading, Writing, and Thinking in the Age of Electronic Literacy." *Literacy and Computers: The Complications of Teaching and Learning with Technology.* New York: Modern Language Association of America, 1994.

APPENDIX B
Examples of Multimodal Rhetoric

There are obviously many different examples of multimodal rhetoric that can be used to facilitate productive conversations in consultant preparation. Here are a few that I have found useful. All of them raise issues of persuasion, design, and culture.

(1) **The Powers of Persuasion: Posters from World War II**
The National Archives Online Exhibit

http://www.archives.gov/exhibits/powers_of_persuasion/powers_of _persuasion_home.html
These posters offer rich opportunities to look at persuasion and culture.

(2) **Eric Blumrich, Grand Theft America**

http://www.ericblumrich.com/gta.html
This is an example of Flash-based multimedia being used to communicate a political message.

(3) **360degrees: Perspectives on the Criminal Justice System**

http://360-degrees.org/
This site offers an interesting counterpoint to the approach of Blumrich; the use of the 360 degree metaphor suggests the need to consider a variety of perspectives.

(4) **The Meatrix**

http://www.themeatrix.com/
Talking animals communicate a serious message.

(5) **CSS Zen Garden**

http://www.csszengarden.com/
This archive of sites all contain the same "content," but take different approaches to design.

(6) **Sree.net**

http://www.sree.net/teaching/photoethics.html
This site contains numerous examples of journalistic photos that have been altered, raising issues of visual ethics.

(7) **Milton Glaser and Mirko Ilic (2005).** *The Design of Dissent.* **Gloucester, MA: Rockport.**

This book collects graphic design artifacts intended to communicate social messages.

(8) **Evolution. Dove Self Esteem Gallery.**

http://www.campaignforrealbeauty.com/dsef07/t5.aspx?id = 7373
This short film demonstrates the pernicious messages women receive from visual culture; it is useful for raising questions of the potentials and dangers of visual representation, including representational practices enabled by digital tools.

APPENDIX C
Cases for Thinking About ML Consulting[5]

(1) John is an experienced web surfer, but has never created a website before. The instructor for his first-year writing course has asked students to make simple home pages in which students represent themselves to a general audience. The assignment counts for a small percentage of the overall grade for the course. Most students in the class are using a free HTML editor that supports basic web design, but lacks the sophistication of a professional grade application such as Dreamweaver. John, however, is excited about the opportunity to make a website and comes to the writing center with a plan for an elaborate website that includes lots of graphics, roll over buttons, and animations. How should the ML consultant negotiate the tensions in this situation between the elaborate vision of the client, on the one hand, and his limited experience and the limited expectations of the instructor on the other? What kinds of planning around resources (software, hardware, and time) should the consultant facilitate? Is there a way to help the client develop realistic expectations without losing the initial sense of possibility and creativity that they bring to this project?

(2) Mary is creating a digital video based on a personal narrative that she has written for a writing course focused on creative nonfiction. She comes to the writing center with a stack of photographs that she needs to scan and seems uninterested in doing anything else. When her ML consultant tries to engage her in a discussion about her project, she grows impatient. She refuses to take questions about audience and purpose seriously. What should the ML consultant do? Is it okay to help the client face the technical challenges of scanning without engaging in a discussion of communication? Are there ways to raise issues about rhetoric and communication without frustrating the client? Is it okay to let Mary stay and use the scanner after her session has finished?

(3) Tony is taking an interdisciplinary urban studies course and is creating a PowerPoint presentation focusing on the city of Detroit. He

---

[5]Sam Dragga provides useful cases for raising issues related to visual ethics in "The Ethics of Delivery" (see especially pp. 83–84).

has spent a substantial amount of time driving around the city, documenting what he sees with a digital camera. He presents this archive of photos to a ML consultant and talks about his plans for composing the slide show.

(3a) The DWC notices that, although there are many photographs that evidence favorable aspects of the city (the houses of Rosedale Park, Albert Khan's skyscrapers downtown, integrated crowds at Belle Isle Zoo, etc.), Tony is only interested in selecting photos that depict negative aspects (boarded up windows, vacant lots, burned-out structures, etc.). Should the ML consultant attempt to engage Tony in a conversation about his method of selecting photographs? What would such a conversation look like?

(3b) Tony has photographed people too—mostly Black residents of the city. (Of course, he made sure that he informed his subjects of the nature of his project and asked them to sign photo-release forms before he took their pictures.) In many cases, because of the lighting conditions and camera settings, the facial features of the subjects are lost to shadows. Should the ML consultant show Tony how to lighten the photograph so that the faces of his subjects are not obscured? What if the original photos are fine, but Tony wants to make them darker to emphasize what he perceives to be the bleak quality of the landscape surrounding his subjects?

(3c) Does it matter if Tony is a Black resident of Detroit or is White and from the affluent suburb of Bloomfield Hills? Does it matter if he is from a different region of the country altogether and has only been to the city one time? Does it matter if his website will actually be posted to the web or if it will only be turned in on a CD?

(4) Allison has created a survey for a political science class. She hopes to make a web version of the survey available that is fully interactive so that respondents can fill it out online and hit a submit button that automatically e-mails the results back to Allison. While Allison, with the help of her ML consultant, easily creates the basic web version of the survey, the interactive functionality proves to be more challenging. Allison does not have time to learn the scripting necessary to provide the interactive functionality. Her consultant, however, knows of a website that provides free resources for web designers, such as uncopyrighted clip art, but-

tons, and scripts. Should the consultant help her download one of these scripts and insert it into her website? What ethical, intellectual property, and pedagogical issues would the consultant need to consider in order to make an informed choice in this situation?

(4b) What if the script was not available on a web resource site, but was actually being used by another survey website? Would it be okay for the ML consultant to have his or her client go to the source code and copy the script for her own page?

(4c) What if the script were not available on the web, but the consultant knew how to write it? Would it be appropriate for him or her to write a script for his or her client? Does it matter that although this particular script might not be available, other scripts that provide common interactive functionality, such as roll-over images and pop-up windows, are included in most web authoring applications and can be inserted automatically? Is it possible to make a distinction between using Dreamweaver to make a roll-over button (which means that it automatically inserts a simple script) and having a consultant create a script for a client?

(5) Phil is taking a cultural studies course focused on representations of class. He has decided to produce a video essay using short clips from Hollywood films that rely on common stereotypes of class. He brings in five VHS tapes, hoping to digitize portions of each. Should the consultant help him digitize the copyrighted materials? What issues surrounding intellectual property, protocols for working with source material in academic contexts, and ethics should the consultant raise? How would a consultant generate a clear understanding of Phil's goals in digitizing the film clips?

APPENDIX D
Template for "Communicating Effectively With . . ." Workshops

The MSU Writing Center offers a series of workshops for writing and writing-intensive classes. These workshops address the opportunities and challenges of different modes and media, from digital video to poster design. The goals for the workshops, however, remain largely the same. We hope participants will gain a deeper understanding of how composing decisions reflect rhetorical context. We introduce a few generative principles aimed at helping composers make effective decisions in a medium that might be new to them. We invite participants to engage in some form of composing so that they can apply the principles we have discussed and can begin to confront the various technologies involved.

To help prepare DWCs to serve as workshop facilitators and to organize the delivery of these workshops, we created a website that serves as the hub of workshop activity. The site includes outlines for all of the workshops, links to any other websites that might be used in the workshop, and links to raw materials and guides that workshop participants can use for work sessions (e.g., images, storyboard templates, and sound clips). For our workshop on PowerPoint, for instance, students could download a presentation containing a poorly designed slide that they are then asked to redesign. Workshop facilitators can access Peter Norvig's famous PowerPoint parody of Lincoln's Gettysburg Address.

Workshop Template

(1) **Critique examples.** Select examples of the media and modes being explored and invite workshop participants to discuss the strengths and weaknesses of each. Ask participants to discuss the appropriateness for various audiences and rhetorical purposes. For instance, workshop facilitators might ask, "Is this a good slide for a professional audience?" Alternatively, facilitators might present three versions of a composition (cf. the CSS Zen Garden) and ask which one is most appropriate for a particular rhetorical context.

(2) **Demonstrate and critique revisions.** Select one or two examples and show revised versions that reflect the principles of communication being explored in the workshop. For instance, a PowerPoint slide might

be redesigned based on Robin Williams' (1994) CRAP principles and/or might be redesigned for a particular rhetorical context.

(3) Invite workshop participants to engage in composing and/or play. In some cases, participants can be asked to design using the target technologies and media. In other cases, participants may need to work with paper-based mockups. Sometimes it is helpful to provide participants with raw materials (such as music and video clips for a workshop on digital video), whereas in other contexts participants can create their own materials. During work sessions, workshop facilitators circulate and answer questions.

(4) Present redesigns. Have students present their designs to the rest of the class and talk about their rhetorical goals. In a workshop we developed for eighth graders, for instance, students created digital videos in iMovie with raw materials that we provided. Presenting these at the end of a 90-minute workshop was always highly satisfying for both participants and facilitators.

(5) Explain the kind of support the writing center can provide.

REFERENCES

Blair, Carole. (1999). Contemporary U.S. memorial sites as exemplars of rhetoric's materiality. In Jack Selzer & Sharon Crowley (Eds.), *Rhetorical bodies* (pp. 16–57). Madison: University of Wisconsin Press.

Blakesley, David. (2004). Defining film rhetoric: The case of Hitchcock's *Vertigo*. In Charles A. Hill & Marguerite Helmers (Eds.), *Defining visual rhetorics* (pp. 111–134). Mahwah, NJ: Erlbaum.

DeVoss, Dànielle. (2002). Computer literacies and the roles of the writing center. In P. Gillespie (Ed.), *Writing center research: Extending the conversation* (pp. 167–185). Mahwah, NJ: Erlbaum.

DeVoss, Dànielle, Cushman, Ellen, & Grabill, Jeff. (2005). Infrastructure and composing: The *when* of new-media writing. *College Composition and Communication, 57*(1), 14–44.

Dragga, Sam. (1993). The ethics of delivery. In John Frederick Reynolds (Ed.), *Rhetorical memory and delivery: Classical concepts for contemporary composition and communication* (pp. 79–95). Hillsdale, NJ: Erlbaum.

Durhams, Sharif. (2000, September 20). UW-Madison doctors photo to stress diversity. *Milwaukee Journal Sentinel.* Retrieved May 13, 2008 from http://www2.jsonline.com:80/news/metro/sep00/uw20091900a.asp

Fiske, John. (1992). Cultural studies and the culture of everyday life. In Lawrence Grossberg (Ed.). *Cultural studies* (pp. 154–173). New York: Routledge.

Griffin, Jo Ann. (2007). Making connections with writing centers. In C. Selfe (Ed.), *Multimodal composition: Resources for teachers* (pp. 153–166). Cresskill, NJ: Hampton.

Haas, Christina, & Neuwirth, Christine M. (1994). Writing the technology that writes us: Research on literacy and the shape of technology. In Cynthia L. Selfe & Susan Hilligoss, (Eds.), *Literacy and computers: The complications of teaching and learning with technology* (pp. 319–335). New York: MLA.

Hilligoss, Susan. (2004). *Handout for* A matter of course: Toward advanced studies in visual rhetoric. San Antonio, TX: CCCC.

Kinneavy, James L. (1986). *Kairos:* A neglected concept in classical rhetoric. In Jean Dietz Moss (Ed.), *Rhetoric and praxis: The contribution of classical rhetoric to practical reasoning* (pp. 79–105). Washington, DC: The Catholic University of America Press.

Kress, Gunther R., & Van Leeuwen, Theo. (2001). *Multimodal discourse: The modes and media of contemporary communication.* London: Arnold.

North, Stephen M. (1984). The idea of a writing center. *College English, 46*(5), 433–446.

Pemberton, Michael. (2003). Planning for hypertexts in the writing center . . . or not. *Writing Center Journal, 24*(1), 9–24.

Ragouzis, Nick. (1997). *Misbegotten rules of web design.* Retrieved May 13, 2008, from http://www.enosis.com/resources/misbegot.html

Rose, Mike. (1980). Rigid rules, inflexible plans, and the stifling of language: A cognitivist analysis of writer's block. *College Composition and Communication, 31*(4), 389–401.

Selber, Stuart A. (2004). Reimagining the functional side of computer literacy. *College Composition and Communication, 55*(3), 470–503.

Selfe, Richard J. (2005). *Sustainable computer environments: Cultures of support in English studies and language arts.* Cresskill, NJ: Hampton.

Sheridan, David M. (2006). Words, images, sounds: Writing centers as multiliteracy centers. In Christina Murphy & Byron Stay (Eds.), *The writing center director's resource book* (pp. 339–350). Mahwah, NJ: Erlbaum.

Sheridan, D. M., Ridolfo, J., & Michel, A. J. (2005). The available means of persuasion: Mapping a theory and pedagogy of multimodal public rhetoric. *JAC, 24*(5), 803–844.

Shipka, Jody. (2005). A multimodal task-based framework for composing. *College Composition and Communication, 57*(2), 277–306.

Stock, Patricia. (2001). Toward a theory of genre in teacher research: Contributions from a reflective practitioner. *English Education, 33*(2), 100–114.

Thomas, Sharon, Hara, Mark, & DeVoss, Dànielle. (2000). In James A. Inman & Donna N. Sewell (Eds.), *Taking flight with OWLs: Examining electronic writing center work* (pp. 65–73). Mahwah, NJ: Erlbaum.

Trimbur, John. (2000). Composition and the circulation of writing. *College Composition and Communication, 52*(2), 188–219.

Trimbur, John. (2004). Delivering the message: Typography and the materiality of writing. In Carolyn Handa (Ed.), *Visual rhetoric in a digital world: A critical sourcebook* (pp. 260–271). Boston: Bedford.

Williams, Robin. (1994). *The non-designer's design book.* Berkeley: Peachpit Press.

Yancey, Kathleen Blake. (2004). Made not only in words: Composition in a new key. *College Composition and Communication, 56*(2), 297–328.

5

ANTICIPATING THE MOMENTUM OF CYBORG COMMUNICATIVE EVENTS

Richard (Dickie) Selfe

Ohio State University

WRITING CENTERS: A SAFE EDUCATIONAL HAVEN

Unlike some of my English studies colleagues interested in communication technologies, I do not see a crisis brewing in the near future (see Yancey, 2004). Those academic professionals and programs that choose to focus on writing and rhetoric, primarily in the alphabetic modality, will do just fine. I am convinced also that Writing Centers and the workers in them (who also focus almost exclusively on the alphabetic production modes) are likely to remain remarkably important to higher educational institutions in the future. If anything, once reluctant disciplines and professionals around us are now more concerned about their students'/employees' writing abilities than ever before (see College Board, 2004; DeVoss, forthcoming; Garay & Bernhardt, 1998). Despite frequently reported needs assessments within and outside the academic setting, however, the hard work that goes on in Writing Centers—repeated close readings and consultations, empathetic listening, collaborative problem solving, assignment translation, institutional orientation, and so on—is unlikely to be taken up to any great extent by others in higher education.

Writing Centers are safe in the sense that they have access to a remarkably important nexus of student learning needs that are not likely to fade in the near future. In this chapter, I do *not* want to suggest that an emphasis on multiple literacies, multimodal communication, digital literacies, or any other trend in English studies should encourage Writing Centers to spend time with name changes (e.g., to multiliteracy centers) or even with major changes in the face-to-face, student-centered, rhetorically based communicative focus that is their traditional strength. Those colleagues and centers that wish to remain committed to the alphabetic, from my perspective, can afford to do so. Others who are intrigued by the implications of multiliteracies and multimodality in our teaching, learning, work, infrastructures, and training might want to read on.

I do want to suggest that Writing Centers are ideally placed to help define what I will call the *anticipatory momentum* that literacy scholars and curriculum designers will need to attend to in the next 10 years. If you have moved on to this paragraph because of an interest in helping with this project—defining and redefining the formation of an anticipatory momentum for literacy scholarship—I assume that I will not offend you if I refer to the physical and online sites where this work might take place as multiliteracy centers (MLCs).

AN OVERVIEW

This chapter has six sections. "Picturing Multimodal Workflows" will attempt to paint a picture of the complexity of the terrain that MLCs can anticipate and then help map for English studies professionals and curriculum designers. Following that, in "A Cyborg, Multiliterate State of Mind," I begin making a case for developing an attitude or approach that attends carefully to human and nonhuman actors in the literacy drama that goes on in MLCs. In the "Cyborg Communicative Events," I suggest a theoretical orientation that might better help us continually redesign the literacy centers we already inhabit to continue anticipating the literacy momentum of our culture. "A Fair Hearing to Human and Nonhuman Alike" tries to demonstrate the kind of conversation we can develop if we listen carefully to the human/nonhuman agents in our communicative dramas. I describe more precisely what anticipatory momentum is and why it seems important for English studies scholars and curriculum designers. Besides defining the following term, "Advanced Literacy Practitioners" describes some important, mundane components of MLCs that will help attract the advanced practitioners we need to support students' multimodal work and illustrate how these practitioners might be integrated into the working practices of an MLC. I conclude by outlining one national project (the Digital Archive of Literacy Narratives), an attempt to create a collection point or repository for the observations that research scholars conduct in our efforts to better understand cyborg communicative events.

PICTURING MULTIMODAL WORKFLOWS

In this collection, the editors are anticipating that our current academic (and professional) momentum will take us toward MLCs regardless of whether the names of these online and/or physical facilities reflect this momentum. They anticipate, rightly I think, that the move toward multimodal workflows will drive the need for those of us in English studies to pay close attention to multiple literacies. The two key terms here for me are *multimodal* and *workflow*. I will take them in reverse order.

When I speak of workflow, I try to expand the attention of English studies professionals. By that I mean that we need to look beyond production (the production of written work, in the alphabetic sense, and beyond the production of video or audio, the production of presentations or graphic representations, etc.). In addition to these modes of production, English studies professionals need to attend to many aspects of literacy work that my interviewees suggest is important in their work. The following list is not intended to be exhaustive, but it does point, I think, to a broader range of literacy activities than those addressed in most writing and composition courses. I follow each point in the workflow description with one or more questions that have implications for changed training and coaching practices in MLCs.

In the literacy interviews of postcollegiate professionals that I have conducted, these recursive activities came up repeatedly:

- Reading, listening, and viewing of materials (intended for all types of people) in many modalities.

  Question: How often do we train coaches to read and support the creation of multimodal compositions: those that their clients create and those that they need to "read" during the research process?

- Gathering, organizing, evaluating materials (information, data, images, audio, video, . . .).

    Questions: Do we often have coaches investigate the processes of gathering, organizing, and evaluating materials and then recommend current advanced practices as they review the work habits of their clients? Do we, as literacy center directors, have some understanding about what these advanced practices might be in the disciplines we service.

- Learning a Living, not earning a living (aka, Marshall McLuhan): As professionals work, they must learn. They have multiple strategies for learning on their own, they learn from each other and on teams, they place themselves in formal and informal learning situations intentionally.

    Questions: Do we explore the learning skills, approaches, and attitudes that our clients bring to their projects and collect strategies from across the disciplines to suggest to those with a less robust set of options? From my interviews with professionals, I wonder how we might encourage the kind of commitment, play, exploration, personal mentoring, and peer problem solving that working professionals seem to have experienced?

- Sharing with stakeholders, discussing or "publishing" multimodal compositions (from the most informal and ephemeral of hallway conversations to the most formal of hardcopy publications).

    Questions: Do we help clients think carefully about other experts (in addition to the teacher), intended audiences, collaborators, and organizational readers of their work? Do we work hard with clients to make sure they understand the copyright conditions of their work and the works they use (for the purposes of publishing)? Do we talk to these authors about the many digital or online publishing/sharing opportunities of which they might take advantage in addition to sharing their work with their teacher? Do we train each other to offer valuable feedback on the visual, aural, and time-based aspects of their compositions that many digital publishing environments make available?

- Discovering additional or new problems or projects to investigate.

  Question: Do we talk about projects in terms of the trajectory that student research might take—that is, talk about their work as one moment in an ongoing intellectual enterprise?

As a short hand, I often think about these sets of literacy practices as a communicative cycle, although I have not deluded myself into thinking that it is at all linear. As my preliminary study of professional literacy practices has indicated, these processes are recursive to the extreme and not sequential. That is the whole point of the research I am suggesting that MLC workers take up. We can help both expand and complicate this multimodal workflow with testimonials from students and professionals. As a result, English studies curriculum designers will have a better sense of where multiple literacies might be taking their teaching practices (and we might be better prepared for the 21st century literacy consulting that we will need in our centers).

But what, then, of multimodality?

At each step in this massively recursive communicative cycle, we are liable, these days, to encounter multimodal materials that include visual, aural, time-based (video/animation), performative, and real-time data representations. My suspicion is that those of us in higher education are having a difficult time understanding the implications of this massively recursive, multimodal communicative cycle, because we have specialized ourselves so thoroughly. I include myself in this group. Other chapters in this volume make the case for multimodality per se, but there is certainly plenty of evidence—CCCC-sponsored research (R. Selfe, 2006), *Chronicle of Higher Education* articles (Monaghan, 2006), and policy statements from MLA Task Force (2006) and NCTE Executive Committee (2005)—that suggests that this is not a passing concern for literacy workers. In addition, my own research (R. Selfe, 2005) indicates that there are likely to be numerous local examples of multimodal literacy work in most English studies departments and programs. We need to explore the multimodal workflow of the disciplines, students, and professionals around us. Why? Because we (English studies faculty) know so little about the complex working conditions of multimodal communicators across the disciplines. Without this cumulative knowledge, we cannot anticipate the needs of academic or professional learner/communicators, much less apply our humanistic attitudes, critical approaches, and ethical concerns to those needs and practices. In other words, using my favorite 1960s vocabulary, we are in danger of making ourselves less relevant and our concerns less important to our students and the curriculum designers at our institutions.

So far, these anecdotes have surfaced within the English studies disciplines that we know so well: composition, literature, professional communication, and so on. But if my experience at Ohio State University (OSU) is any indication, MLCs will encounter students from across the curriculum. Humanities Information Systems, where I work, is in the process of designing an undergraduate computing facility for Humanities majors to be used by the college's 17 departments. We expect to fill that facility with Humanities majors who are working on projects like the ones discussed at faculty seminars during the 2005–2006 school year. Here are a few examples.

- Final papers that consist of large, involved concept maps that explain the interrelationships of Japanese cultural institutions (History);
- English–Spanish translation projects that result in four-color service-learning publications for Spanish-speaking populations in the Columbus, Ohio area (Spanish);
- Online digital portfolios that include video and audio performances (Russian);
- Ethnographic research papers that include coded audio and video clips that can be manipulated and called up in real time (Folklore);
- Data collection from field visits that take the form of audio podcast (using MP4 standards) and include visual, numeric, and alphabetic data (Biology and Agriculture);
- Serial blog "writing" that also incorporates video, audio, and visual materials (Business Communication).

I should mention that none of these activities or projects is entirely digital. They are all associated with human-to-human interactions: presentations, collaborations, and performances. They are, as the NCTE elementary teachers are willing to teach us, multimodal in the broadest sense of the word. In addition, each has both human and nonhuman actors that enrich and constrain the possibilities for communication. These projects are all cyborg in nature, and it is toward that cyborg nature that I turn to next.

A CYBORG, MULTILITERATE STATE OF MIND

It seems commonsensical to claim, then, that MLCs, in all their physical and digital configurations, could indeed be helping English studies programs understand early 21st century literacy practices. That is, they can help with this project when they become MLCs that value and attend to human interactions that are mediated by numerous nonhuman agents.

Many centers have worked and are working hard to recognize and develop the expertise to support the multimodal workflow of their clients: clients who want to take full rhetorical advantage of visual, audio, video, animated, and presentational components of their communication. The MLC, of course, must also attend to the technologies that go along with those multimodal texts. How each center manages the challenges associated with support for multimodal composition will vary from site to site. In this section, I begin to lay out a *state of mind* that goes along with this effort, a state of mind that I hope is transportable, malleable, and even transgressive.

Why a "state of mind" instead of simple advice? Let me try to answer that question briefly. Productive MLCs are not just places or spaces, physical or online. They are those things, certainly, but the work that goes on in these centers has as much to do with the approaches and attitudes of administrators, coaches, and clients as it does with the place and spaces:

- our willingness to consider a changing cultural ecology (Hawisher & C. L. Selfe, 2004) in which both human and nonhuman agents live and thrive;
- our approach to exploring the changing literacies practices we encourage and the new ones we try to understand;
- our ability to think and talk about the changeable local and global technological systems we use (R. Selfe, 2005); and
- our willingness to allow the broadest collective of nonhumans to talk to us: to enter into our planning processes.

This last item is a suggestion that may seem strange to teacher/scholars in Writing Centers across our country who typically have an impressive and important commitment to one-on-one and small-group learning experiences that *appear* to be dominated by interacting humans. In fact, those interactions are not influenced by humans alone; they are, as is always the case, cyborg communicative events. The furniture, the schedule, the lighting, the assignment, and the technology used in completing the assignment are all agents in this drama; they make a difference in the type and quality of the interactions that occur in MLCs. We just assume that all these agents (actants, using Bruno Latour's language) are mute or stable. Neither is the case. The notion that actants can talk to us is an odd practice, but an important one. The following section is an attempt to outline a broad theoretical foundation for this odd practice. Toward the end of the chapter, I illustrate how one might attend to these nonhumans as they enter our conversations.

CYBORG COMMUNICATIVE EVENTS

There can be no doubt that both literate behaviors and communication technologies are thriving and will continue to thrive regardless of whether academic institutions attend to them. Warnings abound of the cumulative results of not paying attention. We will allow social inequities (i.e., class, race, and gender) to continue to haunt our approaches to technoliterate education (C. Selfe, 1999); we are likely to misunderstand increasingly ubiquitous learning environments (i.e., gaming spaces) that shape our students' literacy and cognitive habits (Gee, 2003); and we will simply become less relevant to young people, corporations, and civic groups that are choosing to use powerful, self-sponsored literacy environments (Yancey, 2004). I would suggest that MLC workers have a potentially important role to play in shaping the way the English studies disciplines attend to new literacies, new literacy environments, and the people who stream through our institutions. I believe that what MLCs have to say to English studies will be well received in disciplines across the humanities and the university.

How does one describe the "state of mind" that MLC workers might adopt as they survey the human, technical, and social terrains around them? Cindy Selfe and Gail Hawisher (2004) provide us with useful examples of how to attend to the "cultural ecologies" of those who appear in their *Literate Lives in the Information Age*. The framing of their studies is not foreign to experienced Writing Center workers who have for many decades paid attention to the personal, academic, and social lives of the clients who seek their help with literacy projects. But it is a powerful metaphor reminding those of us studying the *technological* agents and actants at work in these ecologies that there is a "complex web of social forces, historical events, economic patterns, material conditions, and cultural expectations with which both humans and computer technologies coexist" (p. 31).

To gradually take on the "state of mind" that I am suggesting, literacy scholars and social theorists interested in the relationship between technology and humans suggest that we will need to adopt a perpetual curiosity about the human *and* nonhuman actants who are engaged in the communicative events that our students trail behind them as they troop into our MLCs. But first a leading question.

Why do we seem so fixated on multiple literacies these days? Certainly there are reasonable concerns about this fixation—this addiction to literacies of many forms (see Wysocki & Johnson-Eilola, 1999). I would suggest that one of the reasons for our literacy compulsion might be that we are trying to better describe the intimate human relationship to the technologies that are proliferating around us. Those technologies do not grow there without our creative, inventive help, and we do not develop multiple literacies without the force of their existence. We are all cyborgs, of course, and have always been so. What we seem to be trying to do for each other is to update our understandings of literate behavior and to articulate the relationship humans have to the technologies that surround them. In his book *Technics and Time, 1: The Fault of Epimetheus*, Bernard Stiegler (1998) suggests that we have spent too much time articulating the differences between the human and what he calls "technics." Instead, he suggests, "to know the essence of the machine, and thereby understanding the sense of technics in general, is also to know *the place of the human* in 'technical ensembles'" (p. 66).

Stiegler (1998) illustrates, if not a direct connection between human thought and technological development, at least a historical connection that goes back to some of the earliest records of human existence (stone tools). I do not review all that he has to say about Heidegger and his view of technological concerns or what anthropologists say about tools and language, but instead summarize his work this way. One can read Stiegler and still prefer not to believe that humans exist as they do today because they have developed with technologies (from stone tools onward). But it is difficult to remain unaware of the obvious and intimate relationship between our compulsions for technology and literacy. Most people, however, are reluctant to think of themselves as cyborgs perhaps because of our rather fantastic cultural heritage of the cyborg in images in books, movies, and other media. But Stiegler explains our reluctance a different way and rather emphatically:

> Mortals, because they are prosthetic in their very being, are self-destructive [in other places Stiegler calls this self-destructiveness . . . "a constitutive blindness"]. Hence prostheses, when visible, frighten or

fascinate, as marks of mortality. . . . [then later] There is nothing but
prostheses: my glasses, my shoes, the pen, the diary, or the money in
my pocket; and because they are frightening, their visibility is reduced.
(p. 199)

Thus, we find it easy to develop a "constitutive blindness" to our intimate
relationship to technology. The more intimate our relationship, the more
invisible to us those technologies seem. Stiegler suggests, and I agree, that
we can no longer afford the luxury of this blindness as difficult as it is to
shake off.

Of course, other theorists, like Bruno Latour, have explored the human
relationship to technology and the world as a whole. Latour catalogues the
proliferation of "hybrids" or "monsters" and their importance (cf. *We Have
Never Been Modern*). He offers many examples of why the separations
between humans and technologies are debilitating. In his work, *Politics of
Nature: How to Bring the Sciences Into Democracy*, he suggests that our constitutive blindness has led us to adopt impotent processes for dealing with
issues of environmental change. Because of our blindness, we attempt to
draw a bright white line between our understanding of *nature* (matters of
scientific fact) and our human epistemologies or ways of understanding
and explaining the world. According to Latour, in our current *state of mind*,
a few special actors—scientists in most cases—have access to nature and
matters of fact, and the rest of us are relegated to the chattering masses of
rhetorical actors who never come to any conclusions. His objective in that
volume is to create a "political ecology" (p. 246) that will include in its
deliberations both human and nonhuman agents of change and thereby
create a process by which we can hope for a "progressive composition of
the common world" (p. 18).

Yes, he is asking us to invite into our deliberations the discourse of
technological artifacts. I recommend to you the final chapters of *Artemis*
and in *Politics of Nature*, where he illustrates how this might happen and
spare you my description of his work. Instead, I outline a scenario that I
hope makes more sense to MLC workers. Latour's definition of a political
ecology can be adopted by literacy workers who, like me, consider it unac-
ceptable that we make odd distinctions and separations between the
human and nonhuman when talking about technology-rich instruction and
learning. Quite often in the speech acts of technology specialists and curriculum designers, technologies are not intimate actants in the cyborg communicative events that our students bring to MLCs; instead, they are tools,
infrastructures, interfaces, software, hardware, and netware that exist apart
from the real rhetorical work that our students are undertaking. I would

suggest that not only is this not the case, but that distinctions of this sort, as I have claimed elsewhere (*Sustainable Computer Environments*), have led us to enact pedagogies and technology initiatives that are unsustainable. Because we know that multiple and changing literacies are a constant in our worlds, we cannot afford (a) to ignore what the relevant systems have to say, or (b) to underestimate the complexity of their context of use.

A Fair Hearing to Human and NonHuman Alike

How does one apply this odd state of mind to the act of coaching (consulting or tutoring) in a MLC? The following scenarios are real, not exemplary nor complete. But they do describe some of the challenges faced when one attempts to give a reasonable hearing to most available and willing agents and actants in a cyborg communicative event.

Across the country, teachers of rhetoric, composition, and technical communication are taking Aristotle's advice and asking their students from across the curriculum to compose using *all available means of multimodal persuasion* for the sake of specific reading communities. For a snapshot of what some of these undergraduate and graduate assignments and courses might look like, visit the Electronic Written, Aural, and Visual Expressions (E-WAVE wiki) at http://e-wave.wikispaces.com. There you will see and can add to the few (10 as of 4/14/07) examples that emphasize both the multimodal assignments, student work, and student reflections on their project work. It is quite easy to imagine students in these classes taking advantage of a MLC as they develop both the conceptual and textual materials and the rhetorical and technological expertise needed to make their work more persuasive. This small collection of teachers had students working on video and audio podcasts, video documentaries, visual/aural blogs, multimedia wikis, Wikipedia entries, physical scrapbooks, web interface designs, PowerPoint presentations, and game designs. Although this is an impressive array of venues and genres, other disciplines will have their students working in environments as or more diverse than this.

The many genre and diverse composing processes that go along with these projects are a challenge themselves. But I would submit that we are well positioned to adapt and attend to genre and process changes. Most English studies professionals (like Writing Center workers) are perfectly willing to listen to the "voices" of *some* nonhumans—font choice, white space, and information arrangement—as the student develops her print or web-based cyborg communicative artifact. Of course, we are quite fond of listening carefully to the technology of language—voice/tone, word choice, organization, culturally acceptable syntax, and so on—as we work with students' rhetorical efforts. Why attend to some nonhumans while ignoring most others?

What if a student is asked to create a multimodal wiki resource guide for a self-chosen not-for-profit organization (go to http://405c.wikispaces.com/2-minute + Pitch and click on the student names for some examples)? When the student brings this project into an MLC several interesting nonhumans and cyborg systems must speak along with the typical human agents: the coach (advisor, tutor), the teacher, and the student.

It seems important that the coach hear the voice of the actant I would call "student access." In a busy life (that is likely to include kids, other jobs, many classes, and organizational commitments), where, when, and how often does the student have access to the kind of networked workstation necessary to excel at the assignment? Will the multiliteracy coach be able to offer such access or help students find alternative spaces at the institution if the instructor has not provided after-class access (an all too typical situation according to a CCCC research study [C. Selfe, 2006])?

The coach will certainly also need to understand the nature, quality, and quantity of the "expertise cyborg." This is the system of human and online resources that the student might take advantage of as they learn to capture, modify, cite, and publish images, sound files, video clips, or web resources in a rhetorically appropriate manner. Will the MLC provide this expertise? Who else might provide the just-in-time help that students will need? My experience suggests that we need to interrogate the "expertise cyborg."

In most cases, the "access actant" and the "expertise cyborg" are mute during tutoring or consulting sessions. However, MLC directors could set up focus groups of students to translate and speak for these two important stakeholders in the students' projects. From these representatives, you might hear whether their workspaces are safe, convenient, or clean enough, with enough family-friendly hours to complete certain assignments. At one point in 2006, I held such a meeting of this type and heard from a young woman on my campus that the 24/7 lab available to her "smelled like urine" and was in a "spooky" building. The men in the group seemed to accept these shortcomings with little concern. She could not for obvious reasons. When one lets the "access actant" speak (through focus groups), one must be ready for some blunt, contradictory comments. But at least, through a series of focus group discussions, we can accumulate a set of recommendations for access and expertise that will be of great value to students and faculty across the university.

Continuing to engage actants normally left out of our consulting, we might also recruit representatives—the local and central technology support staff, the e-learning specialist, or an advanced practitioner (usually an undergraduate student)—who will be able to speak for the systems in which the students are working—in this case, a wiki site. First, these representatives might suggest that wikis were created to be collaborative environments (as Wikipedia exemplifies), where all or a few people can be invited to revise content. All students in the wiki project mentioned earlier are in the process of creating online content, certainly, but they will, in the end, also need to decide who to invite to continue developing the site. They are, potentially, helping to create an online community that will manage, grow, and update their content. Most wiki systems also provide content creators with a method of "tagging" their work in ways that will make it more likely that search engines will catalogue their pages and site. When a wiki system speaks, it speaks of ease of use, multimodality, collaborative editing choices, and tagging among other affordances. Are MLC workers ready to help students with this type of rhetorical decision making? Are we institutionally inclined to listen to the systems our students are using or asked to use?

We cannot just listen to the space if MLC workers are to help students succeed with digital projects. We also need to hear about the modalities that their spaces encourage or make difficult. In the wiki project, for example, we might let the files generated by each modality speak for themselves. The alphabetic actant would have to admit that they are cheap, measured in kilobytes. Alphabetic rhetoric is a cheap date by professional standards. But images are more expensive and measured in 100s of kilobytes; audio in megabytes; video in gigabytes. Most wiki environments do not allow the uploading of large files. We do not often let files speak for themselves. If we did, we might need to invite translators into our conversations (e.g., videographers). They can speak for the files and systems that they use each day to move gigabytes of data around small networks and where eventually they store their work if they want to share it online. If teachers, students, and coaches agree on video production to deliver their messages, those files and systems might tell us that almost any project will be quite difficult to move around easily and back up in traditional ways. Video files would tell us that most of our students will be constrained to working on a single machine until the production is completed. Even backing up video work is no simple task, although absolutely necessary. Publishing compressed video reduces the file's size, but if our students use a wiki system to display that compressed file, the student will then need an alternative web-based repository on which to store their file (e.g., YouTube). From there. it is possible to link audio and video clips to the wiki site. Are MLC workers ready to help students make decisions about workflow procedures, file formats and sizes, and storage options? They will be if we let key agents and actants speak about the workflow these student clients will need to accommodate.

Okay, but who will speak for our intended online audience? We are now dealing with another form of the "access actant," this time from the "reader's" perspective. Is the intended audience in a connected household (each person with their own computer-sharing DSL connections) or in a differently connected household (one computer in a family of five on 56K phone dialup)? The difference will have substantial implications for receiving and acting on web-based information. A usability testing session with the target clients and audiences might provide an opportunity for the webbed "system of distribution" to speak to our student. Are MLC workers prepared to attend to client-based projects and help the student develop survey/focus group questions for those clients and their specialized audiences? Almost certainly, with real audiences spread across the internet, coaches and other MLC workers will not be able to depend on standard reading practices. A reader is no longer a single person, but many people working on several systems, all having cyborg reading experiences that teachers, students, and MLC workers need to know about. There are other nonhuman actants who might be consulted, but I think it is clear that those we choose to engage and those we choose to ignore will make our student clients' projects more or less rhetorically appropriate.

It is a noisy conversation when we begin letting the human and nonhuman actants participate in discussions about cyborg communicative events. I am certain, as MLC workers begin adopting this cyborg mentality, that the number and character of other human/nonhuman stakeholders will increase. The day-to-day work in MLCs as they grapple with all these agents and actants will give the English studies curricular designers an earful about what students are facing as they take on the multiliterate projects we imagine for them. I would suggest that no one place can do this work alone. As well positioned as MLCs are, they will need to collaborate with others and pool their collected knowledge. Collaborations across academic and technological silos at the institution will have to be instituted, and MLC leadership can be essential to that process. The MLC, with its tradition of penetrating the academic and technological silos of higher education, has one of the best chances of putting together an ongoing "collective" or congress (Latour, 2004) of representatives (human and nonhuman), one of the best chances to help create a culture of support and minimize the dynamic of blame so often associated with technology-rich projects (R. Selfe, 2005).

The MLC is an exemplary space to explore the importance of each agent and actant, document how they fit into the rhetorical context of a project, and talk about the intimate connections between human and technology that we so often overlook.

What possible outcome of importance can result from this type of thinking? An example might help. In the Humanities disciplines at OSU, there is a growing interest in practical, industrial, or journalistic uses for audio and video. However, if one looks around for workspace designed for this media development, students find two choices: They can provide or barter for their own workspace at home or in their dorms or they can make use of centrally managed computer labs on campus. Our central support people on campus do a tremendous job of providing useable lab space (for 55,000 students), but until this year they had no facilities dedicated to media production. Video production, from every actant's point of view, takes a lot of care and careful planning. So if a teacher wanted to create a video assignment for a first-year or technical communication class, they would have to do what the majority of the CCCC survey respondents did: depend on *students* to find their own work space and work time to complete the assignment (R. Selfe, 2006), a result I find both surprising and disappointing. Most of these 46 institutions are 4-year, graduate degree-granting institutions. I am lucky enough to work with people (Humanities Information Systems) who recognized this problem several years ago (long before I came), planned programs, and wrote grants to solve it for Humanities students and teachers. But it seems clear to me that English studies professionals as a whole have not been inviting the nonhumans on which we have all become so dependent into their curricular discussions. As a result those of us encouraging multimodal compositions find our efforts compromised ethically (the poorer students with the least access are less able to meet our assignment's demands) and challenged logistically. We need a constant stream of translators and translations of the nonhumans in our midst if we are to avoid similar situations in the future. MLCs, with the breadth of their vision and contacts, can help immensely.

New Literacies

Will our cultural literacies become less multiple, more coherent, and focused in the near future? If we understand them as highly complex, cyborg events, then the answer is, "No, they will continue to proliferate." Our multiple cultures and disciplines will continue to create Latour's hybrids and monsters into the foreseeable future. Many academics find this a frightening prospect. But I prefer to take it as a promising trend. I do so because those Humanistic academics invested in writing—where writing is seen as taking place in numerous, multimodal venues influenced by many social and technical conditions and forces—can, through their explorations, help us all *anticipate* the necessary skills, attitudes, and approaches important for the next generations of literate citizens. This could well be one of the primary goals of MLCs. Yes, MLCs also help students. Yes, they improve retention statistics, but they can also provide vision for the university.

Anticipation, or rather the anticipatory momentum of MLCs, is an important concept here. How do we generate that momentum and maintain it? In a practical sense, how do admittedly older scholar/teachers come to understand (anticipate) literacy environments or writing systems? How do we find ways to stay in touch with professional and generational contexts: contexts where communities (often newly global in nature), language, acceptable communicative practices, and technologies are all interacting, changing rapidly, and influencing each other as they go? What conditions, over which we have some control, will make our anticipations possible and productive?

As I said earlier, a MLC is an ideal place to explore the values and challenges of new literacy practices because we see them in students' projects, teachers' assignments, and technologists' visions. MLCs also operate in an area of higher education where they are expected to collaborate across disciplines. So assuming that we have the motivation to create a human and nonhuman choir (collective or congress), we also need to continuously recruit and attract all the appropriate agents and actants: technologies (hardware, software, netware, interfaces), specialists (technicians, network engineers, etc.), students with their cyborg communicative projects, teachers, syllabi, and an understanding of the material conditions of student work. English studies needs a cyborg literacy research project, and MLCs, with their scheduled meeting times and comfortable spaces to chat, have an important part to play in that project.

In addition to their space and interdisciplinary inclination, they can hire and train what I call *advanced literacy practitioners*, the most active and useful group of translators of the nonhuman that I have ever encountered. They are key players in what Bruno Latour (2004) calls a collective, "a procedure [not a stable group or thing] for collecting associations of humans and nonhumans" (p. 238).

Advanced Literacy Practitioners

Who are these people? They are the people who Nardi and O'Day (1999) call "gardeners" and the glue that holds together the technocommunities of Brown and Duguid's (2002) communities of practices. They are the student workers whose cumulative explorations keep new knowledge about communicative technologies flowing into our MLCs. Sometimes they are hired outright for these skills, but often they are under the radar: they volunteer; they do additional duty when necessary; they play on the machines; they surprise us with communicative attitudes, approaches, and skills that are often quite sophisticated. They save our butts when our cyborg communicative events go awry.

I have had the privilege since 1984 to collaborate with young people (primarily)—professional staff, graduate, but mostly undergraduate students—who are advanced literacy practitioners. They have helped design, inspire, and support the MLC I worked in during that time: the Center for Computer-Assisted Language Instruction (CCLI) at Michigan Technological University. Groups of advanced literacy practitioners are also helping to design and support another set of literacy centers in the College of Humanities at the OSU.

Over the years of work in these centers, I have noticed some qualities that make them more or less productive sites for our new literacies research project and that make them attractive to advanced literacy practitioners. If we are to understand and adequately accommodate, integrate, and influence literacy practices in the near future, we have to attend to the literacy practices that are walking into our classrooms and centers. In particular, we need to attend to the self-sponsored literacy activities that people develop in academic settings, at home, and in the workplace. Play theorists have, for years, studied the self-sponsored activities of children and young adults and revealed interesting aspects of their motivation to focus and communicate around those playful activities (see Huizinga, 1955). It is not far fetched, then, to imagine that allowing and even encouraging play, gaming, and other self-sponsored collaborations in our MLCs will be an important, if not essential, component of the literacy research we develop. Productive MLCs, then, need to attract advanced literacy practitioners to play in our spaces. To do so, they need to:

- make time and space available for play and other self-sponsored, often collaborative, literacy activities, or at least not ban them outright.
- value students' self-sponsored literate activities overtly and make room for the ongoing study of these cyborg activities.
- respect and learn about the technoliterate practices from across the curriculum and prepare to adapt coaching practices and curriculum suggestions accordingly.

In exchange, we can expect some productive work out of these advanced literacy practitioners. With their support—in exchange for a range of benefits, paid positions being only ONE of these benefits—they can help us incorporate appropriate, academic versions of new literacies into our curriculum. How, for instance, might video blogging and advanced cell phone telephony be productively integrated into English studies? How can advanced search strategies be used productively in official library systems, on the web, and in massive projects like Wikipedia? I suggest here that those understandings should be richly developed descriptions that incorporate the human, the technological, and the social. They can help us teach our students how to live well with technologies and help those students design communication projects that will reinforce the content learning going on in their classes. More to the point of this chapter, they can help us better understand the constantly changing but intimate relationships among humans, technologies, and social contexts that might make our cyborg pedagogies sustainable.

CONCLUDING STATEMENTS
AND THE DALN

MLCs are not simply support or service centers, although they do plenty of that essential and important work. They need to keep reminding themselves that they are or can be research centers that should influence the kinds of literacy practices that are encouraged in higher education across the curriculum. As we learn more about the literacy practices of each generation of students, certainly in collaboration with our writing across the curriculum (WAC) brethren, we need to push that knowledge out into the academic environment so that others—teachers and curriculum designers alike—can take advantage of the many cyborg communicative experiences we see coming our way (anticipatory momentum). MLCs need to push back. Curriculum committees and technical specialists should not be creating a curriculum that forces students to find their own supported work space. They should not be creating curricula that creates problems for economically or physically disadvantaged students. They also should not be banning or ignoring one cyborg communicative experience (cell phones, Wikipedia) over another (hardcopy essay writing) without consulting current best practices in academia that are based on discussions with representative agents and actants.

The most practical advice that I would extract from this chapter would be the following:

1. Get over the human/technology bifurcation in our thinking. We have always been cyborgs and will continue to be so.
2. Set up regular meetings with innovative and effective teachers. Get them to talk to us about the literacy skills and approaches they foster, but also press them to represent the nonhuman actants essential to those skills and approaches.
3. Set up regular meetings with representative agents and actants who can talk with some sophistication about their constituents before announcing support for new literacy assignments.
4. Recruit advanced literacy practitioners (often young technoliterate students) who can train to be multiliteracy consultants or support those already trained, and who can also help keep us aware of the innovative systems being used by each generation of students. They are frequently excellent translators/representatives for the nonhumans among us.
5. More generally, consider the spaces (virtual and physical) around you: labs, classrooms, online sites and systems, research centers, learning centers, and so on. Imagine them operating as MLCs. The creation of these centers is a state of mind (i.e., an approach to the "collective" found in each center). That collective consists of advanced literacy practitioners, consultants, administrators, researchers, technologies, and social and institutional contexts. All of them are active participants in the productive drama that is unfolding there.
6. Finally, contribute to national efforts that are dedicated to better understanding cyborg communicative events.

The complexity of the change suggested here is not something that any one scholar or even one institution can adequately address. We need a space to collect the literacy stories (the nonhuman along with human narratives) that result from our explorations. A national effort to understand the literacy practices growing up around us requires study from many perspectives and many places. One such space is a large scholarly initiative called the Digital Archive of Literacy Narratives (C. Selfe, 2006).

> Digital Archive of Literacy Narratives is a large-scale digital corpus of interviews and artifacts in multiple formats (e.g., print, video, audio) that will trace the literacy practices and values of U.S. citizens and that

will be open to the general public. Individuals will be invited to contribute their literacy narratives and materials to the DALN from home computers, computers in public spaces (e.g., schools, libraries, community centers, [MLCs], etc.), or at a series of DALN Centers where archivists provide both access to technologies (e.g., computers, digital cameras, scanners, audio recorders) and assistance in using technologies. Narratives will be submitted electronically, reviewed by a DALN Board, and posted on the DALN web site.

The formation of such an archive would provide researchers from a range of disciplines a site for studying the changing nature of U.S. literacy practices in the 21st century. Scholars could use the DALN as a site for the historical study of literacy trends and tracing literacy practices and values. Educators and librarians could use the DALN as a site for shaping increasingly effective instruction at all levels (C. Selfe, 2006, p. 1).

This database of narratives is open to literacy practices of all types. It is, for instance, where I will be collecting my professional literacy interviews. I hope that those reading this chapter will consider adding the work that they do with multiliteracy workers and clients to this archive. Of course, I strongly suggest that we each give the nonhuman some voice in this work as we collect it.

REFERENCES

Brown, John Seeley, & Duguid, Paul. (2002). *The social life of information.* Boston, MA: Harvard Business School Press.

College Board. (2004). *Writing: A ticket to work . . . Or a ticket out. A survey of business leaders.* Online. Retrieved August 1, 2006, from http://www.writingcommission.org/prod_downloads/writingcom/writing-ticket-to-work.pdf

DeVoss, Danielle Nicole. (forthcoming). The elements of technical editing. In C. Selfe (Ed.), *Resources in technical communication: Outcomes and approaches.* Amityville, NY: Baywood.

Garay, Mary Sue, & Bernhardt, Stephen A. (Eds.). (1998). *Expanding literacies: English teaching and the new workplace.* Albany: SUNY Press.

Gee, James Paul. (2003). *What video games have to teach us about learning and literacy.* New York: Palgrave Macmillan.

Hawisher, Gail E., & Cynthia L. Selfe, with Brittney Moraski and Melissa Pearson. (June 2004). Becoming literate in the information age: Cultural ecologies and the literacies of technology. *College Composition and Communication, 55*(4), 642–692.

Huizinga, Johan. (1955). *Homo ludens: A study of the play element in culture.* Boston: Beacon.

Latour, Bruno. (1993). *We have never been modern* (Catherine Porter, Trans.). Cambridge, MA: Harvard University Press.

Latour, Bruno. (2004). *Politics of nature: How to bring the sciences into democracy* (Catherine Porter, Trans.). Cambridge, MA: Harvard University Press.

MLA Task Force on Evaluating Scholarship for Tenure and Promotion. (2006, December 7). Retrieved December 10, 2006, from http://www.mla.org/tenure_promotion.

Monaghan, Peter. (2006). More than words: The U. of Southern California trains students how to read—and communicate in—new media. *Chronicle of Higher Education, 52*(45), A33.

Nardi, Bonnie A., & O'Day, Vicki L. (1999). *Information ecology: Using technology with heart.* Cambridge, MA: MIT Press.

NCTE Executive Committee. (2005, November). *National Council of Teachers of English Guidelines: Multimodal literacies.* Retrieved June 22, 2007, from http://www.ncte.org/edpolicy/multimodal/resources/123213.htm.

Selfe, Cynthia. (1999). *Technology and literacy in the twenty-first century: The importance of paying attention.* Carbondale: Southern Illinois University Press.

Selfe, Cynthia L. (2006). National Digital Archive of Literacy Narratives (DALN): Database design and development. *Ohio State University, Grants for Innovation in the Arts and Humanities 2006–07.*

Selfe, Cynthia L., & Hawisher, Gail E. (2004). *Literate lives in the information age: Narratives of literacy from the United States.* Mahwah, NJ: Erlbaum.

Selfe, Richard. (2005) *Sustainable computer environments: Cultures of support for teachers of English and language arts.* Cresskill, NJ: Hampton Press.

Selfe, Richard. (2006, May). Sustainable infrastructure: A report on data from the CCCC. Survey of multimodal pedagogies in writing programs. Conference presentation delivered at *Computers and Writing 2006,* Lubbock, TX.

Selfe, Richard. (forthcoming). Technological activism: Understanding and shaping environments for technology-rich communication. In C. Selfe (Ed.), *Resources in technical communication: Outcomes and approaches.* Amityville, NY: Baywood.

Stiegler, Bernard. (1998). *Technics and Time, 1: The fault of Epimetheus* (Richard Beardsworth & George Collins, Trans.). Stanford, CA: Stanford University Press.

Wysocki, Anne Frances, & Johnson-Eilola, Johndan. (1999). Blinded by the letter: Why are we using literacy as a metaphor for everything else? In Gail E. Hawisher & Cynthia L. Selfe (Eds.), *Passions, pedagogies and 21st century technologies* (pp. 349–368). Urbana, IL: National Council of Teachers of English.

Yancey, Kathleen Blake. (2004, December). Made not only in words: Composition in a new key. *College Composition and Communication, 56*(2), 297–328.

Connections

6

WRITING AIN'T WHAT IT USED TO BE

AN EXERCISE IN COLLEGE MULTILITERACY

George Cooper

University of Michigan

In reviewing Nancy Grimm's (1999) *Good Intentions: Writing Center Work for Post Modern Times*, Harvey Kail (2000) writes that, "As sites for important literacy events, writing centers are at the margins of academic life, yet it turns out that the margins are also the cutting edge" (p. 678). Kail reflects an attitude among Writing Center administrators and theorists that, both physically and conceptually, Writing Centers need to respond to a changing face of literacy. It is not enough to encourage and support academic reading and writing as if they were embodied in one monolithic form. Grimm explains this evolution by distinguishing between modernist and postmodernist definitions of writing. Modernist Writing Centers exist to "improve the clarity, order, and correctness of student writing" (p. 2); modernist literacy practices entail an emphasis on "individual autonomy, rational thinking, and [the] transparent communication structure of the system" (p. 4). In contrast, postmodernist Writing Centers support students' ability

> to simultaneously maintain multiple viewpoints, to make quick shifts in discourse orientation, to handle rapid changes in information technology, to work elbow to elbow with people differently positioned in the university hierarchy, to negotiate cultural and social differences, to handle the inevitable blurring of authorial boundaries, and to regularly renegotiate issues of knowledge, power, and ownership. (p. 2)

Robert W. Barnett and Lois M. Rosen (1999) reflect such a capacious model of a Writing Center, saying that it should be not just a "center," but a "campus-wide writing environment" (p. 1). To this end, they outline "three major elements" that

> form the basis for creating and sustaining a writing environment in which WAC and the Writing Center contribute substantially and in unique ways: (1) building faculty knowledge and establishing the value of writing, (2) providing a support system for faculty and students, and (3) supplying resources for faculty and students. (p. 9)

Support for students includes one-on-one tutoring, "in-class tutoring," and resources such as flyers and handouts. But support is not limited to students. Barnett and Rosen report that their

> WAC/Writing Center partnership works in multiple ways to build faculty understanding of how writing can be used to enhance learning and practical methods that lead to more successful student products. In this, we view ourselves as well informed and experienced colleagues sharing what we know with other faculty members. (p. 10)

Accordingly, their center supports faculty by offering "one-on-one consultations," "workshops" on writing-related topics, "informational visits to classrooms," and various "writing resources (p. 10).

Given the more complex understandings of literacy and Writing Center work, similar to those outlined previously, a contemporary composition course requires resources beyond the typical rhetoric, reader, and handbook that might traditionally have been used. Indeed, it was a more complex understanding of literacy, as well as an unusual set of circumstances that led to the following course description—a kind of *menage a trois* of first-year composition, multiliteracy, and community service:

> Writing ain't what it used to be. Our literate interactions have been deeply influenced through and by computer-aided media, so much so that we sometimes wonder whether the people are running the technology or the technology is running the people. The purpose of this writing course, however, is not to answer a philosophical question of who controls whom. Instead we will study how web-based information systems make demands on our traditional use of the written word.

The Sweetland Writing Center at the University of Michigan had recently initiated a multiliteracy center (MLC), intending to provide a service to the university community that had not yet been established: a technical support unit that was aware of rhetorical principles most often associated with written and oral composition. Its promoters were aware that, like written and oral language, visual images contribute to traditional rhetorical processes. Moreover, regard for the increasingly complex nature of literacy reflects a social and media evolution that The New London Group argues must be accounted for pedagogically. They argue that "literacy pedagogy now must account for the burgeoning variety of text forms associated with information and multimedia technologies" (Cazden et al., 1996, p. 61). Multiliteracy, however, implicates more than the institutional or classroom education because it is central to both "local diversity" and "global connectedness." They argue that

> Dealing with linguistic differences and cultural differences has now become central to the pragmatics of our working, civic, and private lives. Effective citizenship and productive work now require that we interact effectively using multiple languages, multiple Englishes, and communication patterns that more frequently cross cultural, community, and national boundaries. (Cazden et al., 1996, p. 64)

A key word, and one not necessarily self-explanatory, is *effective*, both in its reference to citizenship and to the use of language and the technological apparatuses that provide mediums of communication. In writing about technology and service-learning projects, Melinda Turnley (2007) refers to a recent survey of members of the Association of Teachers of Technical Writing that reported a need for a "critical understanding of technology and the ability to learn what is needed and apply appropriate tools" (as cited in Turnley, 2007, p. 103). Such technical literacy is more than a simple proficiency. "Students," as literacy researcher Kellie Cargile Cook maintains, "need to learn sensitivity toward users and other stakeholders in technical processes and documentation" (as cited in Turnley, 2007, p. 104). As a way to address this need, "technical communication instructors increasingly are turning to service learning as a means to encourage students professional, intellectual, and civic engagement" (Turnley, 2007, p. 104).

* * *

I had been teaching a composition course in conjunction with the Michigan Community Scholars Program (MCSP), a residential learning community that emphasizes "deep learning, engaged community, meaningful civic engagement/community service learning and intercultural understanding and dialogue." The Program's community emphasis had always interested and frustrated me. It interested me because it made sense to draw college students out into the community; although their time in college was relatively brief, it seemed important that they understand Ann Arbor as more than a place to study and party, but as the network of human relationships that define any city. The community emphasis frustrated me because I had found it difficult to get out of my comfort zone as teacher and academic to achieve the community/school interaction that the Program desired.[1] For some years, my students had read memoirs and written their own stories that, as I instructed, were not just illuminations of themselves as individuals, but renderings of the values, times, and places that made incidents worth writing and reading about—a description that I had hoped would turn students' attention outward even as they wrote about themselves. The following few versions of my syllabus reveal oral history as a dominant theme and research technique. Featuring topics of health, sexuality, race, class, and family, the class, in its best realization, took students out of the classroom and into the community to interview people: family, friends, as well as professionals in various relevant fields of work and study.

But it was not enough. I wanted a community partner. The MCSP faculty convened on a regular basis to talk about their work and share stories about teaching and learning. Some of them had begun talking about community partners being matched with their classes and how such partners might help extend our classrooms beyond the limits and expectations typical of the academy. Some of them already HAD partners. At about the same time, David Sheridan, my colleague who worked with others to initiate the Sweetland Writing Center's MLC, suggested that we might work together. He was trying to promote projects that would lead students to seek the kind of help his support unit was initiated to provide. My initial inclination was to resist. I am barely computer literate. I had no ideas about how to develop the curriculum of my freshman composition class in ways that might result in students seeking the help of a consultant in visual literacy. I only wanted a community partner.

Sheridan suggested that we might have my students design websites for area nonprofits—rather than focusing on traditional academic essays,

---

[1] Program policy was, indeed, generous and flexible. My sense that my community curriculum was inadequate was, in the end, entirely my own.

we could stretch the curriculum, trying to achieve a more complex under-standing of 21st-century literacy while maintaining instruction in tradition-al academic writing. I said, "That is easy for you to say." In suggesting this approach, Sheridan was drawing on recent scholarship that suggested a service learning approach offers unique affordances for integrating new-media composition into the writing classroom. Mark Warschauer (1999), for instance, discusses a service learning course designed by Joan Conners at Bay Community College in O'ahu, Hawai'i. The design of Conners' course was informed by "four main themes: (1) real world purpose; (2) dif-ferent genres, different media; (3) decentered classroom; and (4) connec-tion to the community" (pp. 139–140). In this approach, students created websites for nonprofit organizations, allowing them to practice multimodal rhetoric within community contexts. In Warschauer's estimation, "students clearly learned a great deal about writing in new media," including both "technical skills, such as how to scan photos," and "rhetorical skills," such as "how and why to combine certain elements to make an effective pres-entation" (p. 144). Warschauer notes that "consideration of design issues seemed to be heightened by the real-world purposes of the writing. Students learned to take audience into account not only in terms of the text but also in the formatting and the graphics" (p. 144).

In those days, Sheridan offered workshops for faculty about website design, pointing out how visual images contained persuasive possibility. He showed how, in her personal website, a student of his included a photo of herself in the image of Rosie the Riveter, and in that posture suggesting for herself the strength and durability of the WWII icon. Sheridan also spoke about the dangers inherent in not understanding the Internet audience, one far more expansive than we typically engage with, and he cautioned against designs created without regard for that sometimes threatening, impersonal population. In closing, Sheridan said that a cohort of students on the Michigan campus were being trained to work in the MLC, aware of the social, political, and rhetorical vicissitudes of website design, but also knowledgeable about the technology. To assign visual assessments or web-site compositions, faculty need not be technologically savvy. He said, "The multiliteracy center is interested in partnering with faculty on all aspects of teaching with technology, including syllabus design, assignment design, support for faculty development, and one-on-one support for students."

Sheridan's description of the MLC and the support it could provide is familiar to people in composition, in that it evokes images of the process-oriented pedagogy the field has promoted since the late 1960s. The process movement has been criticized recently as overly idealist, assum-ing, as it seems to, that process can be taught as a predictable and transferable method from person to person. At the same time, most teachers of composition will admit that no two people compose alike. Just as important is the fact that, by emphasizing the process of writing, the real exigencies of a high-quality product and, yes, a grade continue to be most important to those seeking help from writing or MLC consultants. Although a product orientation is not so apparent in Sheridan's description, product is clearly apparent in the suggestion to design websites for area nonprofit agencies. Reflecting on the relationship between process and product orientations to composition, John Trimbur (2000) wrote that "the notion of multiliteracies also signals that writing itself has always amounted to the production of visible language and isn't just the invisible composing process we imagine it to be" (p. 30). My association with the MCSP, the emerging MLC, and a community partner was about to influence my teaching practice and philosophy in ways beyond which I had ever imagined.

* * *

Nonprofit Enterprise at Work (NEW) is located in a neo-Romanesque-styled building on the banks of the Huron River, just north of Ann Arbor. It was built on the site of an old junkyard and hailed as part of the vision for an enhanced northern entryway to the city. The organization's mission is "to help nonprofits succeed by strengthening nonprofit management and offering solutions to issues facing our nonprofit community." Dave and I arrived there on a grey November day to speak with Neelav Hajra. Even with a bachelor of science in physics and a Juris Doctor degree from University of Michigan, Hajra enjoyed little satisfaction in the legal department at the Ford Motor Company and decided to bring his talents to the nonprofit sector. He is now Chief Operating Officer of NEW. We brought him a working schedule of my course that, if approved (meaning approved enough to connect us with a nonprofit), we would enact in winter term, a little less than 2 months away.[2]

---

[2]There is some slippage between "I" and "we" in reference to whose course this was. It was my course on the books, and I was responsible for it in the traditional ways that teachers are responsible for their courses and students. But its terms, the language of the syllabus, and even the day-to-day unfolding of the action were generated as a result of conversations with Sheridan and, to some degree, Hajra.

A WORKING SCHEDULE

Project 1 (Concepts and Architecture): January 8–January 22

We set the terms for our work. What is literacy? What is visual literacy? What do websites actually consist of? How are their points established? Is there an argument? What happens to traditional notions of literacy when realized in a website? What are the differences among personal websites, nonprofit websites, and commercial websites? During this time, you will make an appointment with the Sweetland MLC. There you will talk with consultants about website design, and with them you will begin to brainstorm the substance of your first major paper, a critique, comparison, and contrast of various websites (due on the 22nd). In preparation for your next project, make a second appointment at the MLC.

Project 2 (Concept and Design): January 22–January 29

A thematic proposal for your own web page is due January 29. Using rough diagrams supported by a written rationale, write a paper that explains the rhetorical purpose of your website. You will meet once again with the Sweetland Multiliteracy Consultants for this. You will want to include in this proposal a clear sense of what you want your site to achieve rhetorically and conceptually, as well as a rationale for how the specific architecture and design will support your goals. Make a third appointment at the Sweetland MLC for next week to begin your Project 3.

Project 3 (Architecture and Execution): January 29–February 12

For this project, you will construct your own personal website due February 12. During this time, we will share our thoughts in class, critique rough drafts of websites that you are working on, troubleshoot problems, and meet with Sweetland Consultants to best realize your intentions.

Project 4 (Concept): February 12–March 7

Meeting with nonprofits: This initial meeting could very well happen during the time you are working on Project 3. So plan to do some double tasking. This meeting and the work soon following will help you understand

and collaborate in the concept or rhetorical purpose that will best suit your nonprofit organization. Explore the organization. What is its mission? What does it do? How is it staffed? What does it need? Similar to how you began planning for your own website, you will write a paper on this process, in which you critically analyze the concept of the proposed nonprofit website and its relation to how you think the site should be designed physically. Make an appointment with the Sweetland Multiliteracy Consultants for after break to help you brainstorm Project 4.

Week Eight Feb 26 & 28: Winter Break

Project 5 (Architecture and Design): March 5–7

A conceptual rationale for your nonprofit website design is due March 7. During the month of March you will meet a second time, or a first and second time (depending on how the meetings proceed in February) so as to review a mockup of the site you have developed. After you have worked more or less individually in developing the rationale for submission on March 7, you will divide into appropriate groups to share ideas and compose one mockup based on all of your ideas. You will negotiate these ideas with the nonprofit agency in the week of March 11 through 15. Make an appointment at Sweetland for next week to assemble and execute the website.

Project 6: (Execution): March 7–April 4

During this time, you will meet with your group and Sweetland Consultants to execute the nonprofit's website. We will work on these sites both in your groups but also as a whole class. You will also meet with your nonprofit agency to finalize how the design and execution of the website look to them.

Project 7 (Quality Assurance Testing): April 4–23

During this time, you will meet with your nonprofits and show them the site. Because nothing works perfectly and communication is difficult, you can expect to be busy negotiating among the nonprofits, the MLC, and your websites.

* * *

Upon leaving the NEW Center, Dave and I were excited. Hajra had had a lot to say. He asked us plenty of questions, seeking out our commitment and our ability. He was an alumnus of the University of Michigan. He knew the university's resources and came to recognize us among them; on our way to the car, discussing the feedback we had received from Hajra, we understood that we would have not one but two partners to work with in the coming months.

COMMUNITY ORGANIZATION FOR URBAN REVITALIZATION AND SUSTAINABLE ENVIRONMENTS (COURSE)

Arthur Nusbaum and Alan Wasserman are evangelical in their opinions about urban development. They clearly want to persuade people to change their received ideas about how living and working environments are developed, and their organization is a local resource to encourage sound construction and rehabilitation of neighborhoods. Identified by the title "New Urbanism," their philosophy promotes mixed-use zoning, allowing a closer proximity of industry, business and housing. They eschew suburban sprawl, advocating developments that would allow people to live, work, shop and recreate (ideally) within a distance that could be conveniently navigated on foot or bicycle.

Given that many Michigan students come from the suburbs that New Urbanists critique, these two gentlemen presented something of a spectacle. Moreover, teenagers enjoy an intimate romance with the automobile, a vehicle that comes under intense New Urbanist scrutiny, as arguably the single most important technological factor that contributed to suburban sprawl. In a central text of New Urbanist reference, *Suburban Nation: The Rise of Sprawl and the Decline of the American Dream*, Andres Duany, Elizabeth Plater-Zyberk, and Jeff Speck (2000) assert that "what was once our servant has become our master. . . . The problem with cars is not the cars themselves but that they have produced an environment of dependence" (p. 14).

If cognitive dissonance contributes to felicity of learning, then this community partner and these two energetic gentlemen did things for my students that I never could have done alone. Even those students who most defensively rejected new urbanist ideas had to have been impressed with Nusbaum and Wasserman's energy and their commitment to a cause.

Recently, one student from this class wrote in an e-mail, "I learned so much about urbanization and it has really affected my desires when looking for a place to live." Although the substance of their presentation gave my students new and lasting perspectives to think about, there was, in addition, the rhetorical challenge of finding a proper visual and textual representation for the organization's passion and purpose.

HOMELESS EMPOWERMENT RELATIONSHIP ORGANIZATION (HERO)

Marti Rodwell, streetwise and time-tested, has worked with the homeless or near homeless for many years. For her, it all comes down to empowerment: "empowering people who are homeless or at risk of homelessness to attain maximum self-sufficiency through teaching step-by-step goal attainment skills," according to a 2001 newsletter. Attainment skills can be difficult to access because of the psychological hurt put on a person by poverty, social or familial disruption, and, plain and simple, the circumstance of having been homeless or even at risk of homelessness. My students, for the most part—no, from what I knew, all of them—well secured in a house and home with some kind of extended family, had met no one in any way like her.

Rodwell introduced herself and her organization to my class with a kind of word exercise. She asked the class to think of 10 words to describe their positive attributes. She timed us, asking us to put our pens down and turn our attention to her as soon as we finished. Five minutes. Rodwell said that the people with whom she works require much more time to complete such a list. She said that people who are not empowered get scared when close to achieving empowerment, nor do they have the positive self-image (so easily assumed by my college students) required to persist through the obstacles littering the path to achievement. She said she wanted a website that would grab attention and change attitudes, and she wanted visitors to "go through an epiphany—the discovery of the real versus the stereotype or common profile of the homeless."

HERO had a logo (the capital letters of the acronym into the center of which had been inserted a flowing, hand-drawn heart). Rodman was clear about what she wanted a website to do for her and her organization. She wanted a visual image "that creates empathy with the situation." She wanted something that would shock. "I want to inform people that their stereotypes of the homeless are wrong," she said. She was open to controversy, but she didn't want to be so controversial as to be closed down. For the comfortable, university town of Ann Arbor, Michigan, Rodwell wanted a picture of "what is in their own back yard. In this quaint town, you'd be surprised at what you might find." She added that she did not want to offend the Chamber of Commerce.

But then, I get ahead of myself. Our nonprofit visitors came to class during the week of Project 4 (Concept). The concept project intended, in what I think of now as highly idealistic ways, to get students to distill an essence from the people who had come before us, both in character and purpose, and use that essence to provide a theme, motif, or, better yet, rhetorical pose for the websites' compositions. To maintain the hope and idealism attendant to asking students to make a visual representation of a theme derived from a person or organization's character and purpose, some initial groundwork had to have been laid.

* * *

THE BOOKS

Diana Hacker. *A Pocket Style Manual*. Bedford/St. Martin's: Boston, 2000.
Susan Hilligoss and Tharon Howard. *Visual Communication: A Writer's Guide*. Longman: New York, 2002.
Robin Williams and John Tollett. *The Non-Designer's Web Book: An easy guide to creating, designing, and posting your own website*. Peachpit Press: Berkeley, 1998.

The selection of books is more or less self-explanatory: the obligatory freshman comp handbook to be used when students have a problem that they know how to look up; *The Non-Designer's Web Book* to be used as a basic "how-to" guide. But *Visual Communication* is a little different and represents a heady approach to visual forms as basic as a business letter, depicting even standard visual forms as being tied to specific discourse communities. The book contains chapters on genre and perception, on interpreting images and information graphics, and it provides hands-on information about how to plan visual design.

The projects represented keystone assignments for the course and would have, in a traditional writing course, been the, say, five 4- to 5-page papers that would be drafted and revised. But only the first two projects resulted in any traditional kind of written composition work. The first project was a typical comparison and contrast assignment, using websites for its subject matter. Much of our critical language and perspective was obtained from *The Non-Designer's Web Book* and *Visual Literacy*, but this assignment began the cycle of visits to the MLC, where consultants helped students adapt the traditional analytical skills of comparison and contrast to their use on visual material.

Because only two of the keystone assignments involved extended writing, I supplemented each one with what came to be a series of 500-word compositions, trying to provide a rich mix of thinking and writing activity and anticipating the tricky challenge upcoming that would require students to visually represent our nonprofit partners' characters and personalities. This undertaking began in earnest with Project 2, for which students had to write a paper that explained the rhetorical purpose of their own personal website. In conjunction with the longer paper, I asked students to "write a 500 word essay on yourself, emphasizing aspects that you would like to make significant in your own web site." Situated within the framework of the personal essay, I hoped that the experience would prepare them for the later visual representations of HERO and COURSE. But the short assignment reveals how the visual and multiliteracy objectives changed what students did and, more important, what counted as writing. After requesting the short personal essay, the assignment goes on to say, "Acceptable variations on this direction would be to make a 'thick' outline, using a 'bulleted' format that relays information about yourself while at the same time organizing it in a way parallel to how you envision it for your web site." Never would I have allowed a bulleted presentation of information in a typical composition class. Never would I have requested a thick outline.[3]

The shorter paper and its longer companion in Project 2 were important exercises and documents in themselves, as they helped the multiliteracy consultants do their job in facilitating the execution of my students' personal sites. They also represent a considerable effort in what every typical composition class attempts to do—and that is to challenge students to better understand the relationship between an essay's content and its form.

---

[3]Although I wouldn't have accepted the outline format, I am aware there are many professional contexts in which succinct bulleted information is appropriate and even necessary. That I wouldn't have previously asked for such a form is as much the result of my own short-sightedness with regard to the uses of the written word and as it is in the English courses designed to teach them.

In early February, students wrote a short essay that critiqued the layout of any visual composition, using principles contained in our *Visual Communication* text. "Observe subtleties in the visual layout," I instructed. "Choose an image from anywhere you like. . . . (Think of the many flyers you see displayed on campus.) Using the principles explained in chapter 5 of *Visual Communication*, analyze the layout." By instructing to choose an image from anywhere, and even explicitly mentioning the many flyers on campus, I intended students to begin to see the many visual appeals to their attention they experienced every day. The chapter from *Visual Communication* is written as a guide to designing a web page, but we used it inversely as a guide to analyze an image that had been previously assembled. The chapter addresses gestalt-based principles—the use of background space, symmetry and asymmetry, navigation cues, and focal points. Of particular interest is a section on genre-based principles where the text states that "what we expect to see is very much related to what we have seen in the past" (Hilligoss & Howard, 2002, p. 104). The accuracy of the statement cannot be doubted, but at the same time, visual and written design must incorporate some twist or nuance that compels the viewer or reader to continue. If the visual elements that viewers encounter embody only that which they have seen before, they will soon stop looking. In more deeply scrutinizing the images they encountered daily, students might better understand the seductive line drawn between the familiar and the unique.

A week later, after the presentations by HERO and COURSE, students chose one concept regarding the organization that seemed suitable and necessary to be communicated through a website. "Include in this writing some ideas that you have for how technically to communicate the concept visually." In early March, students read a chapter of James Howard Kunstler's book, *The Geography of Nowhere*. Kunstler is an iconic new urbanist writer. He is bombastic, funny, and smart, and he wields his opinion as surely as a samurai sword. In many ways, his energy and linguistic flourish matched that of COURSE directors, Nusbaum and Wasserman. Examine both sides of the issue, I explained to them. "Yes, there is reason to agree with this writer that the current state of land development is scary. And you might also, should also, be able to see a counter side to this, possibly because of some of the unexamined assumptions inherent in the writing, and argue that the current state of development is perhaps not scary at all."

As we might have expected, students found concepts for our nonprofits' presentations in the tension between what they expected and what they heard. For the HERO presentation, students were interested in new definitions of homeless. As one student wrote, "This concept is brand new to me: a homeless person working a full time job." Another one wrote, "Everyone has stereotypes about what homeless people look like, and the first thing the site should have is a way to show the truth." Students were impressed by Rodwell's emphasis on how most homeless are not the soiled, tired, and inebriated souls who jump to mind's eye, but children who go homeless due to a parent's ill health, a parent's poor-paying job, or the lack of affordable housing.

The development of a visual and literal rhetorical concept for COURSE was complicated by two things: (a) the hands-on manner of the nonprofit's cofounders, each of them having a particular design sense that they passionately wanted to see articulated; and (b) the conflict due to COURSE's architectural, urban design philosophy being critical of the homesteads and communities from which most of my 18-year-old students hailed. In response to the James Howard Kunstler essay, one student wrote "I do not think that anybody takes pleasure in sitting in traffic; however, I have never thought the driving distances to all of my necessary destinations to be too far away." Another wrote, "One can reach family members who live thirty miles away in a mere half-hour, helping families maintain a sense of closeness."

Because we had two partners, the class was divided into two groups, each one assigned to either HERO or COURSE. This presented some problems in making assignments to the whole group, insofar as each nonprofit required its own, unique attention. Such dependable and regular classroom routines as reading, critiquing, and essay went by the wayside. Nearly every class was begun with a business meeting to find out what had happened in the interim praiseworthy of note or, in contrast, problematic. I tried to conduct the usual grammar and style lessons using sentences and passages from their own writing to instruct from and reflect on. Competing for class time, however, were committee meetings within each of the two larger groups, troubleshooting compositional and technological issues for each website and conversations about what each student had learned on a recent session with a multiliteracy consultant.

In looking at it now, the short assignment for March 26 shows some of the logistical difficulties. I am including the assignment in its entirety.

> There will be some variation in this assignment depending on your group's needs. In short, you should write something that will appear on your nonprofit's web site. This might very well have something to do with history or background. In fact, I believe most likely it will have something to do with history or background. This assignment might also be fulfilled by doing an interview and transcribing it. My sense is,

however, that we need to provide some kind of historical background for each of these movements or tendencies, if you will, out of which COURSE and HERO have grown. The background and history team should probably delegate and organize this writing, so as to achieve as best as possible some continuity of topics. By this time, they might already have topics to give you. If they don't you need to sit down today and work this out. You will have a week for this, and the little extra time that no class on Thursday provides you. Let's aim for having a kind of historical timeline about homelessness and urban development by next Tuesday that we can add to each website.

I cringe as I read this now, the assignment revealing as it does a sense of desperation, and it is desperation that I well remember. The end of the term is 3 weeks away. At the time, exigencies of final evaluation and fairness arise in all writing courses, such as the subjective nature of writing assessment. However, this assignment reveals me dealing not only with two different groups in my class involved in qualitatively different endeavors, but also with a curriculum that seems to have come up short: I had not prepared for the need for historical timelines.

* * *

Although the experiment in multimodal literacy brought some chaos into my writing classroom and to some degree exposed me at my ill-preparedness worst, it brought with it considerable reward. Some of the students, too, say the right things. In a recent e-mail, now some 5 years after the composition course at issue here, one student wrote:

> Hi Professor Cooper,
> It's good to hear from you again. I do remember the course fondly, but unfortunately do not have anything saved in terms of papers or the backup for the web site.
> However, I still remember your first lecture of rhetoric and our misuse of the term as well as your future lessons on multiple means of communications within both old and new forms of multimedia. I took a lot away from the course and it helped to diversify my focus especially in the field of advertising. I remember the use and importance of not just written English in terms of communication but the methods of non-verbal communication such as the websites that we created/designed.
> Cheers

This student says it well. The methods of nonverbal communication have become increasingly complex and prevalent in our everyday lives and occupations. Managing such methods is not just a matter of technical acuity, but it deserves an understanding of how visual and audio cues fit together in an organized, rhetorical whole. As I indicated earlier, I would not have undertaken this on my own. But I am not certain that I would have undertaken it, either, with only the simple knowledge that there was a multiliteracy center on campus. If left at that remove, I could have been content with the singularly written literacy that my composition course concerned itself with term after term. Because I knew Dave Sheridan, because I had heard him speak on the topic of visual literacy, and because he came to my class and agreed to consult with me through the term, I more readily took on an experiment that I likely would not have otherwise undertaken.

Can fledgling MLCs provide such personal attention and hand-to-hand support? As in the beginning of any enterprise, the new MLCs will have to do a fair amount of education and promotion. This is due, in part, to the considerable change in thinking required of the writing instructor. Although I know something about visual art and have enjoyed greatly the experience of visual stimulation, I never would have thought to incorporate visual elements into my written composition course. My negligence would be due, in part, to my thinking of the already onerous task of bringing young people to a more sophisticated use of language in its own right, bringing them a kind of critical literacy that ostensibly is necessary for their other college courses across the curriculum and in their role of public citizen. No time devoted to the study of language is available to sacrifice to the pleasures of visual elements of persuasion. However, as the student indicated earlier, the kind of literacies he engaged in in the multiliteracy classroom prepared him well for the kind of work he is doing for his career. As much as I adore the written word and the artful and crafty use of it, evolving technologies, many of them based on felicity of communication rather than subtlety of communication, might demand a rethinking of the college writing curriculum. The emerging MLC and its consultants can play a substantial role in that evolution.

My experience suggests that by formally partnering with a MLC over a full semester, composition and rhetoric teachers (as might many others) can engage in innovative teaching practices that might otherwise be impossible. Specifically, MLCs can capitalize on the Writing Center model of providing one-on-one support for students. Each student in this course had a different learning style, brought different technical competencies, and brought different levels of experience with new-media composing. By working with each student in one-on-one conferences, the Sweetland MLC was able to address these differences. This allowed the course to embrace technology, new media, and multimodal rhetoric in ways that would have otherwise been impractical.

The approach adopted by the MLC addressed both technical and rhetorical concerns in the context of individual student projects. One-on-one conferences with students at the MLC were not generic seminars on how to use Dreamweaver or Photoshop. Multiliteracy consultants first asked students to discuss their rhetorical goals; technical issues were addressed in the context of achieving these goals. Moreover, the sustained partnership with the MLC meant that conversations between student composers and tutors were informed by the tutors' deep understanding of the context for the projects on which student composers were working. Tutors knew the details of major assignments, as well as the pedagogical goals of the course, and their conversations with student composers are richer because of this knowledge.

Because of the sustained partnership between this course and the MLC, the arc of learning was longer than it is traditionally when students' interaction with tutors is limited to a single session. This means that conversations between tutors and students could build off of what had happened previously. Some students used the MLC quite regularly over the course of the semester, and MLC tutors got to know them quite well. Tutors had a better sense of the learning styles and comfort levels of these students and could "pick up where they left off."

During this process, my students and I were aware that we were learning together, and to the degree that instructors are willing to take such a risk, the rewards compensate for the demands. By integrating MLC support into their syllabi, instructors can absolve themselves of the burden of being the expert on every aspect of technology-intensive composing (increasingly an impossible task, given the how quickly technologies change). Moreover, the points where students tutor the teacher become moments of genuine empowerment. This course benefited from collaborative planning of syllabus and assignments with MLC faculty, from whole-class workshops given by faculty and MLC tutors, one-on-one instruction, and the real occasion of an instructor learning together with his students.

Although the University of Michigan can be perceived as, and in many ways is, an institution blessed with generous resources, the beginnings of the Sweetland MLC were relatively modest. With the benefit of limited funding through a small internal grant, the MLC accomplished a lot with a little. Consisting of three computers in what had been the office of a single faculty member, the MLC was able to partner in robust ways with my class, as well as our two nonprofit partners, influencing the learning of many students and the life and well-being of members of the community that our partners served.

REFERENCES

Barnett, Robert W., & Rosen, Lois M. (1999). The WAC/writing center partnership: Creating a campus-wide writing environment. In Robert W. Barnett & Jacob S. Blumner (Eds.), *Writing centers and writing across the curriculum programs: Building interdisciplinary partnerships* (pp. 1–12). Westport, CT: Greenwood Press.

Cazden, Courtney, Cope, Bill, Fairclough, Norman, Gee, Jim, Kalantzis, Mary, Kress, Gunther et al. (1996). A pedagogy of multiliteracies: Designing social futures. *Harvard Educational Review, 66*(1), 60–92.

Duany, Andre, Plater-Zyberk, Elizabeth, & Speck, Jeff. (2000). *Suburban nation: The rise of sprawl and the decline of the American dream.* New York: North Point.

Grimm, Nancy. (1999). *Good intentions: Writing center work for post modern times.* Portsmouth: Heinemann Press.

Hacker, Diana. (2000). *A pocket style manual.* Boston: Bedford/St. Martin's.

Hilligoss, Susan, & Howard, Tharon. (2002). *Visual communication: A writer's guide.* New York: Longman.

Kail, Harvey. (2000). [Review of the book *Good Intentions: Writing Center Work For Post Modern Times*]. *College Composition and Communication, 51*(4), 676–678.

Trimbur, John. (2000). Multiliteracies, social futures, and writing centers. *The Writing Center Journal, 20*(2), 29–31.

Turnley, Melinda. (2007). Integrating critical approaches to technology and service-learning projects. *Technical Communication Quarterly, 16*(1), 103–123.

Warschauer, Mark (1999). *Electronic literacies: Language, culture, and power in online education.* Mahwah, NJ: Erlbaum.

Williams, Robin, & Tollett, John. (1998). *The non-designer's web book: An easy guide to creating, designing, and posting your own web site.* Berkeley: Peachpit Press.

7

MULTILITERACIES ACROSS LIFETIMES

ENGAGING K–12 STUDENTS AND TEACHERS THROUGH TECHNOLOGY-BASED OUTREACH

Troy Hicks

Central Michigan University

PROLOGUE

The center, as we would expect, hums with talk about all kinds of writing. Pairs, scattered about the room, gaze over computer screens and discuss essays, slide shows, and web pages. A small group, seated in the kitchen corner, laugh and snack while they discuss teaching strategies from a shared reading. Another small group huddles in the far corner, sitting around one of the more powerful desktop computers in the center, a "creation station," importing digital video and discussing the storyboard for their visual argument. Throughout the room, many people work alone as well: one sits with a laptop and headset, recording a podcast; another sinks into the couch with pen and journal in hand, piles of books and sticky notes scattered around.

Like many writing centers around the world, people here are engaged in the work of writing with both traditional and multiple literacies. Unlike many of these sites, however, most of the people here are not undergraduate or graduate students, although peer consultants are a part of the mix. Instead, as we take a closer look around, we notice a diverse group of teachers—working in grades from kindergarten to college; some just entering their first year as rookies with others nearing retirement—all working diligently as the summer sun pours in through the windows.

INTRODUCTION

This snapshot from a summer institute illustrates the ways in which a vision for a multiliteracies Writing Center outreach effort, when developed with K–12 teachers, can provide a context for "consultative teaching" (Stock, 1997) that centers on collaboration, capacity building, and cross-disciplinary work. Based on my experience as Outreach Coordinator for the Michigan State University (MSU) Writing Center from 2003–2007, I first describe the broader contexts of K–12 multiliteracies work as well as the National Writing Project (NWP). Then, focusing on the work of the Red Cedar Writing Project (RCWP), I provide illustrations of two particular outreach initiatives that I directly facilitated: a project with seven teachers entitled "Digital Portfolios as a Space for Inquiry" and a larger initiative where teachers learned multimodal writing with blogs, wikis, and podcasts, enacted through an NWP "Technology Initiative" grant (< http://www.nwp.org/cs/public/print/programs/ti >). In both examples, I focus attention on how teachers learned multiliteracies, specifically digital literacies, and how the material and pedagogical support of the Writing Center made that work possible. Finally, I close with implications for engaging in multiliteracies work through a discussion of three themes that have emerged over our 15-year history: collaboration, capacity building, and cross-disciplinary teaching and learning. Collaborating with K–12 teachers in multiliteracy-based projects is one of the ways that we, as Writing Center professionals, can have a long-term impact on the quality of writing in our schools, communities, and workplaces. This chapter describes how that vision is enacted in the space of a Writing Center.

THE BROAD VIEW:
K–12 MULTILITERACIES AND THE NWP

To contextualize our work in a broader perspective, I first acknowledge how the field of K–12 teaching continues to inform our outreach efforts. Although a university and its faculty can bring a certain perspective to any outreach work, to ignore these trends would undermine both the philosophy and effectiveness of our work. Our multiliteracies outreach engages teachers and students who teach and learn in K–12 schools that continue to undergo reform efforts and near constant scrutiny. Although it is beyond the scope of this chapter to delve too deeply into the complexities of technology and literacy education in K–12 schools, I offer a few brief points for consideration in light of a multiliteracies outreach effort. First, with regard to technology, many critics rightfully argue that computers in schools do not serve teachers or students well (e.g., Cuban, 1986, 2001; Oppenheimer, 2003). There are complex reasons for this, from the hesitancy or resistance of teachers to use technology in their classrooms, to the hardware and network infrastructure present (or, unfortunately, not present), to the social and political aspects of the institution of schooling (see e.g., Zhao & Frank, 2003; Zhao, Pugh, Sheldon, & Byers, 2002). Although computers, then the Internet, and now the more interactive read/write web that includes wikis and blogs (Richardson, 2006) have all sporadically entered schools, there has been little substantive change in the ways that teaching and learning occurs in most of our country's classrooms. In light of a multiliterate approach to teaching and learning, literacy scholar Donald Leu's (2000) question becomes more resonant: "If educators fail to continually become literate with rapidly changing technologies, how will they help their students become literate?" (p. 763).

Second, in terms of literacy education, the entire field of English and composition studies has been undergoing a shift. Although it has been described in many ways, by many scholars, I oversimplify and summarize the shift here: Once thought of as a neutral, logical, and teachable set of skills, reading and writing today—and as emphasized throughout this entire collection—now imbue a sense of social, cultural, critical, digital, and other competencies (see e.g., Brandt, 2001; Graff, 1991; Heath, 1983; Lankshear & Knobel, 2003; Selfe & Hawisher, 2004; Street, 1984). As The New London Group (2000) reminds us, this vision of multiliteracies can offer another perspective on literacy learning, one that is design-driven and

> connects powerfully to the sort of creative intelligence the best practitioners need in order to be able continually to redesign their activities in the very act of practice. It connects as well to the idea that learning and productivity are the results of designs (the structures) of complex systems of people environments, technology, beliefs, and texts. (pp. 19–20)

Taken in a context of rapidly expanding technologies and literacies, the New London Group's call for design-driven learning provides teachers with a model for how they can engage in their own learning, as well as create learning opportunities for their students. Rather than only reading a text and writing a prompted essay, a design-based approach would encourage students to question the construction of the text, the motivations of the author, and the ways in which they could use similar constructions and motivations in their own composing process. Put another way, current trends in multiliteracies aim for what Selber (2004) calls functional, critical, and rhetorical literacies, a combination that moves beyond basic reading, writing, and computer competency. More than just being able to use computers for utilitarian purposes, Selber argues that a rhetorical approach invites composers to question the ways in which application and document design is developed—and constrained—by the types of interfaces they encounter. This vision of multifaceted, multiliterate practices puts students in the role of designers and teachers in the role of a consultative mentor, much like what we envision for the role of a peer tutor in the Writing Center.

All this—from the realities of schooling to the theoretical shifts in literacy practice—occurs in a context where teachers and students already engage in outreach and multiliteracies. Although the examples are numerous, two recent publications highlight many of the successful programs that currently exist. I cite these to be exemplary, not exhaustive, as numerous others could be shared as well. In other words, I suggest that we as university faculty make ourselves aware of the conversations happening in K–12 scholarship as we begin outreach efforts.

In the first case, Pamela Childers (2006) has edited an issue of *The Clearing House*, in which she argues that secondary school Writing Centers "foster improved student writing, thinking, and learning; support faculty and curriculum development; and enhance collaboration with higher education and the community" (p. 44). Articles in the collection show a variety of perspective on how multiliteracies can inform Writing Center work and collaborations, including selections on high school–university collaborations (Ashley & Shafer, 2006; Barnett, 2006; Jordan, 2006; Littleton, 2006; Tinker, 2006) and implementation of multiliteracies in secondary settings (Elwood, Wolff Murphy, & Cardenas, 2006; Inman, 2006).

In the second case, a recent themed issue of *English Journal* (97.2) focused on "new literacies." Editor Louann Reid (2007) suggested that the editorial board "prompted writers to describe what they do to help students recognize new textual media, understand how texts are created, and think critically about how representation influences meaning and value" (p. 14). Among the many innovative articles in the issue, three were authored by high school English teachers and show how they are using virtual worlds (Arver, 2007), threaded discussions (English, 2007), and multimodal/multigenre writing (Moynihan, 2007) to reimagine their classrooms from a multiliteracies perspective.

This progressive multiliteracies and outreach work parallels another network of teachers and university faculty that has been engaged in collaborative work for more than 30 years: the NWP. Recently cited by Childers (2007) as one of the ways in which K–12 schools and universities can establish productive and sustainable partnerships, the NWP has worked since 1974 to establish a professional development model of "teachers teaching teachers" that stands in contrast to the traditional notions of knowledge and pedagogy flowing from the university to the K–12 schools. Lieberman and Wood (2003), building off an interview with NWP's Co-Director, Elyse Eidman-Aadahl, describe the collaboration as follows:

> Confined neither within universities nor within schools, the NWP brings people, strengths, and concerns from both universities and schools together. . . . While networking educators nationally and regionally, the NWP invites them to bring to the table local concerns and problems for collective dialogue and inquiry. Thus, it foregrounds the everyday, real concerns of educators against a larger horizon of educational issues, and then helps to build knowledge and expertise and distribute them where they are needed. The "third space" of the NWP, then, is both local and remote, grounded in and yet transcendent of particular institutions, and facilitative of both formal professional development experiences and informal personal connections. (p. 88)

In this manner, individual NWP sites work with local teachers and schools to tackle the problems that they face, bringing the latest literacy theories and research into conversation with the day-to-day realities of classrooms. This model respects teacher knowledge and invites them into a conversation, rather than giving them a lecture.

As a site of the NWP, we at the RCWP begin our work in this "third space," knowing that teachers have particular pedagogies and contextual concerns to share in any outreach effort. For such an effort to be successful—especially when layering in multiliteracies—we recognize the strengths, talents, and questions that K–12 teachers bring to the university outreach effort. Return, for a moment, to the snapshot described in the prologue of this chapter, and you get a sense of how the Writing Center looks and feels when this work is in full swing. I will describe how that vision is enacted in our local site's outreach work.

A LOCAL VIEW:
THE MSU WRITING CENTER AND RCWP

> Mindful that literacy is learned through use across contexts and over a lifetime, in addition to working to improve the quality and range of literacy in MSU, the Center reached out to involve itself in the teaching and uses of literacy in both the communities and schools that send students to MSU and the communities and workplaces that students enter when they leave MSU. (Stock, 1997, pp. 11–12)

As teachers spend 4 weeks of their summer in RCWP, they enact the vision of a "consultative teaching" that Patti Stock (1997), founding director of the MSU Writing Center, argued would "produce new knowledge about the teaching, learning, and uses of literacy" (p. 12). Writing center pedagogy relies on peers working with one another to ask questions and seek understandings; when a student works with a writing consultant, the writer remains in control of his or her own work, assisted by a peer knowledgeable about composing practices, genres, and the expectations of college writing. With the material and pedagogical support of the Writing Center, teachers work together to learn how to be better writers and teachers of writing through consultative teaching. In so doing, we believe that they will then return to their schools and offer professional development and support to their local colleagues, all the while considering the effects of newer technologies on the teaching and learning of literacy.

As noted, Writing Centers in higher education have often collaborated successfully with K–12 teachers to establish writing centers in their schools. These are worthwhile endeavors and produce positive results. That said, having a Writing Center in a school may not address the fundamental challenge of how writing is taught in the classrooms that these students return to after their visit to the center. Therefore, when she envisioned the work of the MSU Writing Center, Stock described a different approach to writing center practice, one that would be mindful of a sociocultural perspective on literacy learning and that would work to affect students before, during, and after their time on campus by collaborating directly with teachers.

In her landmark essay, "Reforming Education in the Land-Grant University: Contributions from a Writing Center, " Stock (1997) outlined four "perplexing social challenges" that she hoped the MSU Writing Center would address. These include two specific challenges related to K–12 teachers:

- "to improve the quality of teaching and learning in America's public schools," and

- "to prepare ourselves for living life and making a living in the current and future era" (p. 12).

She then suggests the many ways in which the MSU Writing Center would address those challenges. Like most Writing Centers, MSU established undergraduate and graduate peer consulting. In addition, two additional consultancies emerged. The first was a faculty writing consultancy, consisting of K–12 and university faculty connected through RCWP. This consultative practice aligns with Writing Center pedagogy and offers the MSU Writing Center a unique opportunity to serve as a hub for outreach activity. The first outreach coordinator for the Writing Center, Janet Swenson (who continues to serve as RCWP's director), thus facilitates what Trimbur (2000) noted as the "civic" component of our outreach work.

Alone, the established consultancy of K–12 teachers connected to a Writing Center makes for a mutually beneficial relationship. Yet Stock envisioned another consultancy that began at the same time within the center's group of peer consultants: the Internet writing consultancy. This work is both pedagogical and, by its nature, technical (DeVoss, 2002; Thomas, Hara, & DeVoss, 2000). Our "digital writing consultants" have both a background in peer tutoring as well as the skills related to particular technologies and computer applications so that they can help writers compose nonprint texts, including web pages, slide shows, and digital movies. Because these consultants are available to work with individual and small groups of teachers within our Writing Center during the summer institute and throughout the school year, we have had the unique opportunity to have a multiliteracies approach permeate our outreach work.

Also of note, the MSU Writing Center's outreach occurs within the context of the university's broader mission as a land-grant institution. Outlined in "Points of Distinction: A Guidebook for Planning & Evaluating Quality Outreach" (Michigan State University Committee on Evaluating Quality Outreach, 2000), the university aims to provide outreach to local, state, national, and international constituents that honors nine commitments, including mutuality (collaboration), capacity building, and cross-disciplinary approaches. These commitments guide the types of work in which the Writing Center engages; for RCWP, in particular, these commitments involve a deep trust in the knowledge and experience of teachers, as well as the promise that we will offer them something both theoretically sound and practical for their classrooms.

Yet shifting into a consultative mindset is complicated. To return for a moment to Stock's vision and challenges, for Writing Center outreach efforts in an era of changing literacy practices, this is indeed difficult work.

A multiliteracy center must adopt a different sort of pedagogy; when coupled with the goal of "teachers teaching teachers," this becomes even more challenging. Because technology is such a particular part of our work, it challenges our assumptions about literacy practices. Recently, Anstey and Bull (2006) have summarized the mental shifts involved in rethinking literacy pedagogy:

> [L]iteracy pedagogy must teach students to be flexible, tolerant of different viewpoints, and able to problem solve, analyse situations, and work strategically. They must be able to identify the knowledge and resources they have and combine and recombine them to suit the particular purpose and context. Consequently, school classrooms and teachers' pedagogy must encourage, model, and reflect these sorts of behaviours. (p. 18)

A multiliteracies pedagogy, one that is informed by and respectful of Writing Center pedagogy—stands in contrast to the typical types of pedagogies we sometimes see in schools—pedagogies that enforce the use of restrictive formats for writing, an excessive focus on test-based writing, and a lack of multimodal composing opportunities. I say this not to be critical, although I recognize the undertone it implies. The real constraints of curriculum, administration, or collegial peer pressure may force even master teachers to abandon multiliteracies pedagogy. The MSU Writing Center and RCWP have taken up this challenge to the status quo of how writing is taught in our public schools in a number of ways. The next section expands on the theoretical overview offered by the New London Group as a means to describe how we situate our own teaching and learning of multiliteracies and then describes two particular projects as they illustrate these ideas in action. By exploring these two particular examples, I highlight the ways in which we develop collaboration, capacity building, and a cross-disciplinary approach to our outreach work.

MULTILITERACIES WRITING CENTER OUTREACH IN ACTION

Nearly a decade ago, in a precursor to this collection, Barbara Monroe and her colleagues outlined a vision of a "networked university" and how a Writing Center could contribute to that vision:

The future of education lies, then, with the online, networked university, with its flattened hierarchy and collateral human and electronic networks, connecting schools, universities, businesses, and communities. . . . We have to enter this discursive arena and enter it with entrepreneurial spirit to fulfill our mission as a writing center—that is, to promote a cohesive, highly visible writing program across the curriculum and within the disciplines; to infuse distance learning projects with pedagogical expertise and academic inquiry; and to instill and maintain the public service values of the university. (Monroe, Rickly, Condon, & Butler, 2000, pp. 218–219)

Because the theory and practice of teaching writing has changed over the past decade, writing programs have embraced digital, networked writing (see e.g., Writing in Digital Environments [WIDE] Research Center Collective, 2005; Wysocki, Johnson-Eilola, Selfe, & Sirc, 2004). These trends have influenced the work of the MSU Writing Center and, by natural extension, the work of RCWP. To work as Writing Centers that can meet the goals Monroe et al. outline earlier through outreach work, we have engaged in a number of projects that connect teachers from diverse backgrounds. For instance, in the first years after RCWP was established in 1993, Swenson (2003) began the Write for Your Life Project that connected teachers via e-mail listserv in what she called a "transformative teacher network" that focused on inquiry-based learning where students chose to write about topics related to their health and well-being. As she concluded, "professional development needs to be available to networks of teachers, *at the point of need*, and *fully integrated into teachers' daily practice"* (p. 317; italics original). From this initial work, RCWP has expanded its offerings—with the material and pedagogical support of the MSU Writing Center—into a number of other initiatives.

Before describing two of these initiatives in which I have been personally involved, it is worth noting how we use the work of The New London Group (2000) to frame our outreach projects. These scholars suggest a model of multiliteracy immersion, in which learners (in our case, teachers and, in turn, their students) engage in a series of recursive literacy practices: situated practice, overt instruction, critical framing, and transformed practice. These components "do not constitute a linear hierarchy, nor do they represent stages. Rather, they are components that are related in complex ways" (p. 32). To understand and communicate with new designs of meaning, a learner moves through the four components of this pedagogy in a recursive process. Thus, the "how" of any particular multiliteracy practice becomes more than just technical skills; instead, the entire process can work as a critical and reflective opportunity for teachers examining their own literacy learning in a rhetorical context.

In the practice of Writing Center outreach, then, what does the pedagogy of multiliteracies look like? In what ways can a Writing Center support the kinds of efforts that will lead to systemic change in teaching practice? In a manner that complements the efforts of directors and scholars who set out to transform the teaching and learning of writing through K–12 Writing Centers (e.g., Childers, Fels, & Jordan, 2004), our Writing Center's outreach efforts aim to improve the teaching and learning of writing by engaging teachers in these composing processes so that they, in turn, will transform their teaching practice. By engaging in multiliteracy work, and understanding that process as writers, teachers will take these new understandings back to their classrooms and invite students to do similar work. It is with this in mind that I now turn to a discussion of two particular projects that highlight how a Writing Center that focuses on multiliteracy learning and outreach can influence the teaching and learning of writing in schools at the local, state, and national levels.

Learning Visual Literacy by Designing Digital Portfolios

As part of an NWP Teacher Inquiry Communities Network minigrant, seven RCWP colleagues joined me in a year-long teacher research project where they pursued a topic of interest in their classroom while representing their work through a digital teaching portfolio. Over the course of the year, we met periodically in person and built an online community through a blog, focusing our attention on visual literacy (Burmark, 2002) and web design of digital portfolios (Kimball, 2002). In addition to helping one another throughout the process, we drew on the resources of the Writing Center, in that we met at the center on a regular basis and used its computers for web development. Also, some of the teachers in the project set up appointments with our digital consultants to discuss their work and receive additional assistance.

For instance, one of the teachers, Tara Autrey, had begun working on her website with our group, but needed some additional help to update her site and bring visual cohesion to it. She had built an early draft of the portfolio during one of our group's meetings and sought feedback on it through our blog, yet she still felt as if it was not working exactly the way that she wanted to to. Thus, she scheduled an appointment at the Writing Center with a digital writing consultant and, because she had recently held a class meeting with her students to generate ideas for colors, images, fonts, and contents of her site, she was able to reimagine her portfolio's overall design and purpose. In a collaboratively written article about the project, Tara claimed that,

> Whereas I have been willing to incorporate music, art, movement, and other nontraditional modes of learning into my classroom, technology has almost always been ignored. Until recently, I have been frightened by technology, feeling like my knowledge base was not stable enough to guide students. In addition, our antiquated computer lab had become a daunting place where a neon "enter at your own risk" sign seemed to flash each time I entertained the thought of taking students there. Now, however, not only does my DP [digital portfolio] make using the lab with students necessary but I also have a better understanding of how to access information online and create presentations. Because of this, I am not as fearful about using technology, despite my school's troubled lab. (Autrey et al., 2005, p. 68)

Also, the rhetorical approach that the Writing Center infuses into all of its work permeated our discussions about how and why to set up a website. In a presentation that we offer to numerous undergraduate classes about peer response, our consultants suggest a heuristic for analyzing a rhetorical situation: MAPS. By examining the mode, audience, purpose, and writing situation, a writer can make informed decisions about organization, word choice, design, and other aspects of his or her composition. Teachers in the digital portfolio project used the MAPS heuristic to think about all the potential modes they could incorporate into their portfolios (text, images, videos, hypertext), the potential audiences that they would serve (students, colleagues, administrators, parents), and purposes they might meet (to reflect on teaching, to inform students about curriculum, to document classroom learning). In a second collaborative article that we wrote, Aram Kabodian described this process in the following manner:

> Without this support group of fellow educators, chances are that I would have plodded along in this process of building a website without really looking at the possibilities that lay before me to present my professional and personal life in a concerted, reflective way. I allowed myself the time to think about the implications of my choices and then to mull over those implications within a contemplative group of learners. Listening and responding to the struggles of my peers further developed my concept and purpose for a digital portfolio. I believe the time I spent with the group paid off immensely in the ever-emerging digital portfolio I am constructing. (Hicks et al., 2007, p. 456)

This "critical framing," as The New London Group describes it, allowed the teachers to focus less on the nuts and bolts of building their portfolios— although those skills were important—and more on how they would represent their work to larger audiences.

Thus, the Writing Center and RCWP's work overlapped in generative ways. Teachers were able to rely on the support of digital writing consultants in between our regular group meetings. Of the seven teachers who participated in the project, only three had any background in creating a web page, and that was limited. By working with one another and relying on the personnel and technologies available at the Writing Center, they were able to compose digital portfolios that they then shared with their own students; some even asked students to create multimodal texts of their own as a result of participating in this project. As an outreach effort, this collaboration addressed the K–12 technology and literacy gap as it challenged teachers to reconsider what it means to be literate and how they represent themselves in digital environments.

Engaging in Collaborative Multimodal Writing Through the RCWP Technology Initiative

As part of our NWP Technology Initiative Lead Site grant, we have been able to build on what we learned in the digital portfolio project and engage teachers in multimodal composing for authentic audiences. In the fall of 2005, as we prepared to send a team of RCWP teachers to Pittsburgh for the annual NCTE convention and NWP meeting, Swenson asked me to lead sessions for our teachers on how to compose with read/write web technologies such as blogs, wikis, and podcasts (Richardson, 2006). With blogs having just come into vogue during the 2004 presidential election season, podcasts coming to the fore in the summer of 2005, and *Wikipedia* challenging what it meant to be an expert and collaboratively compose texts, teaching teachers about the nuts and bolts of these technologies and how to critically use them in their own teaching became a central focus for our work at that time.

Building on models of previously successful workshops, we met in the Writing Center and had the support of digital writing consultants as we began our blog and first wiki. Along with the challenges of creating texts, individually and collaboratively, in these web-based applications, teachers also had to begin thinking rhetorically about constructing audio content that would be distributed through podcasts. The goal that we had for teachers was that they would act as "on-the-spot reporters" at the convention for colleagues and students who could not attend, and thus they would produce audio reports that would be suitable for posting on our blog and wiki.

Many of our teachers enjoyed podcasting from the annual meeting, and one in particular, Paul Cryderman, took up the task with gusto. With an iPod and a microphone in hand, he interviewed everyone from fellow teachers to a bartender to a prominent writer of young adult literature, Jerry Spinelli.[1] Podcasting presented a unique composing challenge, in that we had to capture audio, process it with a sound editing program (we used the open source program, Audacity, for our work), and then post that audio file online, as well as embedding it in an accompanying blog post to make it a true podcast. Two of the Writing Center's graduate writing consultants and I helped teachers process and upload their podcasts throughout the weekend in Pittsburgh, and many of them found that having an iPod in their hands gave them a little boost of confidence as they approached famous authors and scholars, inviting them to share their comments with the world.

Having worked at the Writing Center to establish the basics about how to post to the blog and wiki, how to record with the iPod, and how to edit and post a podcast, our work in the field in Pittsburgh (and again the next year in Nashville) went well. Rather than learning on the fly at the conference, we were able to meet comfortably beforehand in the Writing Center, collaborate with one another to learn the applications, and get support from digital writing consultants before attempting to do the same kind of work at a remote location. As we think about how to scaffold teachers in their own multiliteracy learning so that they can then work with their own students to develop these skills, this model of what The New London Group (2000) calls "overt instruction" allowed teachers to become comfortable with the technologies that they were expected to use before they went in the field to use them. Considering the need for teachers to become literate in 21st-century skills, this opportunity to offer them contextual support so they could compose for their own audiences and purposes suggests that they can then engage in similar work with their own students.[2]

---

[1]These podcasts are archived on our blog at: < http://redcedarwritingproject.blogspot.com > . Cryderman's podcast with Spinelli is available at: < http://redcedarwritingproject.blogspot. com/2005/11/interview-with-jerry-spinelli.html >

[2]Our current wiki < http://rcwp.wikispaces.com > remains a centerpiece of our site's work, as teacher consultants collaborate to produce workshop agendas and supporting materials, often working across time and space, yet sometimes together in the Writing Center, too.

IMPLICATIONS

Through our work, we have been reminded of Stock's original vision and the ways that MSU suggests we conduct outreach, especially in the ways that we aim to impact the quality of teaching and learning in K–12 schools. We invite teachers to teach teachers (and, by extension, their students) so as to make a living through writing both today and in the future. Over the 4 years that I was directly involved as RCWP's outreach coordinator, themes from MSU's outreach goals permeated throughout our projects. I suggest three here for Writing Center professionals to consider as they develop their own priorities and goals for a sustained Writing Center outreach effort that focuses on the teaching and learning of multiliteracies in K–12 schools.

As I suggest these themes, I realize that I speak to a variety of audiences from different institutional contexts. As a Writing Center peer consultant, graduate student, or administrator, your institution may—or may not—have an explicit institutional goal for outreach and/or an NWP site with which you could work. My hope is that these general themes and suggested activities will allow you to pursue your own outreach goals within your own institutional context and local community, considering a number of your needs and conditions. Yet I also recognize that Writing Centers, like all academic units, do not work in a vacuum and suggest that you take the necessary steps to ensure partnerships between all involved parties so that your center, your school, and the local schools that you serve all feel that the relationship you will work to develop is mutually beneficial.

Collaboration

By its very nature, multiliteracy learning encourages collaboration. In the examples cited earlier, teachers worked together—sometimes in the space of the MSU Writing Center, sometimes separated by time and distance—to develop collegial relationships and better understand the connections between literacy and technology. Just as the Writing Center provided space and personnel to help the RCWP teachers meet their individual goals, the teachers felt a closer sense of connection to the campus and community because the Writing Center acted as a hub for all activity. When the teachers are at the center, our undergraduate and graduate consultants often work with them on their projects, much in the same way as described in the prologue. In turn, the teachers in the project often present their work, formally and informally, at the Center so that students can get a sense of how technology-infused literacy practices are being enacted in local class-rooms. For instance, last fall, we had a panel of RCWP teachers come for a morning of dialogue and discussion with students from the Writing Center and others enrolled in MSU's English education program. The results are synergistic; any time that an RCWP event occurs, it offers everyone involved the chance to learn about writing in digital environments. Other possibilities for collaboration include:

- Inviting a teacher consultant to bring his or her class to cam-pus, making the visit to the Writing Center a highlight of the trip. Peer consultants could demonstrate response models (pairs, small groups, large groups) for the students.
- Offering open consulting time for local students, perhaps even in a local library or at a school. This would, in turn, be an opportunity to interview students about their experiences as writers in K–12 settings so that their thoughts can inform professional development sessions in the Writing Center.

Capacity Building

Just like Writing Center pedagogy seeks to empower the student writer, our outreach efforts aim to empower the teachers who participate. Like all NWP sites, RCWP is in the business of building teacher leadership. In rela-tion to multiliteracy learning, the Writing Center supports leadership build-ing in a variety of ways. For instance, a few years ago, one of our graduate consultants, Chad O'Neil, taught our elementary writing camp director, Renee Webster, how to record her students with an iPod and create CDs of the students' read-around from the end of camp. He did this over the course of a week and spent time with her each day going over the steps of recording and transferring files, creating playlists, and burning the final CDs. Although our camp director may have been able to figure this out on her own, she lacked the time during camp to do so; also, our consultant could have just made the CDs for her, but wanted to share his experience with her so that she could do it the next year. The two of them worked together to create a project that was meaningful to them both. Much like the time that we spent in the digital portfolio project and the technology initiative work, these moments of consultative teaching—the heart of our mission as a Writing Center—constantly seek to empower the literacy learner. In so doing, we have built a leadership team of more than a dozen teachers who run various youth programs, brief professional development workshops, and week-long summer institutes, all infused with technology and multiliteracy learning. Opportunities for capacity building might include:

- A parent or grandparent attending a "camp" with a child to create digital stories, focusing on both the composition of the narrative as well as the media elements. K–12 teachers would work with Writing Center consultants to ensure that pedagogical and technical goals for the project would be met.
- Peer consultants leading individual or small-group sessions with teachers, focusing on the use of multiliteracies not typically taught in K–12 schools, such as graphic design. Teachers could then model these strategies for their own students and seek feedback from the peer consultant, perhaps even doing so through fully online communications.

Cross-Disciplinarity

Our Writing Center, like many others, thrives on the conversations that move across topics, ideas, and disciplines when consultants and clients discuss their writing. In K–12 writing instruction, a teacher working at any one grade level will have specific objectives for teaching idea development, organization, sentence variety, conventions, peer collaboration, genre, and, of course, writing with technology. When these conversations occur in a multiliteracy center, they are also infused with a broad sense of Writing Center pedagogy and the specific strategies that we use when consulting with technologies. As K–12 teachers begin to bridge the gap between the traditional model of teaching technical skills and instead use networked computers as the unique composing tools that they are, this approach will become more and more important to the work of teaching writing. When teachers are able to discuss genre, purpose, and audience for a variety of texts—print and digital—in an environment that acknowledges and responds to the unique nature of these texts, then these cross-disciplinary conversations become both tangible (in the sense that they can see multiliteracies in action) and practical (in that they can learn from modeling). The MSU Writing Center, in its goal to make betters writers and not just better writing, demonstrates how teaching and learning multiliteracies both recognizes all the traditional aspects of composing (e.g., ideas, conventions) while also layering in the complexities of digital composing (e.g., layout, color, font, images). Ideas for capacity building include:

- Inviting faculty from other departments, such as graphic design, communications, or social science, to talk about the ways that they engage in multiliteracies. Peer consultants, teachers, and students could help plan the event, as well as attend it and lead a discussion session afterward.
- Contacting other departments on campus as well as community organizations that need productions requiring multiliteracies and then engaging partners, peer consultants, teachers, and students in collaborative project-based learning to design and produce texts for these groups.

In considering these three themes—as well as the many other outreach efforts we maintain from year to year, such as a high school writers' retreat, middle-school technology and writing camp, and a digital storytelling workshop for teachers—the MSU Writing Center and the RCWP continue to enact Stock's original vision with the particular focus now on integrating multiple literacies: social, cultural, critical, digital, visual, and local. In so doing, we continue to shift the conversation about how Writing Centers can collaborate with K–12 teachers. Although we have helped establish writing centers in local schools, we also engage in multiliteracies work by inviting teachers into the Writing Center to be learners. Indeed, we aim to engage teachers as learners so they can then transfer that learning to their own classrooms and transform their teaching practice. Through these relationships, projects, and processes, we all continue to become multiliterate across our lifetimes.

REFERENCES

Anstey, Michèle, & Bull, Geoff. (2006). *Teaching and learning multiliteracies: Changing times, changing literacies.* Newark, DE: International Reading Association.

Arver, Cara M. (2007). Are you willing to have your students join Ralph, Jack, and piggy? *English Journal, 97*(1), 37–42.

Ashley, H. M., & Shafer, Lisa Kay. (2006). Writing zones 12.5: Regarding the high school writing center as a gateway to college. *The Clearing House, 80*(2), 83(83).

Autrey, Tara M., O'Berry Edington, Cathy, Hicks, Troy, Kabodian, Aram, Lerg, Nicole, Luft-Gardner, Rebecca et al. (2005). More than just a web site: Representing teacher research through digital portfolios. *English Journal, 95*(2), 65–70.

Barnett, Robert. (2006). Collaboratively establishing high school writing centers in Flint, Michigan, to support the improvement of students' writing skills (Greater

Flint Educational Consortium on Writing Improvement). *The Clearing House,* *80*(2), 80(83).

Brandt, Deborah. (2001). *Literacy in American lives.* New York: Cambridge University Press.

Burmark, Lynell. (2002). *Visual literacy: Learn to see, see to learn.* Alexandria, VA: Association for Supervision and Curriculum Development.

Childers, Pamela B. (2006). Introduction. *The Clearing House, 80*(2), 44(41).

Childers, Pamela. (2007). *Pamela Childers on WAC, CAC, and writing centers in secondary education.* Retrieved September 28, 2007, from http://wac.colostate. edu/atd/secondary/column2007.cfm

Childers, Pamela, Fels, Dawn, & Jordan, Jeanette. (2004). *The secondary school writing center: A place to build confident, competent writers | praxis: A writing center journal.* Retrieved September 28, 2007, from http://projects.uwc.utexas. edu/praxis/?q = node/91

Cuban, Larry. (1986). *Teachers and machines: The classroom use of technology since 1920.* New York: Teachers College Press.

Cuban, Larry. (2001). *Oversold and underused: Computers in the classroom.* Cambridge, MA: Harvard University Press.

DeVoss, Dànielle. (2002). Computer literacies and the roles of the writing center. In P. Gillespie (Ed.), *Writing center research: Extending the conversation* (pp. 167–185). Mahwah, NJ: Erlbaum.

Elwood, Susan, Wolff Murphy, Susan, & Cardenas, Diana. (2006). Enacting multimedia writing center pedagogy in a rural high school. *The Clearing House, 80*(2), 86(83).

English, Cathie. (2007). Finding a voice in a threaded discussion group: Talking about literature online. *English Journal, 97*(1), 56–61.

Graff, Harvey J. (1991). *The literacy myth: Cultural integration and social structure in the nineteenth century.* Piscataway, NJ: Transaction Publishers.

Heath, Shirley Brice. (1983). *Ways with words: Language, life and work in communities and classrooms.* New York: Cambridge University Press.

Hicks, T., Russo, A., Autrey, T., Gardner, R., Kabodian, A., & Edington, C. (2007). Rethinking the purposes and processes for designing digital portfolios. *Journal of Adult and Adolescent Literacy, 50*(6), 450–458.

Inman, James A. (2006). Technologies and the secondary school writing center. *The Clearing House, 80*(2), 74(73).

Jordan, Jeanette. (2006). Change from within: The power of a homegrown writing center. *The Clearing House, 80*(2), 52(53).

Kimball, Miles A. (2002). *The web portfolio guide: Creating electronic portfolios for the web* (1st ed.). New York: Longman.

Lankshear, Colin, & Knobel, Michele. (2003). *New literacies: Changing knowledge and classroom learning.* Buckingham [England]; Philadelphia, PA: Society for Research into Higher Education & Open University Press.

Leu, Donald J., Jr. (2000). Literacy and technology: Deictic consequences for literacy education in an information age. In M. L. Kamil, P. B. Mosenthal, P. D.

Pearson, & R. Barr (Eds.), *Handbook of reading research* (Vol. 3, pp. 743–770). Mahwah, NJ: Erlbaum.

Lieberman, Ann, & Wood, Diane. (2003). *Inside the national writing project: Connecting network learning and classroom teaching.* New York: Teachers College Press.

Littleton, Chad Eric. (2006). Creating connections between secondary and college writing centers. *The Clearing House, 80*(2), 77(72).

Michigan State University Committee on Evaluating Quality Outreach. (2000). *Points of distinction: A guidebook for planning & evaluating quality outreach.* Retrieved September 29, 2007, from http://outreach.msu.edu/pod.pdf

Monroe, Barbara J., Rickly, Rebecca, Condon, William, & Butler, Wayne. (2000). The near and distant futures of owl and the writing center. In J. A. Inman & D. N. Sewell (Eds.), *Taking flight with owls: Examining electronic writing center work* (pp. 211–222). Mahwah, NJ: Erlbaum.

Moynihan, Karen E. (2007). A collectibles project: Engaging students in authentic multimodal research and writing. *English Journal, 97*(1), 69–76.

The New London Group. (2000). A pedagogy of multiliteracies: Designing social futures. In B. Cope & M. Kalantzis (Eds.), *Multiliteracies: Literacy learning and the design of social futures* (pp. 9–37). London; New York: Routledge.

Oppenheimer, Todd. (2003). *The flickering mind: The false promise of technology in the classroom, and how learning can be saved* (1st ed.). New York: Random House.

Reid, Louann. (2007). From the editor. *English Journal, 97*(1), 13–15.

Richardson, Will. (2006). *Blogs, wikis, podcasts, and other powerful web tools for classrooms.* Thousand Oaks, CA: Corwin Press.

Selber, Stuart A. (2004). *Multiliteracies for a digital age.* Carbondale: Southern Illinois University Press.

Selfe, Cynthia L., & Hawisher, Gail E. (2004). *Literate lives in the information age: Narratives of literacy from the United States.* Mahwah, NJ: Erlbaum.

Stock, Patricia Lambert. (1997). Reforming education in the land-grant university: Contributions from a writing center. *The Writing Center Journal, 18*(1).

Street, Brian V. (1984). *Literacy in theory and practice.* Cambridge [Cambridgeshire]; New York: Cambridge University Press.

Swenson, Janet. (2003). Transformative teacher networks, on-line professional development, and the write for your life project. *English Education, 35*(4), 2–62.

Thomas, Sharon, Hara, Mark, & DeVoss, Dànielle. (2000). Writing in the electronic realm: Incorporating a new medium into the work of the writing center. In J. A. Inman & D. N. Sewell (Eds.), *Taking flight with owls: Examining electronic writing center work* (pp. 65–73). Mahwah, NJ: Erlbaum.

Tinker, John. (2006). Generating cultures of writing: Collaborations between the Stanford writing center and high school writing centers. *The Clearing House, 80*(2), 83-89.

Trimbur, John. (2000). Multiliteracies, social futures, and writing centers. *Writing Center Journal, 20*(2), 29–31.

Writing in Digital Environments (WIDE) Research Center Collective. (2005). Why teach digital writing? *Kairos (10.1)*. Retrieved October 15, 2005, from http://english.ttu.edu/kairos/10.1/binder2.html?coverweb/wide/index.html

Wysocki, Anne Frances, Johnson-Eilola, Johndan, Selfe, Cynthia L., & Sirc, Geoffrey. (2004). *Writing new media: Theory and applications for expanding the teaching of composition*. Logan: Utah State University Press.

Zhao, Yong, & Frank, Kenneth A. (2003). Factors affecting technology uses in schools: An ecological perspective. *American Educational Research Journal, 40*(4), 807–840.

Zhao, Yong, Pugh, Kevin, Sheldon, Steve, & Byers, Joe. (2002). *Conditions for classroom technology innovations*. Retrieved November 9, 2003, from http://www.tcrecord.org/pdf/10850.pdf

Production

8

THE FUTURE OF MULTILITERACY CENTERS IN THE E-WORLD

AN EXPLORATION OF CULTURAL NARRATIVES AND CULTURAL TRANSFORMATIONS

Christina Murphy

Marshall University

Lory Hawkes

DeVry University

Brook Thomas (1989) is among many contemporary critics who call for a new historical discourse that enables the modern era to understand its relationship to history as a repetitive texture of change. Within this texture, new ideas replace old ideas as sociopolitical and socioeconomic realities shift frames of understanding and interpretation and, thus, the tensions between ascending and declining paradigms generate the mythologies by which old ideas tenuously cling to power.

For Writing Centers, the course of events has been no different from what Thomas describes as a "new historicism." The process of new paradigms replacing old has been one that has had both beneficial and limiting effects for the development of Writing Centers within academics. The old paradigms have had a decidedly negative effect in devaluing the types of contributions that Writing Centers can make to higher education and thus have worked to keep Writing Centers from reaching their full potential. However, the current century provides new opportunities for Writing Centers to reestablish themselves both within and outside academics as multiliteracy centers focused on the e-literacies of (a) digital technology (digital literacies), (b) images and design (visual literacies), (c) using the Internet to search for information (information literacies), and (d) the capacity to work electronically in international settings and groups (global literacies). Decidedly, the future of the Writing Center will be shaped by its digital awareness and the contributions of digital content specialists to student engagement and instruction via electronic methods.

The significance of this shift in emphases and priorities is highly significant for Writing Centers in that they are the academic units best positioned by their philosophies and histories to capitalize on the importance of e-literacies for the transformation of academics in the 21st century. Thus, the movement from traditional Writing Centers focused on the values and mechanisms of the print culture of the 20th century to multiliteracy centers in the 21st century is truly a significant achievement. It is also a movement that will prove to be transformative for Writing Centers and for the professionals who staff them and that will shape their strategic visions and goals.

One of the most significant changes will be in the ethos that many Writing Centers and Writing Center professionals have demonstrated in the 20th century, specifically in terms of concepts of marginalization and rebellion. Liz Rohan (2002), for example, speaks of the fragile ethos that affects Writing Center professionals who labor within an academy that regards their work as inferior or antithetical to the work of the classroom. In the classroom, teacher scholars teach, create, and discover new knowledge, whereas in the Writing Center, tutors offer sympathy and support, deal with writing problems, and provide instructional services and retention initiatives to the academy. It is no wonder, then, that Stephen North's (1984) essay, "The Idea of a Writing Center," remains the single most famous and most cited essay in Writing Center scholarship largely because, in essence, North's essay is a call for an understanding by the academy of the type of work that Writing Center professionals actually do. North's essay is also a consummate martyrdom narrative in which North is pleading for Writing Center professionals to be understood, accepted, and valued by English departments. Despite that North repudiated this essay in 1994 with "Revisiting 'The Idea of a Writing Center,'" in which North stated that his ideas had been both romantic and naïve, still Writing Center professionals continue to position their discussions and definitions of Writing Center work along the polarities of North's sense of martyrdom and devaluation, or along Kevin Davis' (1995) call to rebellion, in which positioning Writing Centers on the boundary of the academy as subversive agents for change is the most positive direction and philosophical stance that Writing Centers can pursue.

In essence, North and Davis exemplify the long tradition of marginalization and protest against marginalization that has characterized Writing Center work and scholarship for decades. In essence, too, this process has been permitted—if not encouraged—by the fact that, for a number of decades, the debate has been oddly positioned philosophically. Thus, much of Writing Center scholarship and practice have been focused on defending the Writing Center against challenges and questions by other academics or asserting the value of traditional methods of tutoring via one-on-one sessions in a print-culture setting. Little attention has been paid to redefining the tutor as a digital content specialist or the student as one whose learning will be best shaped and best served by electronic methods. In essence, little attention has been paid to finding new academic and cultural paradigms for the Writing Center and its instructional methods and value. Also, the broader national conversation on Writing Centers has not taken into account the instructional implications of changes in societal philosophies.

In essence, Writing Center theorists have not fully explored the implications of social systems theories to Writing Center practices or potentials. Thus, as Victoria E. Bonnell and Lynn Hunt (1999) indicate in their "Introduction" to *Beyond the Cultural Turn*, in the push-pull of ideas and paradigms, it is difficult to determine whether paradigms shape or are shaped by social realities. No doubt there is some interplay, but as Mehdi Farashahi, Taieb Hafsi, and Rick Molz (2005) point out, empirical research and its outcomes drive social realities more than philosophies and paradigms drive the empirical investigations and achievements of science and technology. This conclusion has enormous implications for Writing Center professionals, who must move arguments away from such limited concepts as institutional status—especially within English departments—toward the realities of social change (and thus social roles) driven by science and technology. The ultimate outcome of such a shift in perspective will be the realization that the future of the Writing Center is not as a Writing Center but as a multiliteracy center with expanded pedagogical possibilities and new roles for Writing Center specialists. In this view, Writing Centers will assume their rightful and credible role as a knowledge-making academic resource that fosters the major educational and societal goals of multimodal literacy. Writing Centers will also assume their rightful role as multiliteracy centers engaged in the type of instruction and communication (as well as philosophical and pragmatic design) that Howard Rheingold (1998) describes as "computer-mediated communication that is a many-to-many medium" (p. 121).

If, as David Bawden (2001) contends, the mastery of reading and writing to achieve understanding demonstrates literacy, for decades Writing Center educators have been making the university system of instruction work by diagnosing flaws in reading and writing and in devising creative methods to offer cognitive solutions. All of these initiatives have been pursued amid a growing diversity of students, from students coping with cultural challenges, to learning difference students, to physically challenged students, to academically underprepared students. These educators wisely selected print materials for distribution to students; used dialogue, interpretation, and coaching; and provided feedback in face-to-face and computer-mediated venues to help students learn effective techniques of expression. To be able to deal with the range of students and determine their problems, Writing Center educators have had to be conversant with composition pedagogy as well as with finding effective pragmatic and interpersonal ways to influence students into working through their frustrations with the system of assignments and grading. On the one hand, these educators retaught composition techniques by customizing examples, language exercises, or writing sessions. In doing so, they had to understand the purpose of the composition, align reteaching with the stated goals of the assignment, and yet keep the student writer engaged. These mini-sessions demanded content mastery of composition pedagogy and Writing Center pedagogy as they matched the right approaches to each student's skills, interests, and concerns. As content specialists, Writing Center professionals had the ability to customize information into a hierarchy of learning experiences to promote knowledge building.

Clearly, these modes dominated Writing Center interactions for most of the 20th century; however, in the new paradigm of the 21st century, Writing Center educators become digital content specialists. Drawing on Norman Fairclough's (1993) view of discourse as a socially accepted system of using language to think and act in ways that identify a person as a member of a socially meaningful group, David Bawden (2001) argues that digital literacy provides a means of grasping the nature of that discourse identity and of interacting with others to improve social perspective and standing. By this process, Bawden does not mean merely computer literacy (the ability to wield the processes of the computer to do one's work or accomplish a process) or information literacy (an understanding of how to gain and use information, as well as the societal implications of using technology and accessing information). Instead, he envisions digital literacy as a multimedia fluency of expression based on the ability to acquire and evaluate what one reads and how one chooses to respond in a dynamic cyberenvironment. Citing Paul Gilster's (1999) 10 core competencies for digital literacy, Bawden notes that Gilster and others regard digital literacy as "an essential life skill . . . as a survival skill" (pp. 247–248). Similarly, in "Assessing Multiliteracies and the New Basics," Mary Kalantzis, Bill Cope, and Andrew Harvey (2003) endorse the life-long value of developing multiliteracies and the resultant impact on the individual. They also advocate significant curricular changes:

> The need for flexibility, autonomy, collaboration, problem-solving skills, broad knowledgeability, and diverse intelligence are all underlined by changes to the traditional area of literacy. Yet the trend to multiliteracies is simply a very visible example of broader trends within the new economy, which suggest the need for new orientations to knowledge. Learning will increasingly be about creating a kind of person, with kinds of dispositions and orientations to the world, and not just persons who are in command of a body of knowledge. (p. 23)

A digital content specialist, then, can empower student investigation and knowledge-making by building user interfaces to combine information in an effective presentation and navigational hierarchy. This outcome can be accomplished in two ways to help mediate gaps in understanding and help promote authorship. First, the digital content specialist can customize informational displays to enhance the user's experience. For example, for the visually impaired student who has trouble understanding the concept of privacy for an essay the student is writing, the digital content specialist could create a domain of large typography augmented with sound and slow-moving, simple slide shows to illustrate the concept by juxtaposing key phrases with pictures from recent news stories (also enlarged for easier reading). Second, for the student with learning disabilities who may have trouble reading an assigned essay, the digital content specialist could build an interface that presents the essay in hypertext episodes with a few questions voiced by streaming audio to build comprehension at the end of each episode. The interface would have programmed controls that enabled the student to move slowly or quickly through the essay by touching the screen or selecting a Next button, and these controls would give the student feedback on overall comprehension either textually or aurally with a voice synthesizer.

Four technological innovations will improve the Writing Center's digital self-awareness and make the digital content specialist an important contributor to the well-being of the university by finding ways to use software systems to enhance student learning. The first innovation has already been in place for some time and may include hypertext editors or object-oriented interface development environments (IDEs) that are licensed for use on the university network. These may be high-end software suites, course-delivery systems, proprietary programs, or open-source applications. Although these software products may already exist on many campuses, their use for Writing Centers has not been fully explored. With an editor or an IDE, the digital content specialist can merge pictures with text and imbed sounds to create mood and motivation for further exploration. Using newer animation software, the digital content specialist can portray a process or capture a series of visual images to make a research strategy more vivid. Equally exciting is the improved ability to carry a signal. With improved bandwidth, streaming video and audio are possible. If the student learns better with spoken instructions or attends better to visual demonstration, customized instruction can be crafted to be sent over the university networks or to reside on a Writing Center workstation.

More than ever before, self-paced learning opportunities are possible as a result of object-oriented IDEs. With rudimentary knowledge of hyper-text navigation and scripting language or the use of a high-end scripting editor included in the university's network software, the digital content specialist can provide access to handouts on the university networks juxta-posed with files or handouts from other universities organized by theme, topic, approach, rhetorical or instructional strategy, and so forth. Because self-publishing is also a form of learning and an opportunity to revise and improve written content, digital content specialists can work with students who want to publish their web pages, whether the publication is for personal satisfaction or part of a larger collection of work in a cyber portfolio—which can augment students' resumes for job consideration.

In a similar vein, IDEs also enable digital content specialists to create writing experiences out of everyday things. With an understanding of composition pedagogy and Writing Center pedagogy, a digital content specialist could import an image of Michael Jackson into a text editor, offer a sound clip from a recent broadcast from the pop star, link to his web page and then to a news story about the 2005 trial, and ask the student to write a response based on the combined sensory experience of the media to determine whether the two sites present a biased or unbiased view of the case. The student would be able to experience the news through sight, sound, and text and to create his or her own text to evaluate the given text. The context would have a richness of sensory experience by putting a human face together with differing reports that require responsible, citizen-based judgment. Additionally, the Macromedia Suite, which includes Flash software, provides a simple way to create computer-rendered movies playable on a web page. Thus, a further learning context could be explored by sequencing images from the trial with excerpts from the news headlines and then asking students to express their reactions to the media's influence.

A second digital innovation currently underutilized on university campuses is the large online learning system like WebCT™, Blackboard™, and eCollege™, as well as other open-source systems. These large delivery systems emulate hypertext editors with proprietary programming to provide a visual IDE in which to fashion course syllabi, assignments, and exams. These learning systems have robust multimedia capabilities that can be creatively blended to provide a multisensory learning experience. These learning systems provide liberal storage area for streaming media and graphics. Finally, these learning systems all have color adjustments to increase contrast between the background and foreground text and a means of increasing the size of the typography should visual accommodation be necessary. Because the university network renders files quickly and because students in the university are familiar with the access techniques, digital content specialists could use the Chat feature to stage self-help sessions for study skills, research, and time management. The archived discussions (threaded discussions) could be used as a knowledge management system to offer answers to the most frequently asked questions. The streaming audio and video capabilities could be used as a convenient means to play one of the Writing Center's prerecorded tutorials.

The third technological innovation is wireless technology that permits the broadcast of a signal that is then interpreted and rendered by a personal device, whether that is a cell phone or a personal data assistant. Wireless technology, coupled with the improved vibrant color displays on small monitors, means that learning is both portable and personal. Learning experiences can now become mobile outreaches so that user interfaces developed in hypertext design environments can be downsized, simplified, and broadcast to students on their personal devices and on demand. A digital camera that is connected to a university network could be a streaming media recorder of events simultaneously transmitted by a web cam. These events could be the source and the spur for practice writings. Podcasting, or the use of video transmitted through wireless technology to personal data devices, could be a new way of letting students know what might be available as help in the multiliteracy center.

The fourth technological innovation that is recasting the potential of user interface design in the hands of digital content specialists is both a technology and a social reaction to software gerrymandering. The growth of extensible markup language (XML) web services is remarkable. XML is the new generation of hypertext scripting that enables a designer to concentrate on content so that the designer can customize elements or objects referenced by the script. In essence, the XML scripting language permits the designer to create the interface and the meta-language that produces the interface. XML is the scripting language of choice to produce a reusable code web service that is shared with the larger Internet developer community. The digital content specialist with knowledge of XML, style sheets, and object technology can create tutorials, rich media reports, and utilities that can be shared with colleagues. The Web service, as a module of working code, would be reusable scripting to perform an often repeated function, or it might prove to be a utility program for a much repeated function. Web services can be accessed easily and applied quickly to networks, and web services are resources to the technical community. The model of global sharing of Web services emulates the vision of Ted Nelson, who envisioned the global digital lending library called Xanadu. As both literacy and multi-literacy instruction continues to increase and complexify in this highly tech-nological era and global society, one major question and opportunity for digital content specialists to consider is whether the Xanadu model could be extended to multiliteracy centers and universities that share archives of reusable interfaces categorized by learning experience and user.

The opportunities to advance, customize, and individualize learning experiences through the use of such a design would transform many aspects of student-centered learning and even further permit the multilit-eracy center to address the broad range of issues associated with mediat-ing knowledge in both a global and technological era. Not surprisingly, social theorist Rita Süssmuth (1998) has commented that the potential to mediate knowledge through technology and other means that accomplish socioeconomic ends is an aspect of "the future-capability of society" (p. 27) that educators and all agents within society must be aware of in the design and operation of social systems. Specifically, Süssmuth states that "any attempt to explore the future-capability of society" must be equated with "operative capability" and understood in terms of "the ability to shape events" (p. 27). Reconfirming this premise, she writes, "Most of all, howev-er, future-capability refers to the ability of society and the individual to cope with change and to integrate future framework conditions into human coexistence" (p. 27).

Given the issues that Süssmuth raises, we return to our original ques-tioning of what models and modes of thoughts will best serve Writing Centers in the 21st century, and we find that the question is rooted in a broad range of concerns associated with social transformations. Clearly, Writing Centers are becoming virtual communities, and this progression will mark the dynamic evolution of Writing Centers into multiliteracy cen-ters. This is a progression that is not only predictable, but that is related to other progressions in society. Fundamentally, it is a progression centered in efforts to define what constitutes community in contemporary times, from Robert D. Putnam's (2000) exposition of this issue in his award-winning book, *Bowling Alone: The Collapse and Revival of American Community*, to the discussions of the abstractions that bring communities together via shared concepts and beliefs that Benedict Anderson (1991) explores in *Imagined Communities*. Although social critics Guy Debord (1995) and Jean Baudrillard (1988) question the implications and values of the even more abstract communities created and mediated by technology, their questions and concerns provide a means for the digital content specialists that Writing Center professionals are becoming to design and actualize multiliteracy centers that contribute to the enrichment of communication across an extensive range of settings and experiences. Ultimately, they contribute to community formation and to what Thomas M. Carr, Jr. (1990) calls "the resilience of rhetoric."

Both of these aspects are issues that Sherry Turkle (1984, 1995), a major theorist on e-literacies, explores in *The Second Self: Computers and the Human Spirit* and in *Life on the Screen: Identity in the Age of the Internet*. Turkle's key premises have great significance for Writing Center professionals as they seek to become digital content specialists who use the principles of e-literacies, cognitive theory, and composition pedagogy to carry out their roles within multiliteracy centers. Specifically, Turkle emphasizes that, under earlier models of computer-mediated communication, the boundaries between the computer and the person using the computer were clear and mechanistic. People acted on computers by giving commands to machines—largely so because the vast potential of the computer for different modes of communication and interaction had not yet been fully explored. Within the new model of e-literacies, individuals use computers to enter into dialogues, navigate simulated worlds, and create virtual realities. As a professor in the Program in Science, Technology, and Society at MIT, Turkle exemplifies the types of knowledges and emphases that Writing Center professionals will be exploring in the e-worlds of the 21st century. The connections between technology and society, between the individual's cognitive processes and the cognitive processes required for communicating in the global world of the Internet, and the implications for the types of learners Writing Center professionals will be encountering and instructing are of profound consequence. They will require a deeper understanding not only of our traditional views of what constitutes literacy, but also of our views of identity, knowledge, and community formation. They will also transform our traditional understandings of tutoring and replace them with highly integrated theories of language, learning, and social practices mediated through both the social environment and the various symbol systems of the e-literacies.

The types of social contributions to communication and to community formation that digital content specialists can generate within a multiliteracy center are key aspects of what Nathaniel Branden (1997) describes as knowledge structures in the information age. As Branden indicates,

> We now live in a global economy characterized by rapid change, accelerating scientific and technological breakthroughs, and an unprecedented level of competitiveness. These developments create a demand for higher levels of education and training than were required of previous generations. (p. 221)

Branden further explains that the issue of competency within such times of rapid change and highly complex technologies creates a need for those skilled at responding to and mastering these issues. In other words, it calls for people who can educate others to be responsive to the potentials of technologies to achieve positive and constructive aims within a global society. It calls for digital content specialists who combine multiple perspectives on social cognition and social interaction into a global world made instantly and complexly accessible via technology.

This is the society that Thomas L. Friedman (2005) describes as "flat," in the sense that the digital revolution has created a highly connected world in which rapid and extensive technical advances have instantaneously connected individuals, organizations, and institutions with billions of other people across the planet. To develop, interpret, and structure knowledge within this "flat" and connected world will require expertise beyond the level of traditional instruction provided in today's institutions of higher education. It will also require a rethinking and a transformation of the traditional Writing Center, a task that will fall to theorists and practitioners alike to envision and carry out. It will no longer be productive to be bogged down in the types of arguments over "good intentions" and the types of "noise" that should be coming from the Writing Center, as Nancy Maloney Grimm (1999) and Elizabeth H. Boquet (2002) have called on the Writing Center community to contemplate over the last few years. It will no longer be sufficient to debate issues of marginalization and rebellion within academic structures or to fret over the threat of the outsourcing of writing programs and Writing Centers to corporate entities. What will be necessary are new cultural narratives and cultural transformations for the Writing Center as it becomes the multiliteracy center and thus a major educational resource for the 21st century.

Clearly, many of our most important tasks and contributions for the Writing Center will remain, although modified and enhanced by the requirements of a digital age. By improving outcomes and enriching educational experiences, Writing Center professionals as digital content specialists will continue to contribute to student recruiting/retention and to the significance of universities as community partners and leaders in knowledge creation and dissemination. By helping students achieve their goals, deal with frustrations brought about by literacy inadequacy, or shape new modes of expression, Writing Center professionals as digital content specialists will provide a socioeconomic boost to students who might otherwise fail in the university and consequently fail in their life's aspirations of a degree and a career. Digital content specialists stand at the epicenter of pedagogical transformation to a new world of astounding possibilities brought about by an understanding of their roles in knowledge-making. To act as agents of change within education and educational systems has been a time-honored tradition that Writing Center professionals have fulfilled for well over a century of accomplishment. The next chapter that Writing Center professionals will write in the cultural narrative of the Writing Center will be as digital content specialists who have understood, accepted, and enacted the relationship between social structures and social life—in other words, who have understood the social construction of reality.

They will have understood, too, the value of information and communication technologies to the educational process and will have developed ways in which to integrate this knowledge into their tutoring and pedagogy. Perhaps greatest of all, they will have recognized, as Gunther Kress (2003) points out, the differences between—and different demands of—academic and professional literacies. Academic literacies may well circumscribe and limit definitions of what constitutes literacy and also may well identify these definitions with issues of class, culture, and social control, as Nancy Maloney Grimm (1999) contends. In contrast, professional literacies often work within the broadest of multicultural and multiliteracy contexts to incorporate a vast range of techniques for achieving communication via the integration of language, image, design, and conceptual frameworks. Further, professional literacies provide for more varied means of individualizing communication and learning than do academic literacies and, as such, resonate with what social systems theorist Don Tapscott (1996) envisions as the central social trend of the 21st century—the "molecularization" of knowledge that permits for knowledge and instructional strategies to be highly individualized. The old concept of mass instruction via classrooms and lecture halls is rapidly being replaced by educational methods in which the individual is an active and interactive creator in the instructional process. In a related manner, the actual space of the classroom, lecture hall, or Writing Center is being replaced by virtual space, in which instruction does not need to be located in a physical space, but can be virtually located and universally accessible via the Internet.

What lies ahead for the Writing Center as a multiliteracy center is building on these social systems trends to create highly individualized instructional methods by using technology to respond to each learner's skills and interests and by centering these methods within the e-literacies that will define the 21st century. The implications of a shift like this will be enormous in the impact on Writing Center professionals who will need to become—and be trained to become—digital content specialists who are adept at using technology and who understand the implications of technology for knowledge creation. There is no question this is more than a paradigmatic shift or a philosophical redefinition and refocusing. As social systems theorist Gunther Kress (2003) indicates, it is the emergence of a new era of communication that represents the decline of the print culture and its values, a philosophy and methodology that have held sway over our culture and our educational systems for centuries.

That Writing Center professionals can play a lead role in defining this shift and these revolutionary changes for society is an exciting prospect; it is also a testament to the adaptability, flexibility, and resiliency of Writing Centers in responding to change—a major capability that Don Tapscott and Art Caston (1993) claim is the key to survival and relevance in contemporary times. Tapscott and Caston contend that social institutions responsive to this shift as electronic technologies become the predominant mode of communication and knowledge generation will survive, whereas those that have "severe difficulties embracing the change" or that "remain constrained by traditional approaches" will be doomed to irrelevance and eventual elimination. Fortunately for Writing Centers, the path seems clear, in that the rapid advancement of technology has clearly demonstrated that knowledge of the e-literacies is now an educational imperative for those who wish to operate successfully in academic and professional settings and who wish to contribute to the advancement of society as citizens or civic leaders.

Thus, we end where we began with a focus on the need for a "new historicism" for the Writing Center field. The cultural narrative that needs to be advanced for Writing Centers is of the significant role that Writing Centers can play in centralizing the e-literacies within education. The new cultural narrative must emphasize, too, that the multiliteracy center can emerge from the Writing Center because Writing Centers provide a solid base—in terms of structure, history, and educational values—on which to construct the newer model of writing instruction in a highly technological, global society. Students will need to learn to construct and communicate via multimodal texts, and certainly the instructional models and practices of Writing Centers demonstrate their openness, versatility, and flexibility in responding to educational challenges and opportunities. In the 20th century, Writing Centers demonstrated their enormous ability to respond innovatively to societal shifts that redefined educational emphases and audiences (Murphy, 1991). In the 21st century, this same creativity and authenticity will enable Writing Centers to respond to the societal challenges created by the vast array and broad impact of the information and communication technologies. The best setting and method for responding to these challenges and opportunities will be the development and emergence of the Writing Center as the multiliteracy center in which multimodal instruction and learning can be fostered and explored.

We see the greatest challenge to this vision resting with the training of the Writing Center professionals who will direct and work within the multiliteracy center. Certainly, changes of this sort will produce divisions within the profession as to how the centers should proceed and where the heart and values of such centers should reside. One of the key issues will be, too, how Writing Center professionals will be trained to use the new information and communication technologies wisely and well. There is no question that Writing Center professionals have been adept over the years at shaping their centers to their institutions. Thus, Louise Wetherbee Phelps (1991) is correct in arguing that disciplinary knowledge emerges from practical inquiry and common practice, and this principle is important in recognizing how the training and common practice of Writing Center professionals as digital content specialists will occur. It is a question of institutional identity and purpose, and these facets will guide the transformation of the Writing Center into the multiliteracy center, as well as shape and guide the types of local knowledge that multiliteracy center professionals will need in developing their programs, responding to various audiences and constituencies, and navigating the often turbulent waters of defining a meaningful and effective institutional role in times of rapid societal and educational change. In other words, in those times in which a "new historicism" is emerging that redefines potential and enables the actualization of an even greater level of achievement.

REFERENCES

Anderson, Benedict. (1991). *Imagined communities: Reflections on the origin and spread of nationalism.* London and New York: Verso.
Baudrillard, Jean. (1988). In Mark Poster (Ed.), *Selected writings.* Palo Alto, CA: Stanford University Press.

Bawden, David. (2001). Progress in documentation Information and digital literacies: A review of concepts. *Journal of Documentation, 57*(2), 218–259.

Bonnell, Victoria E., & Hunt, Lynn. (1999). Introduction. In Victoria E. Bonnell & Lynn Hunt (Eds.), *Beyond the cultural turn* (pp. 1–34). Berkeley: University of California Press.

Boquet, Elizabeth H. (2002). *Noise from the writing center.* Logan: Utah State University Press.

Branden, Nathaniel. (1997). Self-esteem in the information age. In Frances Hesselbein, Marshall Goldsmith, & Richard Beckhard (Eds.), *The organization of the future* (pp. 221–229). San Francisco: Jossey-Bass.

Carr, Thomas M., Jr. (1990) *Descartes and the resilience of rhetoric.* Carbondale: Southern Illinois University Press.

Davis, Kevin. (1995). Life outside the boundary: History and direction in the writing center. *Writing Lab Newsletter, 20*(2), 5–7.

Debord, Guy. (1995). *The society of the spectacle* (Donald Nicholson-Smith, Trans.). Cambridge, MA: Zone Books.

Fairclough, Norman. (1993). *Discourse and social change.* Cambridge: Polity Press.

Farashahi, Medhi, Hafsi, Taieb, & Molz, Rick. (2005). Institutionalized norms of conducting research and social realities: A research synthesis of empirical works from 1983 to 2002. *International Journal of Management Reviews, 7*(1), 1–24.

Friedman, Thomas L. (2005). *The world is flat: A brief history of the twenty-first century.* New York: Farrar, Strauss, & Giroux.

Gilster, Paul. (1999). *Digital literacy.* New York: Wiley.

Grimm, Nancy Maloney. (1999). *Good intentions: Writing center work for postmodern times.* Portsmouth, NH: Heinemann-Boynton/Cook.

Kalantzis, Mary, Cope, Bill, & Harvey, Andrew. (2003). Assessing multiliteracies and the new basics. *Assessment in Education, 10*(1), 15–26.

Kress, Gunther. (2003). *Literacy in the new media age.* New York: Routledge.

Murphy, Christina. (1991). Writing centers in context: Responding to current educational theory. In Ray Wallace & Jeanne Simpson (Eds.), *The writing center: New directions* (pp. 276–288). New York: Garland.

North, Stephen. (1984). The idea of a writing center. *College English, 46*(5), 433–446.

North, Stephen. (1994). Revisiting "the idea of a writing center." *The Writing Center Journal, 15*(1), 7–19.

Phelps, Louise Wetherbee. (1991). Practical wisdom and the geography of knowledge in composition. *College English, 53*(8), 863–885.

Putnam, Robert D. (2000). *Bowling alone: The collapse and revival of American community.* New York: Simon & Schuster.

Rheingold, Howard. (1998). Virtual communities. In Frances Hesselbein, Marshall Goldsmith, Richard Beckhard, & Richard F. Schubert (Eds.), *The community of the future* (pp. 115–122). San Francisco: Jossey-Bass.

Rohan, Liz. (2002). Hostesses of literacy: Librarians, writing teachers, writing centers, and a historical quest for ethos. *Composition Studies, 30*(2) 60–77.

Süssmuth, Rita. (1998). The future-capability of society. In Frances Hesselbein, Marshall Goldsmith, Richard Beckhard, & Richard F. Schubert (Eds.), *The community of the future* (pp. 27–33). San Francisco: Jossey-Bass.

Tapscott, Don. (1996). *The digital economy: Promise and peril in the age of networked intelligence.* New York: McGraw-Hill.

Tapscott, Don, & Caston, Art. (1993). *Paradigm shift: The new promise of information technology.* New York: McGraw-Hill.

Thomas, Brook. (1989). The new historicism and other old-fashioned topics. In H. Aram Veeser (Ed.), *The new historicism* (pp. 182–203). New York: Routledge.

Turkle, Sherry. (1984). *The second self: Computers and the human spirit.* New York: Simon & Schuster.

Turkle, Sherry. (1995). *Life on the screen: Identity in the age of the internet.* New York: Simon & Schuster.

9

MULTILITERACY CENTERS AS CONTENT PRODUCERS

DESIGNING ONLINE LEARNING EXPERIENCES FOR WRITERS[1]

David M. Sheridan

Michigan State University

In their chapter for this collection, Christina Murphy and Lory Hawkes (chap. 8) outline a vision in which multiliteracy centers serve as important sites for the development of instructional resources. In this reconfiguration, multiliteracy center workers are not just consultants who help others produce, but rather are producers who create sophisticated tools to support students working on both digital and nondigital projects. Peer tutors are reconfigured as "digital content specialists" who "use the principles of e-literacies, cognitive theory, and composition pedagogy" to design multimodal learning environments customized to the needs of individual learners. Digital content specialists "can empower student investigation and knowledge-making by building user interfaces to combine information in an effective presentation and navigational hierarchy." The current chapter explores one experiment aimed at implementing the model of digital content specialists that Murphy and Hawkes describe. It focuses on the development of an online learning module that attempts to exploit the visual, aural, and interactive potentials of new media in order to operationalize fundamental aspects of writing center pedagogy.

---

[1]This chapter discusses an online learning module that resulted from the collaboration of dozens of individuals associated with the MSU Writing Center. I am grateful to all of them for all of their contributions and for all that they taught me throughout the collaborative process. Although it would take up too much space to list all of their names here, it is important to note that Michael McLeod did most of the programming and HTML coding for the module, Timothy Gunn directed the movie that is the module's centerpiece, and the project benefited greatly from the involvement of Janet Swenson, then director of the MSU Writing Center.

MODELS OF LEARNING AND THE ECONOMY
OF WRITING CENTERS

Although writing centers strive to serve all writers at their respective institutions, realities of time, funding, people, and space often limit the amount of support they can actually provide. At Michigan State University (MSU), we are mindful that we cannot work with all 45,000 MSU students over the course of a single year, to say nothing of faculty and staff, whom we also serve. Given these limitations, writing centers have looked to emergent technologies, especially Internet-related technologies, to provide ways of maximizing their resources. Most uses of the Internet by centers fall into one of two broad categories: (a) online archives of information for writers, or (b) online consulting services. Eric Hobson (1998) addresses problems associated with the former in his introduction to *Wiring the Writing Center*. Hobson describes

> a situation I find distressing and entertainingly ironic: in their first forays online, many writing centers are creating themselves in the form of their antithesis, that nemesis writing lab. Put bluntly, many OWL's consist primarily of the contents of old filing cabinets and handbooks—worksheets, drill activities, guides to form—pulled out of the mothballs, dusted off, and digitized. (p. xvii)

As Hobson points out, the kind of instruction that writing centers can most easily provide through the Internet is in many ways opposed to the pedagogy that centers have come to embrace, which is based on active learning and dialogue. As online filing cabinets, writing centers risk positioning students in the passive role of information consumers and risk presenting writing as a matter of memorizing rules, conventions, and forms (see also Miraglia & Norris, 2000).

Online consulting services hold more promise for using the Internet in ways that are consistent with writing center practice (see Inman & Sewell, 2000; Gresham, chap.2 this volume). Although online consulting may help solve problems of distance and time, it does not fundamentally change the economics of delivering writing center services because it still requires a consultant for every client. In fact, the costs involved in extra training, administration, and setup may make online consulting services more expensive than face-to-face services.

The trade-off, then, seems to be this: Centers can provide unlimited support to writers through online handouts, but that support is inconsistent with principles of consulting that many centers consider fundamental. Centers can offer more dialogic and interactive forms of support using online consulting, but that support is severely limited by the resources allocated to the them. What we need is a third way.

THE PROMISE OF DIGITAL MEDIA

As Murphy and Hawkes suggest, the interactive and multimodal affordances of digital media might provide centers with this third way. We came to similar conclusions at MSU, conclusions that emerged out of our Composing and Teaching in Digital Environments (CTDE) Program. In implementing our CTDE Program, we had invested in an array of media production hardware and software. We had recruited consultants from a variety of relevant disciplines and backgrounds, including web designers, interactive media producers, and a semiprofessional film director/producer/editor. Working together, we routinely produced web pages, flyers, posters, and other resources to support the mission of the Writing Center and were used to soliciting from each other critiques of projects that we were working on in our own personal and professional lives.

As a multiliteracy center, then, our local culture was defined by conversations and collaborations focused on issues of new media and digital rhetoric, and this culture shaped our responses to the exigency of serving larger numbers of writers through the Internet. One response was to partner with MSU's Writing in Digital Environments (WIDE) Research Center to develop an online, interactive module to support writers.[2] WIDE was willing to contribute a small amount of its funding to support quarter-time graduate teaching assistantships for a programmer/web designer and a digital video producer/director, as well as a course release for me, who at the time was the associate director of MSU's Writing Center. This support meant that we were able to develop our module without diverting resources from other areas of our work.

Despite our enthusiasm for new media, we approached the task of designing this module with a degree of skepticism, feeling that it would be difficult or impossible to translate the kind of consulting pedagogy that we have come to value into an unstaffed virtual learning environment. We had no illusions about artificial intelligence or the ability of computers to somehow evaluate or respond to writing on their own.

---

[2]http://wide.msu.edu/

As we sought models for the kind of online interactivity we hoped to provide, we found the *Training for Tough Tutorials (TTT)* module that Joe Essid and consultants developed at University of Richmond's Writing Center particularly suggestive.[3] Although aimed at consultants, not writers, *TTT* takes an interactive and multimodal approach, combining video clips of consulting sessions with spaces for online critique. Due, in large part, to its online video components embedded within a framework that encourages critical reflection, *TTT* functions as a powerful resource that learners can access whenever necessary. We also were attracted to the "Writing Activities" included in Colorado State University's Writing@CSU website.[4] Rather than merely presenting information, these writing activities guide writers through the process of writing by offering sequenced, online composing spaces. These examples illustrate Murphy and Hawkes' observation that, because of the special affordances of new media, "more than ever before, self-paced learning opportunities are possible." Models like these suggested to us that digital media have the potential for offering highly interactive, engaging, and media-rich learning opportunities for writers.

Over the course of about 8 months, we developed *Getting Started: Analytical Writing in the Humanities*, which focuses on constructing interpretive arguments about cultural texts and artifacts (see Fig. 9.1).[5] This choice was motivated in part by the reality that at that time one of our largest constituencies was comprised of students enrolled in Integrated Arts and Humanities 201, a required, writing-intensive course. IAH201 asks students to write about a wide range of primary sources, including poems, novels, legal documents, letters, presidential speeches, photographs, and paintings. But many other courses at MSU and elsewhere ask students to analyze cultural artifacts as well. So this seemed like a good focus for our first module, offering an opportunity to address the needs of a large group of learners.

Getting Started focuses on the initial concerns that writers enrolled in humanities classes face, such as assessing the rhetorical situation, identifying an intellectual problem, and developing a thesis statement. In addition to traditional written guides, the module provides a palette of interactive components and tools, including writing spaces, note-taking tools, digital animations, and video elements.

Feeling that digital video is a powerful teaching tool, we devoted considerable resources to producing a 20-minute video narrative that serves as

---

[3]http://writing2.richmond.edu/training/tough/
[4]Michael Palmquist is listed as the Writing@CSU and Writing Studio Development Director, see http://writing.colostate.edu/about.cfm.
[5]http://writing.msu.edu/interactive/humanities/

the centerpiece of the module. "The Thesis Reloaded" offers a fictional account of a student named Eleanor who is searching for an appropriate thesis statement (see Fig. 9.2). The video dramatizes the writing process, focusing on strategies for invention. Eleanor has been asked by her professor to write about the film *The Matrix Reloaded*. The assignment specifies that she needs to have a clear thesis statement as well as an argument that connects the movie to the themes of the course. Eleanor is frustrated because she does not understand what it means to construct an argument about a film. She originally proposes to argue that the film is an "awesome movie," but after talking about the paper with friends, a writing consultant, and her instructor, she develops a thesis that argues for a particular interpretation of the film. TJ, the writing consultant in the film, also serves as the tour guide of the module, appearing in short video clips that introduce the other components of the module.

Murphy and Hawkes claim that digital content specialists develop instructional resources that are informed by writing center pedagogy. Does *Getting Started* achieve this goal? Answering this question is not an easy task. In the remainder of this discussion, I concentrate on a small part of that answer: I interrogate the design of the module in an attempt to show how it operationalizes certain pedagogical values that define writing center pedagogy. As those of us involved in this project defined for each other the

Figure 9.1. The menu page for *Getting Started: Analytical Writing in the Humanities* presents learners with multiple options.

Figure 9.2. "The Thesis Reloaded" is a short video narrative in which Eleanor engages in conversations with friends, a writing consultant, and her instructor as she attempts to generate an effective thesis statement.

distinguishing pedagogical assets of the Writing Center, we found ourselves continuously emphasizing that peer consulting is *student-centered, active, process-oriented*, and, above all, *dialogic*. In the following sections, I discuss our attempts to exploit the affordances of digital media to preserve these fundamental aspects of the writing center approach.

DESIGNING STUDENT-CENTERED SPACES

Writing centers are student-centered spaces in multiple senses. Those of us who work in writing centers know that peer consultants can facilitate collaborative learning precisely because they are peers, because they share a cultural space with the writers they serve. As John Trimbur (1987) writes, writing centers are "efforts by educators to tap the identification of student with student as a potentially powerful source of learning" (p. 24). Noting that "student culture" is "the social medium of co-learning" (p. 27), Trimbur claims that "we need to treat peer tutors as students, not as para-professionals or preprofessionals, and to recognize that their community is not necessarily ours" (p. 27). Likewise, Marilyn Cooper (1994) notes that peer consultants can serve as "radical" or "organic" intellectuals "by virtue of their constant contact with institutional constraints *and* with students' lived experiences" (p. 103). As mediator between institutional and student cultures, peer consultants can help writers develop a critical awareness of academic practice without disrespecting writers' cultural identities as students.

One of the key hallmarks of academic practice is, of course, a commitment to writing itself, to the written word as the privileged form of communication—a commitment not necessarily shared by nonacademic cultures. *Getting Started* attempts to honor students by adopting modes and media valued by student culture. In our experience, students at MSU appreciate the dynamic, multisensory experiences afforded by digital media. Early designs of the module called for a heavier reliance on the written word, but students we consulted critiqued that decision, labeling our approach boring and traditional. They suggested ways of integrating more video elements and made suggestions about visual style. The film, the video introductions to individual sections of the module, and the multimedia overviews of the module all reflect our attempt to adopt semiotic forms valued by students at MSU.

Educational psychologist Kym Buchanan (2003) has foregrounded the use of student-valued technologies in his writing on "co-opting":

> As our students fearlessly embrace new technologies for communication and entertainment, educators can be change agents or change victims. Many "toy" technologies are extraordinary low-threshold opportunities for "serious" learning. Rather than barricade the door, educators should co-opt the technologies students already play with. (p. 10)

yes!

Buchanan echoes literacy theorists like Patricia Dunn who critique the academy's practice of constructing the multimedia literacies that students bring with them as inherently inferior and lacking educational value (Dunn, 2001; see also Dyson, 2003; Wade & Moje, 2000).

In addition to emphasizing modes and media favored by students, the approach of the module is student-centered in the way that it honors the different needs and learning styles of individual students. The first thing to note about *Getting Started* is that, as a hypertext, it "permits readers to choose their own paths through a set of possibilities" (Landow, 1994, p. 33). It offers a menu of options and allows readers to select ones that best meet their needs at any given point in time.

One set of needs relates not to content, but to learning style. Attending to different learning styles has been a key writing center value and is an important dimension of the goal of individualized instruction that Murphy and Hawkes outline. Elizabeth Konstant (1992) describes visual, auditory, kinesthetic, and multisensory techniques for consulting with writers. Although Konstant's specific focus is students with learning disabilities, she announces from the beginning that "we all have our own preferred ways of learning" (p. 6), and her advice to "do what works with each individual" (p. 7) is consistent with the student-centered approach that writing centers take in all consulting sessions.

Accordingly, *Getting Started* offers students choices between various ways of interacting with the material, from text-only versions that can be processed by the screen readers of sight-impaired students to multimedia and interactive approaches appropriate for users who favor more visual, auditory, or tactile ways of learning. We see this attempt to provide a range of options as consistent with Gardner's (1999) "multiple intelligences" and Felder and Silverman's (1988) "learning styles." We find particularly compelling Patricia Dunn's (2001) summary of Paulo Freire's (1993) "multiple channels of communication" (p. 49; cited in Dunn, 2001, p. 37). Dunn argues that the importance of multiple channels in Freire's method—his use of slides, visuals, dialogues, and documents—has often been ignored. According to Dunn, scholars often fail to "emphasize the harm done by written-word-based pedagogies to students whose primary ways of knowing are spatial, aural, or kinesthetic" (p. 47). In designing the module, we had in mind the "richness of sensory experience" that Murphy and Hawkes identify as a key asset of digital content.

Coming from a technical-writing framework, Mike Markel (1998) confirms the importance of the visual for certain learners: "Research clearly suggests . . . that people learn better and more quickly if the information includes visual cues beyond traditional typography, and that some people are significantly better at processing visual information than verbal information" (p. 49). Markel outlines a strategy of "media redundancy"—the practice of providing information in more than one medium. Embracing the concept of media redundancy, the module presents concepts like "thesis statements," "argument," and "textual evidence" through written guides, video narratives, digital animations, and online spaces for guided writing.

Our decision to adopt a specifically narrative use of video (as opposed to, for example, video lectures) was informed by a growing body of research that supports the use of narrative as a learning and thinking tool. Summarizing this research, educational theorist Marsha Rossiter (2002) writes that a "narrative orientation to education is grounded in an understanding of narrative as a primary structure of human meaning and narrative as metaphor for the developing self" (p. 5). Likewise, psychologist

Donald Polkinghorne (1988) observes, "narrative is the fundamental scheme for linking individual human actions and events into interrelated aspects of an understandable composite" (p. 13). Although narrative is sometimes forsaken by the academy in favor of more abstract and argumentative forms, it is a rhetorical mode valued by cultures outside the academy and one particularly well suited to presenting writing as a process that involves actions and interactions over time.

The narrative presented in "The Thesis Reloaded" was designed as an affirmation of student culture and student literacies. Eleanor learns by talking with peers (a roommate, a peer consultant, and a friend) in student-centered spaces (a dorm room, the Writing Center, and a coffee bar). Consistent with the affordances of peer consulting sessions that Muriel Harris (1995) outlines in "Talking in the Middle," the students with whom Eleanor interacts "inhabit a middle ground where their role is that of translator or interpreter, turning teacher language into student language" (p. 37). In focusing on these conversations and settings, we dramatize the reality that the classroom is not the exclusive domain of learning; we offer an image of invention that affirms the value of peer-to-peer collaboration and the essential reality that writing is often, in the broadest sense, a collaborative endeavor.

In both form and content, then, *Getting Started* was designed as a student-centered space, emphasizing forms of discourse, media, modes, and learning styles that are valued by students.

DESIGNING ACTIVE, PROCESS-ORIENTED SPACES

Jeff Brooks (1991) famously argues that peer consultants should aim to make their clients "do all the work" (p. 1). Although Brooks' brief article is somewhat reductive, Brooks' fundamental point is important: One of the strengths of the writing center approach is that it encourages students to play an intensely active role in their own learning. Effective writing consultants devise approaches that keep their clients emotionally, intellectually, and often physically engaged. They ask questions, request alternate presentations of ideas, and provide opportunities for clients to write. Brooks usefully, if implicitly, locates writing centers in a larger tradition of "active learning" that stems from Jean Piaget, John Dewey, and others, and that characterizes an important—if loosely defined—cluster of ideas in contemporary learning theory. As Charles Bonwell and James Eison (1991) explain,

Surprisingly, educators' use of the term 'active-learning' has relied more on intuitive understanding than a common definition. Consequently, many faculty assert that all learning is inherently active and that students are therefore actively involved while listening to formal presentations in the classroom. Analysis of the research literature . . . , however, suggests that students must do more than just listen: They must read, write, discuss, or be engaged in solving problems. Most important, to be actively involved, students must engage in such higher-order thinking tasks as analysis, synthesis, and evaluation. (p. iii)

To illustrate how the module reflects this definition of active learning, I describe in detail one guided writing sequence we call "The Thesis Tester" (see Fig. 9.3). In this writing sequence, TJ—the consultant that Eleanor is assigned when she visits the Writing Center—appears in short video clips that lead users through the process of generating a thesis statement, describing their target audience, and summarizing the evidence they will use to persuade their audience that their thesis is valid. The writing that students produce is synthesized and presented back to them in the following frame:

In this paper you will attempt to convince [target audience] that [thesis statement] by presenting evidence like [description of evidence].

Figure 9.3. In the "Thesis Tester," video prompts from TJ guide users through the process of generating a thesis statement, describing their target audience, and summarizing the evidence they will use to persuade their audience that their thesis is valid.

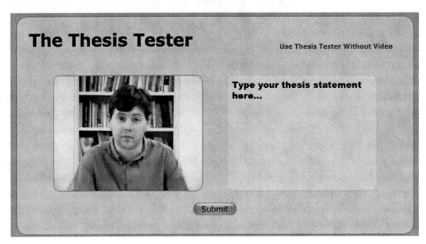

This presentation is followed by a set of heuristic questions for assessing the effectiveness of the thesis statement:

1. Is it possible to convince your target audience that your thesis is valid or are the attitudes, beliefs and values of your audience such that no amount of persuasion will be effective?
2. Does your audience need to be convinced that your thesis is valid or do they already accept it as true?
3. Is the evidence that you plan to use appropriate?
4. Does your thesis enable you to contribute to ongoing conversations?

Each of these questions are in turn linked to detailed explanations.

Moving beyond plot summary to rich analysis of texts and artifacts is one of the key challenges that students face in the kind of writing they are asked to do in humanities courses. Instructors who teach the IAH 201 course here at MSU continually observe that when writing about Frederick Douglass' *My Bondage and My Freedom*, for instance, students have a hard time moving beyond statements like "Frederick Douglass was oppressed" or "Slavery was wrong." "The Thesis Tester" writing sequence is designed to help students go beyond obvious claims by integrating their proposed thesis statements into a summary of an intellectual project that delineates the relationships among thesis, audience, and evidence. If a user writes, for instance, that her thesis is "Frederick Douglass was oppressed," describes her audiences as "instructor and classmates," and lists her evidence as "Douglass' experiences in *My Bondage and My Freedom*," her responses will be integrated into the following statement:

> In this paper you will attempt to convince instructor and classmates that Frederick Douglass was oppressed by presenting evidence like Douglass' experiences in *My Bondage and My Freedom*.

Because this thesis is close to a summary of Douglass' text, the audience that the student identifies will not need to be convinced of it. Inserting the proposed thesis into this frame helps to reveal the need for revision.

The approach taken by "The Thesis Tester," then, is different from a handout that lists criteria for or provides models of good thesis statements. The Tester engages students in writing, reframes the writing they generate in a way that prompts them to see their task differently, and then guides them through an assessment process. The writer is forced, as Brooks says, to do all the work. Other components of the module reflect this approach as well. Students are guided through the process of assessing the rhetorical context, are given various examples of thesis statements to critique and are invited to compare their responses with others, and are invited to compare their interpretation of *The Thesis Reloaded* with running commentary by others.

DESIGNING DIALOGIC SPACES

Dialogue is fundamental to the writing center approach. "What the peer tutor and tutee do together," writes Kenneth Bruffee (1984), "is not write or edit, or least of all proofread. What they do is converse" (p. 10). More poetically, Alice Gillam (1991) observes, "like a fertile, overgrown garden, the writing center breeds conversations between writer and tutor which grow and spread in directions neither consciously intends" (p. 3).

The approach adopted in the module is fundamentally dialogic in its rhetorical structure. Although some information is provided in the form of more traditional guides, the core components of the module do not make use of directive comments delivered with the voice of an expert. A component like "The Thesis Tester" is patterned after the kind of turn-taking one might find in a consulting session. A writer is asked to provide a thesis statement and other information relevant to it. This information is synthesized into a new statement in the way that a consultant might say, "Let me summarize what I hear you saying." This synthesis is followed by a number of questions, which in turn prompt the writer to reflect and revise.

The video components of the module are also dialogic. "The Thesis Reloaded," for instance, is comprised of a series of conversations about writing. Students are not subjected to a lecture in which a teacher attempts to impart knowledge, but instead are given a narrative meant to invite reflection and extrapolation. Rather than create a handout that attempts to monolithically describe the components of effective thesis statements, we offer (in a separate video component) a conversation in which two experienced instructors discuss at length a set of sample thesis statements. As the instructors articulate what they perceive to be the merits and limitations of each thesis, there are points of consensus and disagreement. Students can see that there is no single authoritative understanding of writing, but that different readers bring different expectations and that writers need to understand these expectations to write effectively.

I realize that some readers will feel that I am reaching when I characterize these elements as dialogic. Clearly, the richness of a live exchange—of two or more copresent interlocutors responding to each other in the moment—is not literally replicated in the components of the module that I have just discussed. My argument rests on a more metaphoric understanding of dialogue.

Getting Started does, however, include a more literal integration of dialogue: Each component of the module is linked to a separate thread in an online discussion forum. All visitors are invited to read and participate in this ongoing conversation. Visitors can therefore provide perspectives that we leave out, critique any feature in or information provided by the module, and ask questions of each other.

These threaded discussion spaces are similar to the "dialogic spaces" that Eric Miraglia and Joel Norris (2000) describe in relation to Washington State University's (WSU's) Writers' Exchange. Miraglia and Norris describe WSU's desire "to avoid the authority-laden, monolithic, responses of expert-to-novice email exchanges in favor of more open-ended, discursive dialogues derived from multiple authorized and unauthorized voices" (p. 97). They sought a "public forum" characterized by a "one-to-many or many-to-many paradigm in place of the e-mail OWL's one-to-one paradigm" (p. 92). In this model, visitors would share and comment on each other's writing instead of submitting it to a single consultant. *Getting Started* does not ask students to share papers, but instead asks them to make an inquiry into the nature of academic discourse. We have seeded this inquiry with guides, video dialogues and narratives, and other interactive elements, but surrounding all of these elements is space open to anyone who wishes to explore the nature of analytical writing in the humanities.

At work here are multiple and overlapping models of dialogue inspired by prominent discussions of writing centers and peer consulting, such as Kenneth Bruffee's (1984) deployment of Michael Oakshott's "conversation of mankind," Andrea Lunsford's (1991) use of Kenneth Burke's "parlor," and Alice Gilliam's (1991) application of Mikhail Bakhtin's "dialogism." In all three of these models, the specific exchange between writer and consultant is a single instantiation of a much broader set of overlapping conversations that develop across time and space. The module we have designed provides users with meaningful glimpses of this larger conversation—students talking with students, instructors talking with instructors, and instructors talking with students—and invites them to join in. *Getting Started* does not attempt to replicate a practice of submitting a draft to and receiving comments from a peer consultant. Instead, it helps writers become aware of how their writing relates to and participates in broader conversations and discourse communities.

TOWARD A SUSTAINABLE CULTURE OF WRITING CENTER INNOVATION IN ONLINE SPACES

In her examination of the Internet as a public space, Irene Ward (1997) cites Electronic Frontier Foundation cofounder John Perry Barlow's (1996) comment that "whatever the human mind may create can be reproduced and distributed infinitely at no cost" via the Web (cited in Ward, 1997, p. 372). Ward considers the possibility that the Web will democratize education by making content available to people who otherwise might not have access to it. But Ward is skeptical about the likelihood of this prospect:

> Is it really feasible for each school to produce its own instructional material? Given the cost, will institutions cooperate in producing material? How will such projects be funded? (p. 372)

But in recent years, we have witnessed the substantial production of free online educational resources. Wikipedia, for instance, is a compendium of 2,373,483 articles (just counting the ones in English), all of which were written by volunteers. One could name hundreds of other resources—dictionaries, encyclopedias, guides, articles, interactive modules, educational TV shows, films, blogs, and podcasts—that are freely available on the Internet. Murphy and Hawkes' reconfiguration of centers as content producers offers a way of thinking about how writing centers can make unique contributions to the public space of the Internet. As centers embrace the multiliteracy center model, they will increasingly be staffed by individuals who have the skill sets and experiences necessary to facilitate the innovative appropriation of online spaces.

REFERENCES

Barlow, John Perry. (1996). *A declaration of the independence of cyberspace.* Retrieved September 12, 2005, from < http://homes.eff.org/ ~ barlow/ Declaration-Final.html >

Bonwell, Charles C., & Eison, James A. (1991). *Active learning: Creating excitement in the classroom* (ASHE-ERIC Higher Education Report No. 1, 1992). Washington, DC: The George Washington University.

Brooks, Jeff. (1991). Minimalist tutoring: Making the student do all the work. *Writing Lab Newsletter, 15*(6), 1–4.

Bruffee, Kenneth A. (1984). Peer tutoring and the "conversation of mankind." In Gary A. Olson (Ed.), *Writing centers: Theory and administration* (pp. 3–15). Urbana, IL: National Council of Teachers of English.

Buchanan, Kym. (2003, October). Opportunity knocking: Co-opting and games. *Association for Learning Technology Newsletter,* pp. 10–11.

Cooper, Marilyn. (1994). Really useful knowledge: A cultural studies agenda for writing centers. *The Writing Center Journal, 14,* 97–111.

Dunn, Patricia A. (2001). *Talking, sketching, moving: Multiple literacies in the teaching of writing.* Portsmouth: Boynton/Cook.

Dyson, Anne Haas. (2003). *The brothers and sisters learn to write: Popular literacies in childhood and school cultures.* New York: Teachers College Press.

Felder, Richard M., & Silverman, Linda. (1988). Learning and teaching styles in engineering education. *Engineering Education, 78*(7), 674–681.

Freire, Paulo. (1993). *Education for critical consciousness.* New York: Continuum.

Gardner, Howard. (1999). *Intelligence reframed: Multiple intelligences for the 21st century.* New York: Basic Books.

Gillam, Alice M. (1991). Writing center ecology: A Bakhtinian perspective. *The Writing Center Journal, 11*(2), 3–11.

Harris, Muriel. (1995). Talking in the middle: Why writers need writing tutors. *College English, 57*(1), 27–42.

Hobson, Eric H. (1998). *Wiring the writing center.* Logan: Utah University Press.

Inman, James A., & Sewell, Donna N. (Eds.). (2000). *Taking flight with OWLs: Examining electronic writing center work* (pp. 85–103). Mahwah, NJ: Erlbaum.

Konstant, Shoshona Beth. (1992). Multi-sensory tutoring for multi-sensory learners. *Writing Lab Newsletter, 16*(9–10), 6–8.

Landow, George P. (1994). *Hyper/text/theory.* Baltimore: Johns Hopkins University Press.

Lunsford, Andrea. (1991). Collaboration, control, and the idea of a writing center. *The Writing Center Journal, 12*(1), 3–10.

Markel, Mike. (1998). Testing visual-based modules for teaching writing. *Technical Communication, 45*(1), 47–76.

Miraglia, Eric, & Norris, Joel. (2000). Cyberspace and sofas: Dialogic spaces and the making of an online writing lab. In James A. Inman & Donna N. Sewell (Eds.), *Taking flight with OWLs: Examining electronic writing center work* (pp. 85–103). Mahwah, NJ: Erlbaum.

Polkinghorne, Donald. (1988). *Narrative knowing and the human sciences.* Albany, NY: SUNY Press.

Rossiter, Marsha. (2002). Narrative and stories in adult teaching and learning. 1–5 ERIC Digest. First Search. ED473147. September 5, 2005. < http://www.ericdigests.org/2003–4/adult-teaching.html > .

Trimbur, John. (1987). Peer tutoring: A contradiction in terms? *The Writing Center Journal, 7*(2), 21–27.

Wade, Suzanne E., & Moje, Elizabeth B. (2000). The role of text in classroom learning. In Michael L. Kamil et al. (Eds.), *Handbook of reading research, Vol. III* (pp. 609–627). Mahwah, NJ: Erlbaum

Ward, Irene. (1997). How democratic can we get? The internet, the public sphere, and public discourse. *JAC: A Journal of Composition Theory, 17*(3), 365–379.

Reality Check

10

THE NEW MEDIA (R)EVOLUTION

MULTIPLE MODELS FOR MULTILITERACIES

Jackie Grutsch McKinney

Ball State University

In Writing Center scholarship, there are two seemingly contradictory tropes used with some frequency: (a) every center is different and context changes everything, and (b) certain practices and theories are universal to all Writing Centers. Although on the surface, these tenets might be incompatible, it takes no great leap of imagination to see that they are not mutually exclusive. Consider something innocuous as tutoring manuals like *The Bedford Guide for Writing Tutors* (Ryan & Zimmerelli, 2006) or *The Allyn and Bacon Guide to Peer Tutoring* (Gillespie & Lerner, 2004). Many Writing Centers are able to use these sorts of texts even with their different staffs and contexts because there is enough in common in practices, beliefs, epistemological assumptions, and theoretical grounding among those who identify with Writing Centers to be a discourse community. Discourse communities do not need absolute consensus; rather, those participating in the conversation have just enough in common to be able to communicate with one another, which is in turn enriched by all that participants do not have in common.

Enter multiliteracy centers. The early centers that have developed in the past decade have been largely similar in practice and theory; as such, we can begin to see a model emerging for addressing multiliteracies in a peer tutoring setting. At this formative stage, multiliteracy practices and theories are emerging that might set the course—the conversation—for future generations. Therefore, it seems important to look closely at this model now to see how it addresses multiliteracies and how it might or might not work in particular contexts. To this end, this chapter aims to define this emerging model and trace its theoretical lineage, discuss the difficulties of enacting this model, and reveal consequences of not adopting it using my own institution as an example. In doing so, my hope is to keep the conversation of multiliteracy centers from narrowing to a set of practices that comprises just one possible model of addressing multiliteracies in a peer tutoring setting by naming this set of practices and imagining others. To be sure, pioneers in multiliteracy centers have not wanted to limit the conversation of multiliteracies in particular ways—in fact, they are most invested in having the conversation expand. This is one small attempt to do so.

THE ALL-IN-ONE
MULTILITERACY CENTER MODEL

The New London Group (1996) was the first to discuss multiliteracies in order to emphasize their concern for addressing linguistic diversity of the global economy and the multiple modes used for composition at the turn of the century. They contrast the idea of "multiliteracies" with "mere literacy" (pp. 63–64). Mere literacy "remains centered on language only, and usually on a singular national form of language at that, which is conceived as a stable system based on rules such as mastering sound-letter correspondence" (p. 64). In their self-proclaimed programmatic manifesto, "A Pedagogy of Multiliteracies: Designing Social Futures" (1996), the group forwards *design* as the key term, naming six "areas" that literacy educators should attend to: "Linguistic Design, Visual Design, Audio Design, Gestural Design, Spatial Design, and Multimodal Design" (p. 78). The New London Group also asserts that teachers of writing can help students become multiliterate by "Situated Practice," "Overt Instruction," "Critical Framing," and "Transformed Practice" (p. 65). These varied ways of designing learning experiences, they believe, will prepare students for the literacies necessary to communicate at a moment in history defined by an "increasing complexity and inter-relationship of different modes of meaning" (p. 78).

Stuart Selber (2004) has a slightly different notion of multiliteracy in *Multiliteracy for a Digital Age*, in which he argues literacy teachers must teach computer literacy in writing classes. In doing so, he joins Cynthia Selfe (1999), Lee Ann Kastman Breuch (2004), and Laura J. Gurak (1999), among others, in asserting that writing with technology has become so prevalent that one should not attempt to teach one (writing) without the other (technology). He names three technological literacies that we should help students obtain: functional, critical, and rhetorical. Students who obtain functional literacy understand how to use hardware and software; they are proficient *users* of technology. Students who obtain critical technology literacy understand the political, cultural, and economic ramifications of using technology; they are critics of technology. Rhetorical literacy mediates between critical and functional literacy. Students with rhetorical literacy know how to choose among competing technologies to achieve their rhetorical ends; they are savvy *producers* of technology (also see Selber, 2005).

Selber (2004) believes that teachers of writing are more likely to address critical or rhetorical literacies over functional. That is, they are more likely to talk with students about the political implications of using technology or the rhetorical choices involved in composing with technology than they are likely to teach students how to use hardware and software. There is a general disdain for functional literacy in the humanities, according to Selber, "for functional literacy often becomes a blunt tool with which ruling classes create minimally skilled workers" (p. 33). However, he sees it as irresponsible not to teach students the full range of literacies.

This move is similar to the argument that Cynthia Selfe (1999) makes in *Technology and Literacy in the Twenty-First Century*, where she comments on the government initiative, "Getting America's Students Ready," which defines technological literacy as having "computer skills and the ability to use computers and other technology to improve learning, productivity, and performance" (p. 10). Like Selber (2004), she wants to stretch earlier notions of technological literacy. She writes:

> technological literacy refers to a complex set of socially and culturally situated values, practices, and skills involved in operating linguistically within the context of electronic environments, including reading, writing and communicating. The term further refers to the linking of technology and literacy at fundamental levels of both conception and social practice. In this context, technological literacy refers to social and cultural contexts for discourse and communication, as well as the social and linguistic products and practices of communication and the ways in which electronic communication environments have become essential parts of our cultural understanding of what it means to be literate. (p. 11)

Thus, Selfe argues that the notion of being "literate" is now tied to technology.

None of these discussions—The New London Group, Selber, or Selfe—named the Writing Center as a possible site for multiliteracy instruction, but Writing Center scholars have. For instance, John Trimbur (2000) notes that Worcester Polytechnic Institute (WPI), where he worked, had recently renamed its center The Center for Communication Across the Curriculum "to signify the Center's commitment not just to writing but to multiliteracies" (p. 29). He says he thinks this change at WPI is "fairly indicative of recent trends in Writing Center theory and practice to see literacy as multimodal activity in which oral, written, and visual communication intertwine and interact" (p. 29).[1] Along with Trimbur, James Inman (2001), Danielle DeVoss (2002), Krista H. Millar (2004), and David Sheridan (2006) have described multiliteracy work at other Writing Centers.

Each of these centers (WPI, Michigan State, University of Michigan, and Furman University) has adopted a similar way of multimodal tutoring, which I see as the emerging model of the multiliteracy center despite their differences in actual names. At this point, it does not seem necessary for a center to call itself a multiliteracy center in order to work under this model—in a similar way, I suppose, to the way that many Writing Centers are, in fact, called labs, clinics, studios, workshops, and so forth. There are three characteristics that constitute this multiliteracy center model as I see it, which I will call the all-in-one (AIO) model.

The first of these involves how new media writing is isolated from other writing and tutored by specialty tutors. For example, Trimbur (2000) notes at the center at WPI, they have separate workshops (tutorials) for writing, oral presentation, and visual design. DeVoss (2002) writes about the Internet Writing Consultancy at Michigan State, which was a specialty tutoring cohort trained to help students write for the web. According to Sheridan (2006), this tutoring team is now called the digital writing consultancy. Likewise, the Multiliteracy Center within Sweetland Writing Center at University of Michigan[2] held special sessions just for new media writing (Millar, 2004). At Michigan State and University of Michigan, tutors begin as regular writing tutors and take an additional semester-long training course to become multiliteracy tutors (Millar, 2004; Sheridan, 2006). Using special-

---

[1] He writes about the First World-ist mistake of offering writing help in only English, too. This is one of the few mentions of a multiliteracy center in a Writing Center context that alludes to both definitions of multiliteracy intended by The New London Group.

[2] The Multiliteracy Center at Sweetland was created under an internal technology grant; the center lasted 3 years (2000–2003).

ty tutors like this is one of the ways that Michael Pemberton (2003) discussed that Writing Centers could accommodate hypertexts. Alternatively, he also supposed that Writing Centers could treat hypertexts like all other texts, train all tutors to work with new media, or decide not to work with hypertexts.

Second, in the AIO multiliteracy model, tutors participate in overt instruction in functional technology literacy. They teach students how to work with software and hardware, and they engage students in rhetorical and critical literacy activities, too. As Sheridan (2006) explains, a tutor at a multiliteracy center might sit down with a student and ask about goals, purpose, and audience for a particular webtext. Then the tutor and student might move to a computer where the tutor can show a student how to do things without taking over.

The third defining characteristic of the AIO model is that the center is equipped with appropriate hardware and software for how-to tutoring of new media. Because new media writing may take many forms, the equipment list might be long (more on this later), although at least one center (Click & Magruder, 2006) limited what kind of new media texts (e-portfolios) and what kind of software (Dreamweaver) it would support, thus making the seemingly endless possible equipment list much more manageable.

Having the equipment, specialized tutors, and functional computer literacy instruction is appropriate given the goal of helping students with multimodal texts (The New London Group definition of multiliteracy) and teaching with and about technology (the Stuart Selber notion of multiliteracy). However, this is not the model for multiliteracies we have in place at my current institution. Here, we use a model that has any tutor at any session prepared to respond to all genres of writing—new media or not. In this model, the center does not segregate texts that are or are not multimodal. To do this, our Writing Center model prepares all tutors to respond to multimodal texts; this is consistent with how Writing Centers have historically worked with a wide range of genres. As this model prepares tutors to respond to multimodal texts, it meets the ends of the New London Group's notion of multiliteracy. However, this model does not require the technology or overt training on the technology that Selber sees as essential under his umbrella of multiliteracy. If we buy the literacy prescriptions of Selber (2004) and others and that they would apply to nonclassroom spaces like the Writing Center, then we probably would see the AIO model as the optimal model. But this does not mean that the multiliteracy center model will come easily for us.

WHAT'S DIFFICULT
ABOUT EMPLOYING THE AIO MODEL?

Many institutional, economical, and rhetorical factors can play a role in deciding whether one can adopt an AIO model. There are several obstacles that block the path for me. I do not want to imply that they are insurmountable, but only that navigating around them makes the road less direct and immediate. As Jo Ann Griffin (2007) notes, "In most institutions, Writing Center resources are stretched thin, and many Writing Center directors, when faced with the prospect of helping teachers and students on multimodal composition assignments, will express concerns about time, attention, and material resources" (p. 153). I do not have concerns about working with multimodal texts—I think we have to—but I do have concerns about the AIO multiliteracy model.

My first concern is probably the most obvious: Where do I get the money to do this right? As Selfe (1999) reminds us, "It remains a fact that high-quality programs in computer literacy cannot be built or sustained on the backs of unsupported teachers" (p. 224). If we are to be prepared to work with students on any type of text, we need equipment, lots of equipment. At this point in time, we might feasibly see students working in various modes (audio, video, image, color, text), for various media (computer screen, projector, paper, TV screen, speaker), using various programs (word processors, Photoshop, Dreamweaver, InDesign, Flash, Final Cut). True, some things we might already have. Most Writing Centers have computers. We might already have some programs or might be able to get them for no or low-cost through our institutional agreements or alternatives as freeware. Still, in my estimate, if I wanted to equip three tutoring stations for multiliteracy tutoring, assuming I have the space and furniture already, I still would request nearly $15,000 (see Appendix A)—and I am imagining requesting less than what Sheridan states could be appropriate in his introduction to this collection. In making the case for this equipment with either the department chair, dean, or granting agency—I do not have the budget for this currently—I would have to ask for both the start-up amount and maintenance costs. Given how quickly technology changes, it would be reasonable to expect to upgrade the equipment and software at least once every 3 or 4 years.

Another cost related to equipping the center is support staff for doing technology maintenance and troubleshooting. My department has a full-time technology support person, so we have this resource available to us.

Others may not. Notice, too, that I have listed lock changes on my equipment list. Costly equipment requires costly protective majors that we have been able to avoid up to this point. One way around technology equipment costs is to require students to bring in laptops with the necessary hardware and applications. This could work if students are already required to have laptops; only certain majors do at Ball State. But even if all the students had laptops, the tutors would not be able to train and experiment on the various applications if the center is not equipped.

Equipment is only one part of the funding issue. The other major one is staffing. The multiliteracy model employs specialized tutors for specialized sessions. Unless a Writing Center is operating under capacity and has extra money in its tutoring budget, adding a multiliteracy center component means making a case for more tutoring funds. Further, if the multiliteracy center tutors are a more highly trained force, they probably should be paid more than regular writing tutors.

Sheridan (chap. 9, this volume) says that "the hard truth" is that multiliteracy consultants are a kind of supertutor. I believe this to be true, and training under this model would require supertraining or superrecruiting (see Sheridan, Introduction, this volume). Ball State typically staffs 10 to 15 tutors. Most of these are undergraduate peer tutors; many are English education students. We do not have a required tutoring class because no such course officially exists. I have taught a tutoring class twice in the last 5 years as a special topics course, but because of the infrequency of its offering, I cannot require it as a condition for hire. Instead, we have bimonthly training meetings throughout the year to work with the staff on tutoring issues.

It would be difficult to fit software and hardware training into this current arrangement. With orientation sessions and an observational period where the tutor observes other tutors, the initial training of tutors takes weeks—sometimes over a month. The time we have in training meetings would not be sufficient to also provide tutors with a functional technological literacy. Increasing the frequency of training meetings, which are paid, would necessitate a cut in the number of available tutoring hours; it is the same budget. However, the school does subscribe to online tutorials on certain software programs, so I could require these during the tutor's orientation/observation period. These self-guided lessons are time-intensive, however. Learning one program could take 20 to 30 hours.

I know there is a cliché about the current generation of students being hyper-technoliterate, some referring to them as digital natives (Prensky, 2001). To be sure, many young people are more comfortable with certain technologies than older generations, the so-called "digital immigrants." However, in my experience, teaching multimodal texts, web, and document design to this generation reveals that the technocompetency of this generation is decidedly mixed. (Why would we need multiliteracy centers if it were not?) In fact, in 5 years as a director, I think I have had two or three tutors total (less than one per year) who would come in with enough of the basics or enough interest in technology to pursue further training to become a multiliteracy consultant.[3]

Certainly, with a finite time frame and budget, directors need to make choices that reflect their priorities. There is no getting around the fact that directors who want to prepare tutors for multimodal tutoring will probably have to reevaluate how to best use their time and resources in this new media age. Adding multimodal tutoring to a training agenda might feel like a monumental shift and another drain on resources, which is one reason that Pemberton (2003) suggests some centers might just decide not to.

Another problem could be the one that Fishman (chap. 3, this volume) describes at Clemson: when you offer functional tutoring, that may be all that students want. If we become associated with the how-to aspect of technology literacy, then students might be frustrated when, to them, we veer off course to ask about their rhetorical vision or goals. Fishman says her students want a Kinkos, not another teacher (p. 62). So, figuring out how a multiliteracy center might support functional literacy and yet maintain an identity as a tutoring center rather than a fix-it shop is a challenge.

Likewise, other campus entities might feel like we are inching in on their turf if we start tutoring on technology. Our university, like many others, already has substantial technology support services that help students purchase and install software, troubleshoot issues with their own computers and programs, and provide training sessions for further development of skills. Because university resources are historically tight, replicating (or nearly replicating) a service that exists elsewhere on campus puts one in competition with other campus entities when the next administrator wants to cut costs.

---

[3]It is also worth mentioning here that, like many other centers, we operate with both face-to-face and online, synchronous tutoring (currently we use WConline, which includes a text chat, whiteboard, and video/audio chat). I am not aware of any interface that allows synchronous editing on other multimodal files—websites, video essays, podcasts, and so forth. If it is difficult for us to read and respond to these sorts of texts online, I cannot imagine how we would also help students with the technology without being able to see what they are doing. Perhaps that technology is not far away, but for now it would be an insurmountable training issue.

CONSEQUENCES OF NOT BEING AN AIO CENTER

Clearly, there are reasons that moving to an AIO multiliteracy model is a complicated decision, one that may not be entirely our own. It might seem easiest to use another model. However, that choice is not without its own consequences, to which I can attest. By not having specialized tutors and equipment, and by not offering how-to technology help, we create other problems.

One of the results of not being prepared to help students with their functional technological literacy in the creation of new media texts is that others will step into that role. Students need to know how to use programs, and the need becomes intensified when the new media text is a high-stakes assignment. At Ball State, since 2002, each teaching major has had to create, maintain, and update a digital teaching portfolio at several "decision points" throughout his or her time in the degree. Failure to meet the assignment criteria can, ultimately, be cause for the student to not pass a decision point or not qualify for graduation or licensure.

To help students with this assignment, the Teachers College has created a Digital Portfolio Center, which is open more than 50 hours a week. A supporting website is indicative of the functional literacy approach that the center takes. From the front page, "all majors" are instructed to follow a link to "start here." This link leads to a page that provides a list of things to do first: set up campus web space and download an ftp application, a free web-composing application, and a third application necessary to publish using the campus wireless connection (Teacher Education Digital Portfolios, "Getting Started"). The instructions are thorough and linear—and telling. The student is not to begin by thinking about the genre of the portfolio or encouraged to think what they might want to include in such a project first as they might be at the center Sheridan (2006) describes. Instead, because they have little choice in completing or designing the portfolio, they are just told how to do it.

The website also has several example portfolios, which are templates rather than actual student portfolios. Fig. 10.1 shows the example given for secondary education students (Teacher Education Digital Portfolios, "Secondary"). The sample shows a title, center-aligned, with a spot to put in a name. Then there is one of Ball State's logos, center aligned, followed by a visible bordered table with linked text taking the reader to each of the 10 required elements in the portfolio. Teaching majors must match their required "artifacts"—usually school papers—to the Interstate New Teacher Assessment and Support Consortium (INTASC) principles. What is concern-

Figure 10.1. Sample Digital Teaching Portfolio from Digital Portfolio Center.

Professional Teaching Portfolio for

Insert your name here!

BALL STATE
UNIVERSITY.

INTASC 1	INTASC 2	INTASC 3	INTASC 4	INTASC 5
INTASC 6	INTASC 7	INTASC 8	INTASC 9	INTASC 10

ing about this sample, to me, is that it is poorly designed: The interface is hard to use, it means nothing except to a specialized audience, it violates basic web design principles such as avoiding center alignment and turning off borders in tables, and it does not take advantage of possibilities of the genre. This design is dated; it looks like the earliest self-published websites from the 1990s. Even more concerning is that most of the actual student digital teaching portfolios I have seen look similar to, if not exactly the same as, this one.

Now, in the students' defense and in defense of the Digital Portfolio Center, the actual assignment is prescriptive. Students are expected to make a portfolio that looks like this sample. They are told they must have an index page and exactly 10 INTASC pages ("Introduction"). The students get little class time to develop functional literacy and are not expected to think through the genre, software, design, multimodality, and so forth of the assignment. They are expected just to replicate this website. Further, students who did put effort into making creative sites were frustrated when they found local school districts would not initially accept digital teaching portfolios as application materials. In all, students are usually not interested in their own teaching portfolios because they do not have much rhetorical power, are not given much teacher support, and receive little feedback on their efforts aside from a check on their degree checklist.

I emphasize all of this not to make a point about the ridiculousness of the constraints (okay, maybe a little bit), but to use this as one example of a multimodal assignment and support center for that assignment that does not encourage multiliteracies in either the sense intended by The New London Group (1996) or Selber (2004). The lesson in this for me is that if we are unwilling to support functional literacy, someone else probably will. This is potentially a good thing; functional literacy skills should be encouraged in both classroom spaces and nonclassroom services. But if we are not willing or able to support functional literacy, we cannot really complain about how others do it.

Although it is nearly impossible to track the clients who are not coming to a center, I am certain that we could help more students if we were an AIO center. We know that some students need functional literacy help. We also know that Writing Program faculty who are assigning new media texts ask whether we can do this for their students. So, I am pretty confident in supposing that if we were an AIO center, we would attract more students with how-to questions.

Moreover, I think there is a chance that some students who would come in for how-to help would be asked to think about other issues in the texts they are working with that might make them return for critical or rhetorical feedback on other new media or old media texts. We know this happens with students who are required to come for writing help. Many are resentful or skeptical about needing to be there, yet every semester we have converts—students who end up praising the Writing Center and returning for help of their own volition later in the term. In this sense, our consultations are our best advertisements; thus, the more consultations, the more consultations.

The other consequence of not being equipped for functional technology tutoring is that it is terribly inconvenient to not be able to respond to the full range of questions a student has about a text. Tutors have tried to be flexible and inventive; on more than one occasion, a tutor has taken a student downstairs to a computer lab, which has Dreamweaver and the Adobe Creative Suite installed, to help a student revise. The other option is to send the student to a computer help desk on campus. It is easy to see how this would interrupt the flow of a session. Let's say a tutor makes a suggestion for a student to embed a video into a web page to make a more explicit argument. and the student thinks this is a great idea and asks how it is done. If the tutor does not know, the student might go for help elsewhere or might decide just to do something else (also see Sheridan, 2006).

I began this chapter suggesting that there is enough that Writing Center professionals have in common that they are able to participate in a discourse community with one another, and, also, there is something to be said for keeping individual contexts in mind. Likewise, the emerging AIO model and the model for multiliteracy that I employ certainly have common ground—they are in the same general conversation. But through illustrating my specific constraints, concerns, and consequences, I hope that I have been able to show that context plays a role in how centers address multiliteracy, too. I have not tried to speak to others' exact issues, but have just wanted to enable the growing conversation to stay large enough to hear the disparateness of all of our voices.

Some of us may not have exactly the same goals in addressing multiliteracies in a peer tutoring setting because the idea of multiliteracy is used in different ways by theorists. As I have noted, The New London Group (1996) has used the term to talk about teaching students to be able to read and write texts that consist of more than just words. Selber (2004) uses the term to discuss different types of computer literacy. The difference reminds me of what Janet Eldred (2006) notes in her review essay "To Code or Not to Code, or, If I Can't Program a Computer, Why Am I Teaching Writing?" when she describes two paths opening before writing teachers:

> Down one path, we see "teachers of digital communication," a vision that entails some code making (programming). Down the other, we see "teachers of visual rhetoric," a vision, which, while it certainly can embrace a variety of new technologies, can also be accomplished with the old tools of scissors, glue, drawing pencils, and paper. (p. 120)

The so-called "teachers of visual rhetoric" work to promote multimodality with their students by teaching about the affordances of different modes and how to make rhetorically sound composing choices among those modes. Multimodal compositions do not have to be digital; clearly, there were multimodal texts long before there were personal computers. In *Writing New Media*, one of the books Eldred is reviewing, there are several sample new media writing assignments that do not require a computer or digital composing skills. In contrast, Eldred's "teachers of digital communication" include Selber and others who want students in writing classes to be competent producers of technology. Because most texts today (multimodal or not) are produced with computers, this group sees computer literacy as fundamental to composing. The question might be: Is the fundamental skill in writing today understanding multimodality or understanding technology? The teachers of visual rhetoric start with multimodality in first-year writing, and the teachers of digital communication start with technology.

The two multiliteracy center models I have discussed here seem to mimic those two paths to some degree. The model I use asks tutors, first and foremost, to be teachers of visual rhetoric; the AIO model has tutors as teachers of digital communication. Part of me would like to suggest this reading as a tidy ending to this discussion, to say that both models thereby accomplish their goals and that is that. However, I am not entirely comfortable with that ending because I am haunted by the persuasive line of scholars (Gurak, 1999; Kastman Bruech, 2004; Selber, 2004; Selfe, 1999) who insist that the most responsible way to teach writing is to also teach technology. With that in mind, the AIO model seems more responsible because of its comprehensiveness.

In addition, advocating a model that has tutors respond to multimodal texts but does not help students compose those texts could also be seen as problematic. In "Visual Rhetoric in a Culture of Fear: Impediments to Multimedia Production," Steve Westbrook (2006) critiques the passive role encouraged in the humanities that often asks students to be consumers and critics of new media, but not producers. Likewise, Selber (2004) critiques an instrumental view of technology that celebrates technology as long as it does not change textual production (p. 11). Both of these critiques might make me think I am not doing enough by having tutors teach multimodality in absence of instruction on technology. So, where does that leave us if we desire to help students with multimodal texts and we believe that teaching writing also means teaching students the technology necessary for digital compositions, but we are unable in our institutional contexts to create AIO centers?

Well, for one, no one expects Writing Centers to do it alone. Instead, we can be a part of the new media ecology on our campuses, doing what we can. Because most Writing Centers are equipped with computers, viewing and responding to screen-based documents is probably within our reach; having Photoshop, Acrobat, Flash, Dreamweaver, Final Cut, and InDesign as well as expertise in composing in each of these may not be. If no one else on campus is helping students with these programs, we might consider strongly taking up the cause. If others are already doing this sort of how-to help, we might see how we can make the lines of support more visible for students. Perhaps we can form new media alliances and join together in marketing and educational campaigns to let campus entities know what we do individually and jointly.

Further, there is nothing stopping us from building toward an AIO model slowly. If we have an annual technology or equipment budget, we can use that to meet the most immediate needs of our particular institution first. There is no reason that we cannot start with one program, one genre, or one technology expert first and build from there. Then we resist the pressure to be experts in everything all at once. In a sense, we could be informally, under the radar, building toward a more comprehensive model and maintaining typical Writing Center services simultaneously. We do not have to pick one route over the other. In fact, if we are to make multimodality a sustainable project at our institutions, Richard Selfe (2007) suggests we both build communal support and we obtain the technology.

Every Writing Center will have to imagine the possibilities in addressing multiliteracies at their individual institutions. The AIO model certainly has its appeal theoretically, if not practically. More time, more research, and more conversation will allow us to further refine our work with new media in Writing Center settings.

APPENDIX A
Estimated Multiliteracy Center Start-Up Costs

	QUANTITY	ESTIMATED PRICE
Hardware		
Mac Pro w/ 30" display	1	$5,100
Gateway® One ZX190	2	$3,000
Projector	1	$700
Webcams	3	3 x $75 = $225
Microphones	3	3 x $50 = $150
Speaker System	3	3 x $50 = $150
Scanner	1	$500
Software (Education Price)		
Adobe Creative Suite 4	3	$600 x 3 = $1,800
Microsoft Office 2007/2008	3	$150 x 3 = $450
Final Cut Studio 2	1	$1,300
Room Upgrades		
Card key locks on door	1	$2,000
Wall-mounted Screen	1	$50
		TOTAL: $15,425

REFERENCES

Click, Ben, & Magruder, Sarah. (2006). Implementing electronic portfolios as part of the writing center: Connections, benefits, cautions, and strategies. In Christina Murphy & Byron L. Stay (Eds.), *The writing center director's resource book* (pp. 359–370). Mahwah, NJ: Erlbaum.

DeVoss, Dànielle. (2002). Computer literacies and the roles of the writing center. In Paula Gillespie, Byron L. Stay, Alice Gillam, & Lady Falls Brown (Eds.), *Writing center research: Extending the conversation* (pp.167–186). Mahwah, NJ: Erlbaum.

Eldred, Janet. (2006). To code or not to code, or, if I can't program a computer, why am I teaching writing? *CCC 58*(1), 199–207.

Gillespie, Paula, & Lerner, Neal. (2004). *The Allyn and Bacon guide to peer tutoring* (2nd ed.). New York: Longman.

Griffin, Jo Ann. (2007). Making connections with writing centers. In Cynthia Selfe (Ed.), *Multimodal composition: Resources for teachers* (pp. 153–166). Cresskill, NJ: Hampton.

Gurak, Laura J. (2003). *Cyberliteracy: Navigating the Internet with awareness*. New Haven, CT: Yale University Press.

Inman, James. (2001). At first site: Lessons from Furman University's Center for Collaborative Learning and Communication. *academic.writing 2*. Retrieved March 1, 2008, from http://wac.colostate.edu/aw/articles/inman2001/

Kastman Breuch, Lee Ann. (2004). *Virtual peer review*. Albany: SUNY Press.

Millar, Krista H. (2004). David Sheridan on building a multiliteracy center. *Kairos 9*(1). Retrieved March 1, 2008, from http://english.ttu.edu/kairos/9.1/binder.html?interviews/sheridan/index.htm

The New London Group. (1996). A pedagogy of multiliteracies: Designing social futures. *Harvard Educational Review, 66*(1), 60–92.

Pemberton, Michael. (2003). Planning for hypertexts in the writing center . . . or not. *The Writing Center Journal, 24*(1), 9–24.

Prensky, Marc. (2001). Digital natives, digital immigrants [Electronic Version]. *On the Horizon, 9*(5), 1–6.

Ryan, Leigh, & Zimmerelli, Lisa. (2006). *The Bedford guide for writing tutors* (4th ed.). Boston, MA: Bedford/St. Martin.

Selber, Stuart. (2004). *Multiliteracies for a digital age*. Carbondale: Southern Illinois University Press.

Selber, Stuart. (2005). Postcritical perspectives on literacy technologies. *College English, 67*(3), 331–339.

Selfe, Cynthia. (1999). *Technology and literacy in the twenty-first century: The importance of paying attention*. Carbondale: Southern Illinois University Press.

Selfe, Richard. (2007) Sustaining multimodal composition. In C. Selfe (Ed.), *Multimodal composition: Resources for teachers* (pp. 167–180). Cresskill, NJ: Hampton.

Sheridan, David. (2006). Words, images, sounds: Writing centers as multiliteracy centers. In Christina Murphy & Byron L. Stay (Eds.), *The writing center director's resource book* (pp. 339–350). Mahwah, NJ: Erlbaum.

Teacher Education Digital Portfolios. (n.d.). *Getting started with your digital portfolio: Beginning steps.* Retrieved March 11, 2008, from http://portfolio.iweb.bsu.edu/start1.html

Teacher Education Digital Portfolios. (n.d.). *Secondary education sample.* Retrieved March 11, 2008, from http://portfolio.iweb.bsu.edu/SECED/index.html

Trimbur, John. (2000). Multiliteracies, social futures, and writing centers. *The Writing Center Journal, 20*(2), 29–31.

Westbrook, Steve. (2006). Visual rhetoric in a culture of fear: Impediments to multimedia production. *College English, 68*(5), 457–480.

CONTRIBUTORS

George Cooper is a lecturer at the University of Michigan, where he teaches composition as well as training courses for peer tutors at the Sweetland Writing Center. He is currently part of a research team trying to put qualitative and quantitative measurements on the behaviors and benefits of one-to-one conferences.

Teddi Fishman currently serves as the Director of the Center for Academic Integrity, housed in the Rutland Institute for Ethics at Clemson University. Her experience with writing and multimedia tutoring began at Purdue University, where she worked first as a writing center tutor and later as the coordinator of the Online Writing Lab (OWL). Her current research interests include digital portfolios and identity issues in online education.

S. Morgan Gresham is an assistant professor of English and Writing Program Coordinator at the University of South Florida, St. Petersburg. Her research interests include digital composing spaces, assessment of digital compositions, and feminist administration. With Roxanne Kirkwood, she is currently working on a manuscript on academic family trees.

Lory Hawkes is a senior professor in the Liberal Arts and Sciences department at DeVry University (Dallas Metro). She serves as the Honors Council Chair working with faculty and students to improve the curriculum and promote the honors program in the liberal arts core as well as encourage student membership in national honor societies. Always fascinated with the cognitive adaptation of human processes in working with technological systems, she has written or co-authored books, essays, and conference papers on the implications of technology. She holds a PhD in English from Texas Christian University, and is nearing completion of a Master of Information Systems from Keller Graduate School of Business with an emphasis on Internet technology tools. She holds the rank of Fellow in the Society for Technical Communication, and she is a former member of the board of directors of that organization.

Troy Hicks is an assistant professor of English at Central Michigan University where he teaches writing methods courses to pre-service teachers and is also the founding director of the Chippewa River Writing Project. A former middle school teacher and co-director of the Red Cedar Writing Project at Michigan State University, his research interests include composition, the teaching of writing, and writing with newer literacies and technologies. He is currently authoring a book for secondary teachers about creating a digital writing classroom as well as co-authoring a book about digital writing in K-12 classrooms that is being produced in conjunction with the National Writing Project. His blog can be found at http://hickstro.org.

James A. Inman is at the University of Tennessee. His books include *Technology and English Studies: Innovative Professional Paths* (with Beth L. Hewett, 2005); *Computers and Writing: The Cyborg Era* (2004), *Electronic Collaboration in the Humanities: Issues and Options* (with Cheryl Reed and Peter Sands, 2004), and *Taking Flight with OWLs: Examining Electronic Writing Center Work* (with Donna N. Sewell, 2000).

Jackie Grutsch McKinney has been an assistant professor of English and writing center director at Ball State University since 2003. She teaches graduate and undergraduate courses in rhetoric and composition. She has articles and chapters published and forthcoming in several journals and edited collections including the *Writing Center Journal* and *WPA: The Journal of the Council of Writing Program Administrators*. Currently, she is exploring how the emergence of new media and Web 2.0 complicates writing center work.

Christina Murphy is the former Dean of the College of Liberal Arts and Professor of English at Marshall University in Huntington, West Virginia. Dr. Murphy has published extensively on administrative issues in higher education and is the author of eight books and more than fifty articles and book chapters. Her most current books include the third edition of *The St. Martin's Sourcebook for Writing Tutors* (with Steve Sherwood) and *The Writing Center Director's Resource Book* (with Byron L. Stay). Dr. Murphy has won national awards for her scholarly publications and has also received national recognition for her work as the editor of the scholarly journals *Composition Studies* and *Studies in Psychoanalytic Theory*.

After 20 years of work in digital literacy and literacy acquisition, **Richard (Dickie) Selfe** is now Director of the Center for the Study and Teaching of Writing (CSTW) in the College of Humanities at Ohio State University. The CSTW houses OSU's Writing Center, the Writing Across the Curriculum program, a Professional Writing Minor, a series of K-12 and community Writing Outreach projects, a research initiative on Writing in 21st Century Contexts, and the Student Technology Consultant program. His scholarly interests lie at the intersection of communication pedagogies, programmatic curricula, and the social/institutional influences of digital systems. His most recent book-length project is entitled *Sustainable Communication Practices: Creating a Culture of Support for Technology-Rich Education*. He is currently working on another collection with Danielle DeVoss and Heidi McKee called *Technological Ecologies and Sustainability*.

David M. Sheridan is an assistant professor in Michigan State University's Residential College in the Arts and Humanities. His research interests include digital and visual rhetoric (especially as these intersect with public rhetoric), alternative learning spaces for writing, and educational games. "'The Available Means of Persuasion': Mapping a Theory and Pedagogy of Multimodal Public Rhetoric" (with Jim Ridolfo and Anthony Michel) is included in *Plugged In: Technology, Rhetoric and Culture in a Posthuman Age* (Eds. Lynn Worsham and Gary A. Olson, 2008); "Words, Images, Sounds: Writing Centers as Multiliteracy Centers" is included in *The Writing Center Director's Resource Book* (Eds. Christina Murphy and Byron Stay, 2006). He is currently co-authoring (with Jim Ridolfo and Anthony Michel) a book that explores the potentials of multimodal rhetoric in the public sphere.

AUTHOR INDEX

229

SUBJECT INDEX

LaVergne, TN USA
20 November 2010

205737LV00003B/56/P